D1527379

Death and Drama in Renaissance England

Death and Drama in Renaissance England

Shades of Memory

WILLIAM E. ENGEL

OXFORD
UNIVERSITY PRESS

OXFORD

UNIVERSITY PRESS

Great Clarendon Street, Oxford OX2 6DP

Oxford University Press is a department of the University of Oxford.
It furthers the University's objective of excellence in research, scholarship,
and education by publishing worldwide in

Oxford New York

Auckland Bangkok Buenos Aires Cape Town Chennai
Dar es Salaam Delhi Hong Kong Istanbul Karachi Kolkata
Kuala Lumpur Madrid Melbourne Mexico City Mumbai Nairobi
São Paulo Shanghai Taipei Tokyo Toronto

Oxford is a registered trade mark of Oxford University Press
in the UK and in certain other countries

Published in the United States
by Oxford University Press Inc., New York

© William E. Engel 2002

British Library Cataloguing in Publication Data

Data available

Library of Congress Cataloging in Publication Data

Data available

ISBN 0-19-925762-0

1 3 5 7 9 10 8 6 4 2

Typeset in Sabon
by SNP Best-set Typesetter Ltd., Hong Kong
Printed in Great Britain
on acid-free paper by
Biddles Ltd.,
Guildford and King's Lyn

FOR KAAREN:
Otiosi videmur, et non sumus.
(Some think we are in retirement, and yet we are not.)
(Seneca, *Epistles*, LVI. 11)

The problem of the Renaissance now presents itself as that of the metamorphosis of the energy of the human and individual self-awareness caused by the polarization due to the re-instatement of the memory images of energy-peaks in the classical past—more briefly, 'dynamic polarization through restored memory'.

(Aby Warburg, *Diaries*, 1907)

[M]*agic* seems to stir up in everyone some hidden mental forces, some lingering hopes in the miraculous, some dormant beliefs in man's mysterious possibilities. Witness to this is the power which the words, *magic, spell, charm, to bewitch*, and *to enchant*, possess in poetry, where the inner value of words, the emotional forces which they still release, survive longest and are revealed most clearly.

(Bronislaw Malinowski, *Magic, Science, and Religion*, 1925)

'This spectacle of the world, how it is fallen! how changed! how defaced! The path of victory is obliterated in vines, and the benches of the senators are concealed by a dunghill.' . . . The art of man is able to construct monuments far more permanent than the narrow span of his own existence: yet these monuments, like himself, are perishable and frail; and in the boundless annals of time his life and his labours must equally be measured as a fleeting moment.

(Edward Gibbon, *The Decline and Fall of the Roman Empire*, ch. 71)

Acknowledgements

FIRST, I WANT TO THANK MY CHILDREN, Zoë, Simon, and Iris, for understanding when I travel to faraway places for long stretches of time. I am indebted to Ruth and Marvin Engel for making select emblem books readily available, and to Barbara and Basil Hirschowitz for bringing Ralegh and Ross into my home. Sophie Goldsworthy, Sarah Hyland, and Frances Whistler, along with proofreader Andrew Hawkey, at Oxford University Press have been exemplary in every respect; sincere thanks go to copy-editor Jeff New, an able classicist and gifted stylist.

As an independent scholar, I am especially grateful to those who graciously have taken the time to offer helpful suggestions: on the Introduction, Barbara Bowen, Mary Carruthers, Leah Marcus, Anne Lake Prescott, Phoebe Spinrad; on Part I, Michael Bath, Stephen Greenblatt, S. K. Heninger, Jr., Karl Höltgen, Clark Hulse, Frederick Kiefer, Kurt Koenigsberger, John Manning; on Part II, Tom Conley, Arthur Kinney, Luigi Monga; on Part III, Ward Allen, Emerson Brown, Stephen Orgel, Tim Raylor, Hal Weatherby; and on the Conclusion, Paul Gehl, Inge Leimberg, Grant Williams, Carla Zecher.

Jonas Barish helped me launch this project, but passed away before he could cast his critical eye over the final draft; this book would have benefited immeasurably from his pencil-comments, admonishing me to be more direct. Alastair Fowler made a timely intervention that has kept me on track, and later offered invaluable suggestions about how I could present my argument more clearly and persuasively, thus earning my enduring gratitude.

Earlier versions of several sections of this book have appeared in Peter Daly and John Manning (eds.), *Aspects of Renaissance and Baroque Symbol Theory, 1500–1700* (New York: AMS, 1999); in Luigi Monga (ed.), *Annali d'italianistica* 14 (1996), and also, by agreement, *Bollettino del Centro Interuniversitario di Recerche sul 'Viaggio in Italia'* (Torino, 1995); and in Rita Wilson and Carlotta von Maltzan (eds.), *Spaces and Crossings: Essays on Literature and Culture in Africa and Beyond* (Frankfurt: Peter Lang, 2001). I am grateful to the editors and publishers for permission to reuse some of this material.

Contents

x   *Contents*

List of Illustrations

Note on Conventions

Punctuation and spelling in dramas follow the modern editions cited; prose works are given in their original forms, but printing-house contractions and anomalies have been silently expanded.

Prologue

> Some place is chosen of the largest possible extent and characterised by the utmost possible variety, such as a spacious house divided into a number of rooms . . . all these places are visited in turn and the various deposits are demanded from their custodians, as the sight of each recalls the respective details. . . . We require, therefore, places, real or imaginary, and images or symbols, which we must, of course, invent for ourselves.
>
> (Quintilian, *Institutio Oratoria*, XI. ii. 18–21)

The spirit of decline haunting the Renaissance imagination left its mark on dramas, dictionaries, and historical compendia. These various forms of literary expression all shared a common principle of organization. Each was decidedly at odds with oblivion, and drew from reservoirs of the culture's collective memory—namely from emblems, proverbs, and *exempla*. These repositories of accrued commonplaces and perennial wisdom were staples of the classical Memory Arts, which enjoyed a revival during the period. This was especially the case with respect to theatre and its metaphors, as expressed through tragedies, phrase-books, and histories.

This book contends that the Art of Memory gave shape to, and animated, these different ways of recording and responding to the extremes of human experience and the extent of mortal knowledge. Examining them in this light opens up new possibilities for understanding early modern intellectual life. Therefore this book looks at how mortal temporality was figured and reconfigured between 1570 and 1670 from three perspectives.

Part I, where the main concern is with emblems, demonstrates the instrumentality of the Memory Arts for reconstructing the aesthetic and affective conditions giving rise to certain framing mechanisms in English Tragedy that self-consciously extended the limits of theatre's magic. Special attention will be given to scenes from *Friar Bacon, Doctor Faustus, The Spanish Tragedy, The Revenger's Tragedy, Bussy D'Ambois, Hamlet, The White Devil,* and *The Broken Heart*, which used cunning, initially mute, staged spectacles that evoked images of fatal destiny. Part II, concentrating on proverbs, examines the psychological and philological links forged by the Memory Arts. The focus here will be on John Florio, whose language books dramatized the double truth of simulated speech through highly mannered vignettes of a traveller's everyday routine abroad. Part III, where the main concern is *exempla*, looks at how metaphors of the stage were translated into a body of work which sought to characterize and portray the soul of history. The focus here is on Walter Ralegh's *History of the World* and on Alexander Ross's efforts to digest and correct, and then to continue and complete, Ralegh's monumental project.

The works discussed all contain resonant messages that would remain obscure were it not for the critical approach to encoded mnemonic designs that is developed and applied in this book. With the Art of Memory as our interpretive key, we can gain access to what these exemplary works of Renaissance drama, the language arts, and history have to say about the place of oblivion in our lives. For, as Thomas Browne reflected in his meditation on burial urns: 'But the iniquity of oblivion blindly scattereth her poppy, and deals with the memory of men without distinction to merit of perpetuity. . . . Oblivion is not to be hired: The greater part must be content to be as though they had not been.'

Death and Drama thus concludes with a parting glance at the monument scene in Shakespeare's *The Winter's Tale* and at English translations concerning the restless dead, namely those who are apparently beyond life though not yet beyond the reach of art and language. This will crystallize how Renaissance memory images came to store and disclose, and to translate and revive, their symbolic contents and backlog of cultural meanings. They did so, finally, with respect to an overarching Aesthetic of Decline. Seen in this way, we can recover, in their original contexts, certain shades of memory, from just this side of oblivion, and attend to what they still have to tell us about living artfully in the face of death.

Introduction
'Take away but one letter':
The Spirit of Decline

Ombra, any shadow or shade, the shadow of anything, the shadow that Painters give to their works, or the first draft in painting, before it be finished; by met. Darkness, or privation of light; also a ghost, a spirit, or vision of any person; used also for an inking of suspicion, or least colour of unkindness or jealousie.

(Giovanni Torriano, *Vocabolario*, 1688)

Oblivion. Dark, dusky, dusty, moldy, gloomy, rusty, musty, rude, thankless, shady, discourteous, unkind, lazy, dull.

(Josua Poole, *The English Parnassus*, 1677)

Shall not the portion of my dayes come soone to an end? Let him withdrawe himselfe quickly, that I may take my breath agayne. Before I go into the countrie of darknesse and into the shadowe of death, from whence there is no returning agayne. Into the darke countrie where there is nothing but darknesse, even thicke darknesse where there is nothing but disorder, and when it should shine, there is nothing but darkness.

(Job 10: 20–1)[1]

SAMPLING JOB

The spirit of the subtitle of this book, 'Shades of Memory', is embodied in these three citations. The first comes from an Italian–English dictionary, and covers the range of meanings associated with the word for 'shade' in the Renaissance. The second

---

[1] *Sermons of Master John Calvin, upon the Booke of IOB translated out of the French by Arthur Golding* (London, 1574), sig. M7v.

citation, taken from a thesaurus, identifies the word 'shady' as being one of the many possible epithets an aspiring poet might use with 'oblivion'. The first speaks of art as well as of nature, and concerns the supernatural ('a ghost, a spirit') as well as antisocial behaviour ('unkindness or jealousie'). The second citation, regarding oblivion, reiterates the movement between the natural and the social worlds (dark to rude, moldy to unkind). And the third brings together and expands on the idea of 'privation of light' from the first, and notions of 'shady' oblivion from the second. This passage from Job brings home the melancholy implications lurking within the darkness that shades off from 'ombra' into 'oblivion', which is to say, the inevitable prospect of our going into 'the shadowe of death, from whence there is no returning agayne'.

These three citations also can be taken to sum up each part of this book, which, broadly speaking, concerns: (1) shadows of things in the world represented on the stage, but which turn into shades of a different sort; (2) the 'dusky, dusty . . . rusty, musty' poetic way of thinking and speaking that can be associated with a dictionary maker's and translator's linking of meanings through sounds no less than semantic implications—after all, we speak of a translation catching the spirit of the original; and (3) the way an individual's history can be expressed through, and in terms of, the history of the world and that of humanity universally. This double sense of history is haunted, even as it is directed, by the biting question: 'Shall not the portion of my dayes come soone to an end?' And so it is: 'rude, thankless, shady, discourteous, unkind;' we rail at fate much in the way Job did before he came around to seeing the bigger picture—and, for the purposes of this book, it will be seen in terms of being a memory-picture.

Such a picture of history was vouchsafed to the likes of Job. For this reason it is especially apt to begin this book with Job; and moreover, because Job, perhaps more succinctly and universally than other books of holy writ recording similar laments of loss, exile, or decline, gave convenient expression to the sense of world-weariness prevalent in Stuart England.[2] Thomas Browne summed

---

[2] Christopher Hill, *Intellectual Origins of the English Revolution* (1965; repr. Oxford: Clarendon Press, 1982), 4, 11; and, on 'biblical poetics', especially as it pertains to Job, see Barbara Kiefer Lewalski, *Milton's Brief Epic: The Genre,*

up this commonplace attitude, with special relevance as it relates to the futility of our striving in the face of mortality, implied in the 'portion of our days':

'Tis too late to be ambitious. The great mutations of the world are acted, our time may be too short for our designes. To extend our memories by Monuments, whose death we dayly pray for, and whose duration we cannot hope, without injury to our expectations in the advent of the last day, were a contradiction to our beliefs. We whose generations are ordained in this setting part of time, are providentially taken off from such imaginations. And being necessitated to eye the remaining particle of futurity, are naturally constituted unto thoughts of the next world, and cannot excusably decline the consideration of that duration, which maketh Pyramids pillars of snow, and all that's past a moment. . . . Oblivion is not to be hired: The greater part must be content to be as though they had not been, to be found in the Register of God, not the record of man.[3]

This melancholy view of history as having peaked and begun to reach for its ending, is more complicated than it appears at first glance. By virtue of how Browne formulates the issue, we are induced to consider another way in which we fall further away from perfection, and thereby discover ourselves to be further in decline than we had realized. It occurs even as we acknowledge the truth of the decay of all things (and most especially of the world itself), for we confront our inability to see the extent of this truth within the sweeping context of God's grand, providential, design. And yet, what else could be expected from people who, both individually and as a culture, are doomed and who are—so to speak—living on borrowed time? Further, how are we to give voice to our despair stemming from this realization as well as from our not being able to express adequately, let alone conceptualize accurately, our place in such a grand design? The Book of Job provokes just such a chain of questions.

During the Renaissance and Reformation, Job was not merely an example but something to be sampled. The trials and lesson

Meaning, and Art of 'Paradise Regained' (Providence: Brown University Press, 1966), 10–36.

[3] *The Works of Sir Thomas Browne*, ed. Geoffrey Keynes (1928; repr. edn., Chicago: University of Chicago Press, 1964), i. 166–7.

of the Book of Job, no less than the proverbial patience of the character of Job, gave ready expression to some deep-seated, everyday concerns. It shows up time and again in letters, sermons, and epitaphs. Calvin based his sermons on Job so frequently that when they were collected and published in English by Arthur Golding they ran to 750 folio pages.[4] Beyond the Book of Job's powerful statement about our diminutive status in the presence of God, it echoes the common lament that our speech is inadequate to express the depth of our feelings—including and especially our anguish at not being able to give voice to the extent of our sorrow over this very condition. This accounts in part for a steady movement back to the words of the ancients as a way of expressing what I will be discussing shortly in terms of an overriding Aesthetic of Decline.

The ancients could be made to speak for the humanists, to intercede on their behalf, and, as it were, to catapult their impoverished words beyond the realm of ordinary speech and thought. For example, as was often cited and referred to by commentators, 'Augustine the bishop, flying like an eagle over the mountain peaks and not attending to what is at their foot, discoursed in clear language about the broad spaces of the heavens, the length and breadth of the lands, and the circle of the seas'.[5] Edgar Wind has remarked about this theme of 'translatability' (a principal concern in Part II), of looking to the words of ancients so as to make a broad appeal without losing its depth of meaning, that 'the principle of "the whole in the part" permitted so many kinds of foreshadowings and foreshortenings that the speculative phases of the argument could remain hidden in the clouds, and yet be accurately "mirrored" in a practical adage'.[6]

The casting about for and finding just such an indispensable word, Wind concludes, 'fulfilled the prerequisite for any philosophy fashionable in its day'. And, with this end in mind,

---

[4] Copies of the first edition of Golding's translation of Calvin's sermons on Job are scarce, but the importance and popularity of this book is attested by the fact that no fewer than two variants were printed in 1574, two in 1580, and again two in 1584.
[5] Jacobus de Voragine, *The Golden Legend*, trans. William Granger Ryan (Princeton: Princeton University Press, 1993), ii. 127.
[6] Edgar Wind, *Pagan Mysteries in the Renaissance* (1958; repr. New York: W. W. Norton, 1968), 97.

the humanists looked to the Church Fathers for 'the practical adage'—which could just as easily concern Job as thorny points of doctrine, or both. For example, as humanists in the Renaissance would have known, Gregory wrote to Innocent (prefect of Africa): 'I am gratified by your interest and your request that I send you my commentary on holy Job but if you wish to gorge yourself on delicious fare, read the treatise of blessed Augustine.'[7] Furthermore, they looked to classical voices like Seneca and Plutarch, who were favoured among humanists for their eloquent and easily extracted passages on the vagaries of fortune and fate. And, more frequently than not, they looked to biblical voices like Job, and like Solomon, for the Book of 'Ecclesiastes, or the Preacher' likewise was a popular and ready way to express the vanity of mortal strivings (a principal concern of Part III).

By the middle of the seventeenth century Job had come to be a coded byword for certain values and views. For example, 'like Job on a Dunghill', and similar references, had passed from the proverbial into the vernacular.[8] For example, words from Job were favourite epigraphs on title-pages, particularly on tracts relating to the times of plague, like Benjamin Spenser's *Vox Civitatis* (1635). The citation from Job 19: 21, 'Have pittie upon me, have pittie upon me, oh yee my friends, for the hand of God hath touched me', was so familiar to readers that it could show up without quotation marks, without a gloss, and without even a reference to its source, and be recognized as speaking both for Job and, in this case, for London—and, by extension, for all of us: 'because God hath touched me' (sig. D3ᵛ). This phrase is glossed at length by Calvin, and was popularized further by Arthur Golding.[9] The result of having been thus touched, though, is far from salubrious: 'once the Phoenix, now the Owle; once the Paragon of beautie, now a Patterne of deformitie; lately the crown and pride of great Britaine, now a skarcrow and scorn' (sig. B1).

One needed only to quote a short passage, or simply refer to it in its abbreviated form in the margin, when wanting to evoke the compound motif of being tossed about in the 'theatre of the

---

[7] Voragine, *Golden Legend*, 'Saint Augustine', ii. 127.
[8] Benjamin Spenser, *Vox Civitatis, or Londons Complaint against her Children in the Countrey* (London, 1636), sig. B3ᵛ.
[9] *Sermons of Calvin* (London, 1574), sig. X7.

world' and subjected to God's inscrutable judgement. In fact, such citations, as a kind of cultural shorthand, often were the basis for edifying expositions of the theme, which at times were accompanied by moral emblems illustrating some aspect of the *theatrum mundi*.[10]

Job thus stands both as an example of an assimilated humanist commonplace and also, more particularly, as a sample of the Aesthetic of Decline typical of the period. This notion brings together what Michael Neill has referred to as an 'aesthetic of death' during the period and what, in my earlier work, I discussed in terms of an aesthetic of anamnesis.[11] The idea of an Aesthetic of Decline can help us bridge these two conceptual realms, death and memory, through a judicious sampling of select forms of cultural expression which share similar underlying principles. The aesthetic in question, during the Renaissance, was concerned with representing the recognition and inevitability of the dark and mysterious night of nothing that will overtake us all, and of a realm beyond the pale of ordinary existence as we know it.

While this theme was hardly unique to seventeenth-century English literary and spiritual life, what is remarkable during this period is the appearance of a variety of related ways that were ideally suited for expressing this theme.[12] Accordingly, each part of this study is concerned, respectively, with drama, with dictionaries, and with dates; to put it more specifically, with emblematic

---

[10] On the place of this motif during the period, though without necessarily being glossed in terms of Job's trials, see Frances A. Yates, *Theatre of the World* (Chicago: University of Chicago, 1969); José Antonio Maravall, *Culture of the Baroque: Analysis of a Historical Structure*, trans. Terry Cochran (1975; repr. Minneapolis: University of Minnesota Press, 1986), 199–202; James V. Mirollo, *Mannerism and Renaissance Poetry: Concept, Mode, Inner Design* (New Haven: Yale University Press, 1984).

[11] Cf. Michael Neill, *Issues of Death: Mortality and Identity in English Renaissance Tragedy* (Oxford: Clarendon Press, 1997), 356, 363; and William E. Engel, *Mapping Mortality: The Persistence of Memory and Melancholy in Early Modern England* (Amherst: University of Massachusetts Press, 1995), 12, 112, 118, 121, 195, 199–202.

[12] See Robert J. Clements, *Picta Poesis: Literary and Humanistic Theory in Renaissance Emblem Books* (Rome: Edizioni di Storia e Letteratura, 1960), 194–207; and Wind, *Pagan Mysteries*, 218–35. Cf. Stanley Fish, *Self-Consuming Artifacts: The Experience of Seventeenth-Century Literature* (Berkeley: University of California Press, 1972), 371–2.

devices and theatrical conventions, with translation theory as it is put into literary practice, and with the efforts to organize and orchestrate what comes to pass as the truths of history. Each of these three main areas—drama, dictionaries, and dates—corresponds to the following domains of knowledge: philosophy, poetry, and history. Each finds its proper, rudimentary commonplace in emblems, proverbs, and *exampla*.[13] Drama, for the purposes of this investigation, belongs to the province of philosophy, with its faculty being Reason, insofar as tragedy presents precepts and, in so doing, depicts the social dynamics and extreme consequences of our being in the world. Dictionaries, translations, and phrasebooks line up with poetry, with its corresponding faculty being Imagination, owing to the reliance on similitudes and the invention of conceits. And historical writing, while it may exemplify many of the traits of poetry and rely on metaphors of the stage, and while it may, overall, evoke the ethos of the theatre, finally is concerned with examples taken from the sayings and deeds of those who have run their course in the world. Its proper faculty is Memory.

The story of Job brings together, and partakes of, all three domains of knowledge. And yet there is a fundamental bit of knowledge concealed from Job, which is out of his reach but which, owing to the narrative design, is available to the reader. As with medieval religious dramas, here the audience is given access to a scene to which no mortal could be privy. In so doing, the spectators are left with the uneasy feeling concerning just how much more then must be concealed from them in their own lives. Still, the person who reads what Job discovers through great hardship is left wondering whether she or he will fare any better for knowing Job's case. The bit of information, unknown to Job, involves a wager that takes place off-stage, as it were. It sets the plot in motion and propels the main character into a vortex of misery mirroring his mortality. The wager is played out through words passed between the Adversary and God. God's testing of Job was incited by the taunting words of Satan, according to the King James Version of 1611 (Job 1: 11–12): 'But put foorth thine hand

[13] Cf. Engel, *Mapping Mortality*, 97.

now, and touch all that he hath, and he will curse thee to thy face.
| And the Lord said unto Satan, Behold all that hee hath is in thy
power, onely upon himselfe put not foorth thine hand.'

The same passage provides the focal drama to Francis Quarles's
poetic meditation *Job Militant*, in words that presage Milton's 'I
cannot praise a fugitive and cloistered virtue, unexercised and un-
breathed, that never sallies out and sees her adversary, but slinks
out of the race where that immortal garland is to be run for, not
without dust and heat'.[14]

> True Lord (reply'd the Fiend) thy Champion hath
> A strong and fervent (yet a crafty) Faith,
> A forced love needs no such great applause,
> He loves but ill, that loves not for a cause.
>
> .   .   .   .
>
> But small's the triall of a Faith, in this,
> If thou support him, tis thy strength, not his.
> Can then my power, that stands by thy permission,
> Encounter, where Thou mak'st an Opposition?
> Stretch forth thy Hand, and smite but what he hath,
> And prove thou then the temper of his Faith.[15]

Fully grasping the dramatic potential of the situation, Goethe
provided additional nuances to the wager implicit in this agreement in terms of a 'Prologue in Heaven', regarding the testing of
Faust, who is cast as a Job-figure: 'About my bet I have no hesita-
tion, | And when I win, concede your stake | And let me triumph
with a swelling breast: | Dust he shall eat, and with zest, | As my
relation does, the famous snake.'[16] And it is in this respect that my
study is situated between two poles, or responses: the approach
to life as a contest or game, and living life as a journey toward
death—expressed in more academic terms as *Homo Ludens* and
Homo Necans.[17]

---

[14] *John Milton, Complete Poems and Major Prose*, ed. Merritt Y. Hughes
(Indianapolis and New York: Bobbs-Merrill, 1957), 728.

[15] Francis Quarles, *Divine Poems* (London, 1632), sigs. N2ᵛ–N3.

[16] *Goethe's 'Faust'*, trans. Walter Kaufmann (New York: Doubleday, 1961),
88–9.

[17] Johan Huizinga, *Homo Ludens: A Study of the Play Element in Culture*
(1944; repr. Beacon, 1955), and Walter Burkert, *Homo Necans: The Anthropology of Ancient Greek Sacrificial Ritual and Myth*, trans. Peter Bing (1972; repr.
Berkeley: University of California Press, 1983).

The sentiments expressed in the passage cited from Job show up in, among other places, the devotional works of John Featley (or Fairclough), who styled himself 'the least of the Apostles & Chaplaine of his Majesty' (Charles I). He was the nephew of the more eminent Daniel Featley, who disputed learnedly with King James during the monarch's last days and published the 'scholastick duel' as *Cygnea Cantio* (1629). John Featley, like his uncle, was a popular preacher for the Crown's cause. From 1639 on he was chaplain to Charles I, and after the Restoration in 1660 was named 'Chaplain extraordinary to the King'. While in exile on the continent during the civil strife, he published among other tracts *A Fountain of Teares* (1646).[18] In it he used Job to further his extended meditation on the timely themes of lamentation and consolation, 'for the benefit of all that are in affliction; and particularly in these distressed times of warre'. The main text for this sermon, though, and one paralleled by many comparable passages in Job, comes from Jeremiah 9: 1: 'O that mine head were waters, and mine eyes a Fountaine of tears, that I might weep day and night for the slaine of the daughter of my people.'[19] His opening cry ('O that mine head . . .') creates a sense of urgency and despair, lending to the lament a tone of epic and dramatic appeal. It gives a guiding context to the words that follow, and which, as Featley proposes, are intended to induce 'Teares of Godly sorrow, or devout Melancholy'. Elsewhere, he calls on the exclamation explicitly to wring from the passage additional meanings appropriate to the intense, and intensified, grief about which he speaks: 'My teares are many; my pangs increase, and *double* and *treble* themselves upon mee. One O is not enough to cry; but as if my short life were onely to be imployed in accents of sorrow, I lengthen my exclamations, and I cry *o o o o o o* &c: as if my paine waxe the lesser when I make my complaints either lowder, or longer' (sig. O12v, p. 336).

Through his words then (or, more correctly, by virtue of a phonic repetition, which conduces to a silent play of wit), we move

[18] John Featley, *A Fountaine of Teares* (Amsterdam, 1646), sig. 2D6. Another edition was printed in London in 1683.

[19] Among the more notable uses of this recurring image, see Petrarch, *Sonnetto, In vita*, 153, 191–5; Thomas Kyd, *Spanish Tragedy*, 3.2; and Crashaw's *The Weeper*, stanzas 19 and 23.

through a special kind of 'declension'. Specifically, as we listen to the dramatic cry, and try to imagine what this, or any, chaplain would sound like while making such a woeful cry of despair without sounding forced or foolish,[20] and then fit ourselves into the pattern of his homily, we are implicated in its theme and become part of a symbolic—indeed, a mortal—syntax: we move from high to low, and fall through the case. To follow the conceit to its conclusion, we fall from the nominative case (specifically, from the subject, from one who is sorely troubled and whose voice speaks for each of us) to the exclamation itself, understood as a sound which communicates a feeling without necessarily having any fixed content, though in this case it is marked as denoting a special kind of despair linked to not being able to express adequately the extent of one's sorrow. And so it falls to us, literally, to give voice and spirit to the declension in question, even as we recognize that it is our own declination we are (or should be) lamenting. Such an understanding gives added meaning to the view that symbols are sensible signs, capable of being actualized.[21]

A similar phonetic display of wit along the lines of what we follow, and fall into, with Featley's homily shows up in the work of his more famous uncle, Daniel Featley, also chaplain to a king.[22] His lament traces a movement away from the word of woe, by virtue of slip of thought, to a series of repetitions using a single sound to indicate subtle differences in meaning.

In my discourse of our later end, to draw towards an end, before the destruction of the holy City, the Temple, *Josephus* writeth of a man afflicted in minde, that ran about the City crying, Wo to the City, wo to

[20]   Cf. Shakespeare, *Venus and Adonis*. ll. 833–4.

[21]   Charles Sanders Peirce, *Selected Philosophical Writings, Volume 1 (1867–1893)*, ed. Christian Kloesel and Nathan Houser (Bloomington and Indianapolis: University of Indiana Press, 1992), 5, 7–9, 225–6. On Peirce's applicability to a discussion of Renaissance symbol theory, see Albert Tricomi, *Reading Tudor-Stuart Texts Through Cultural Historicism* (Gainesville: University of Florida Press, 1996), 7.

[22]   Daniel Featley, *Clavis Mystica* (London, 1636), 'Philip his MEMENTO MORI or, The Passing Bell' (sigs. 2B2ᵛ–2C2), which takes as its text Deut. 32: 29: 'O that they were wise, then they would understand thus, they would consider their latter end.' This sermon had a strange enduring quality that led it to be reprinted as late as 1708, as a pamphlet, and to be sold 'for the benefit of the poor'.

the Temple, wo to the Priests, wo to the people, and last of all wo to my selfe; at which words he was slaine on the walls by a stone out of a sling. Let us take away but one letter, turning wo in O, and his prophesie for the future may be our admonition, and the application of this observation for the present. O that the world, O that this Kingdome in the world, O that this City in this Kingdome, O that we in this City here present were wise, then would wee understand this: this spectacle of our nature, this embleme of our frailty, this mirrour of our mortality, and in it consider our later end, which cannot bee farre off. For our deceased brother is here arrested before our eyes for a debt of nature, in which wee are as deeply ingaged as hee. (p. 289)

In addition to taking away one letter so as to acquire and run with the new exlamative formation while still carrying along with it the previous and ordinary sense of sorrow, Featley's florid rhetoric conjures up a series of evocative images, all of which reinforce and expand his meaning. These techniques are fairly standard for sermons of the day, and yet this particular example reveals something a little unusual about the author's ingenuity, and which can be used to introduce the main argument of this book, linking the chapters and resolved in the Conclusion. The deceased about whom the sermon is constructed ceases to be in more ways than one. In death his individuality disappears, and he becomes fair game, metaphorically speaking, to stand quite generally for anyone and everyone. The corpse does so (though still carrying along in the mind of the auditor the previous identity of the deceased) and thereby becomes a dreadful spectacle of our own nature, an emblem of our frailty, and a mirror of our mortality. Through the words which breathe life into the symbolic value now accorded to the corpse, it becomes not just a corpse but a visible, to some extent legible, token of our decline and implied future dissolution. But, as this study endeavours to examine critically: just how legible is such an emblem on its own, without contextualizing commentary? Legible with respect to what manner of lexicon?

In becoming a rhetorical mirror of 'to what we all must come', the body of the deceased thus is made to speak a specific lesson. Building on the recognition that we are already in a state of decline, from youth to age, Featley further sets up in the chambers of our memory an aurally resonant echo of our mortality in the form of a body further along in its decay than our own. But there is still another, more complicated, mirror of mortality that is set up for us to see ourselves at a time when we will have passed beyond our materiality. The other mirror, which reflects our translation from this body and this life into another, shows up in the vocalized lament. Just as we can be made to see ourselves as spectacles, emblems, and mirrors—as shades of what we have known ourselves to be—so too, we catch a glimpse of our implied future passing in the sliding from 'wo' to 'o, o, o, o.' The repeated 'o, o, o, o,' like 'wo' moving to 'o' allows for and, to some extent, enables the conceptual transmission and transformation of the letter to the spirit.

DEATH'S COMMONPLACES

The decline and decay of every individual, like the abasement and bringing low of mankind, is an old theme with many ways of being expressed during the Renaissance. One fairly common version shows up as the penultimate entry in Geoffrey Whitney's benchmark collection of emblems, dedicated to Robert Dudley, Earl of Leicester (Fig. 1). The Latin title, 'Ex maximo minimum', indicates the ultimate declension in human existence, the slip from the greatest to the least. The explanatory poem beneath leaves no doubt about how we are to understand this *memento mori* emblem. And the full effect of its words concerning the great translation depends on a paradoxical twisting of conventional logic: we are asked to imagine something from the point of view of a time when we no longer have a mind with which to think even this thought (a theme resumed in the Conclusion).[23] The emblem proposes the obliteration of one's faculty to make sense. The seat of Reason, which discerns precepts, is shown here as that which is brought low in the face of death, and which thus, iconographically, becomes the face of Death, and existentially, the faceless face of each of us after death.

---

[23] Rosalie L. Colie, *Paradoxia Epidemica: The Renaissance Tradition of Paradox* (Princeton: Princeton University Press, 1966), 396–423.

Ex maximo minimum.

Fig. 1. The seat of sacred reason

> WHERE liuely once, GODS image was expreste,
>   Wherin, sometime was sacred reason plac'de,
> The head, I meane, that is so ritchly bleste,
> With sight, with smell, with hearinge, and with taste.
>   Lo, nowe a skull, both rotten, bare, and drye,
>   A relicke meete in charnell house to lye . . .

And yet the pictorial elements move us away from the charnel house for, nearby, a flower has sprung up, nourished by the decaying matter of what once was a person. According to the implicit Christian allegory of the resurrection, such a new life can await us as well.[24] Further, whereas God's image once was so lively expressed in the body of the one who now is dead, the emblem now serves as a body or receptacle for—and is a lively expression of—a timely warning about our mortality.

The theme of this great translation, as we decline—and are declined—'by this to that', shows up prominently in Quarles's book of moral verse (Fig. 2). We can go from the one to the other (from mortal life to an incorruptible crown) only through and by means

---

[24] Caroline Walker Bynum, *The Resurrection of the Body in Western Christianity, 200–1336* (New York: Columbia University Press, 1995).

Fig. 2. The brief of man's estate

of death—risking oblivion. The closing lines of 'The Minde of the Frontispiece' explain it this way:

> Th'one points to Death, the t'other to a Crowne,
> Who THIS attains, must tread the OTHER down:
> All which denotes the Briefe of MANS estate,
> That HEE's to go from HENCE, by THIS to THAT.

From hence by this to that . . . a phrase that will be repeated in a variety of ways before this book reaches its conclusion. For it is in the moment spanning 'this' and 'that', in the movement from hence, that the transformation takes place—the great translation of our mortal bodies and identities to . . . that which is other than being.[25]

What exactly transpires, and who is eligible to be thus translated, was hotly contested during the period. What will command our attention, though, are the framing and the emblematic staging of an instant where something potentially mysterious takes place. No matter which side of the religious, polemical divide one found oneself, there was rarely debate over the fact that something miraculous takes place in the movement 'from hence by this to that'. What goes on in between 'this' and 'that' is integral to the definition we give to ourselves about our being in the world. It is integral, further, to how we come to figure, and reconfigure, ourselves as being in the world in such a way that we come to envision ourselves to *be* in terms of a mode of being that is other than being.[26]

Whatever else happens to us after death, physically at least we all will become what the emblem depicts, as Whitney puts it: 'a skull, both rotten, bare, and drye, | A relicke meete in charnell house to lye.' The emblem reduces complex philosophical notions to a simple play of wit, and makes us call to mind a time when, ironically, our mind—our most prized way to apprehend the truth of our being—will be no more. And so, like Job's lament about the portion of our days, this points the way toward our recognizing a

---

[25] Emmanuel Lévinas, *Autrement qu'être ou au-delà de l'essence* (Dordrecht: Martinus Nijhoff, 1974), 171.

[26] Emmanuel Lévinas, *Time and the Other*, trans. Richard A. Cohen (Pittsburgh: Duquesne University Press, 1987), 74.

truth of the projected event of our eventual undoing, at that time when we can project nothing more, by making us entertain the possibility of a mode of being outside reason, cut off from language and vision and light. It thus evokes a special sense of dread regarding what awaits us by setting up a paradoxical way of understanding a mode of being that is other than being,[27] along the lines lamented by Job: 'Into the darke countrie where there is nothing but darknesse, even thicke darknesse where there is nothing but disorder, and when it should shine, there is nothing but darkness.'

We cannot come to know it through simple discursive practices; paradoxically though, *this truth* can be known to us. In fact, knowing *this* may well be a defining characteristic both of our being and also how we come to figure the nature of death—of our own death. Thus Whitney's 'relicke' bereft of life, like the one glossed by George Wither in which the token is referred to as being 'the fleshless ruines of a *rotten Skull*' (Fig. 3), has no voice of its own but manages to speak to us about our mortality through the emblem, figured as a resonant echo from beyond the grave.

Other allegorical tableaux partaking of the same visual conventions likewise show Death as an animated skeleton, like the one on the title-page of Arthur Warwicke's *Spare Minutes or Resolved Meditations* of 1637 (Fig. 4). This somewhat more lively mirror of our mortality is depicted extinguishing the flame of life. The poem accompanying the emblematic frontispiece is quaintly glossed to direct our attention toward what comes after Death's fatal breath has been blown: 'Death puft this Light; and his earth-banisht Flame | Flew up to heav'n, and so a Starre became.' The commonplace message notwithstanding, the medium deserves our attention as well, namely, the mechanism by which the declination of our being, 'from hence, by this to that', is presented. The allegorical power of this potentially trite image, like Quarles's somewhat more doctrinally derived one, is based on a tacit but simple theme: the power to which the emblem alludes is invisible and yet its effects in the world manifestly are real. The skeleton blowing out the light of life, more so than other similar allegories

<hr>

[27] Lévinas, *Time and the Other*, 75.

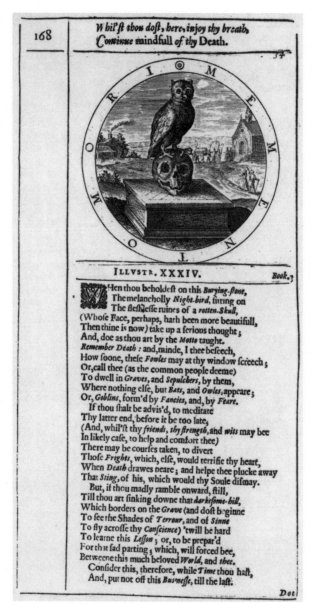

Fig. 3. Remember death

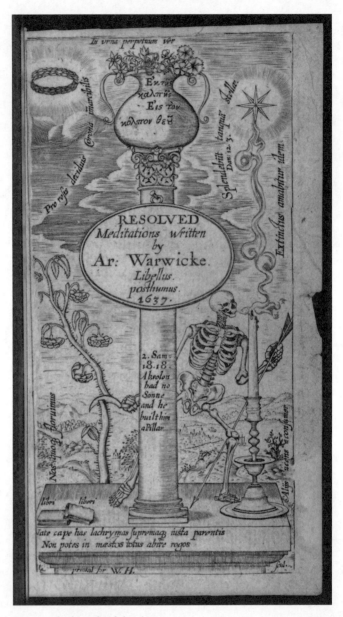

Fig. 4. The breath of death

of *vanitas*, is exemplary of the central paradox animating, and revealed by, the conventions of the mode of representation that is put on display here.[28] How is it that air or wind or breath can be coming from that hollow ribcage? What force generates and pushes air through that empty cavity and out the rictus mouth? A series of easy, though not altogether satisfying, answers to these questions present themselves immediately. The illustration obviously is not meant to represent faithfully, to the life, every detail; and, anyway, it is just a symbol, in this case, of our mortality. Realism is hardly the final aim of an iconic depiction; and yet it is the hint of realism that suggests the way the viewer should be thinking about the image, and doing so with a larger picture or message in mind. No one would ever mistake a picture of a unicorn or a dragon for anything that lives in the world, so we should not even consider that skeletons really walk; this is just a fanciful picture, an image with no real correspondence in the world. Viewers simply take in the cheat, the visual wit, and move on to glean the moral from the allegorical image. What goes on in this movement, in this winking, however, is what my study wishes to open up for critical investigation.

For although there is truth in all of the responses just given, they all still presume that something is amiss that needs explaining. A step seems to be missing from this to that, from one epistemological field to another way of thinking about and knowing what is intended. An instructive way of conceptualizing this cognitive rift, which is another instantiation of how we come to think about the movement from 'this to that', is described as 'mention-selection':

Mention-selection points up certain features of the learning process. The clearest illustration of this fact is provided by terms with null denotation. Such terms cannot be acquired by pointing to the things they apply to. There are no unicorns to point to in teaching a child to use the word unicorn. . . . Here we have recourse to other, related representations, to pictures of unicorns. . . . [T]he picture is itself no unicorn.[29]

[28] In asking the next set of questions, I am mindful of, and concur with, Neill, *Issues of Death*, 15: 'The bizarre liveliness of the figures of Death, on which viewers invariably comment, serves only to underline their impersonal sameness stressing the paradox that to envisage death is to personify a radical defacement.'

[29] Israel Scheffler, 'Words and Pictures—Mention-selection and Mental Process', *Language of Design*, 3 (1995), 46.

While we have recourse to realistically rendered pictures of static corpses and to allegorical images of dynamic skeletons used to convey death, there is nothing actually walking in the world to which we can point that will teach us what death is. Still, some kind of mental transfer, as part of a recognition process, takes place when such an illustration, like the title-page of Warwicke's book, is confronted. Israel Scheffler's description of what happens when children play can be extended to apply to what happens when adults partake of the perhaps more sophisticated play involving allegorical images. '[T]he broomstick indeed signifies, stands for, or denotes horses. . . . In galloping along on his broomstick, the child fantasizes himself as riding on a horse, not a stick, even though he knows he is straddling a stick, not a horse. The representative character of the stick enables him thus to use it in play' (p. 51).

Johan Huizinga has addressed this theme with respect to how images and rituals, like religious allegories, take hold of us and transform not only our thoughts but also how we experience and make sense of the world.[30]

Whether one is a sorcerer or sorcerized, one is always knower and dupe at once. But one chooses to be the dupe. The savage is a good actor who can be quite absorbed in his role, like a child at play; and also like a child, a good spectator who can be frightened to death by the roaring of something he knows perfectly well to be no 'real' lion. The native, says Malinowski, feels and fears his belief rather than formulates it clearly to himself.[31]

Huizinga goes on to say that 'despite this partial consciousness of things "not being real" in magic and supernatural phenomena generally, these authorities still warn us against drawing the inference that the whole system of beliefs and practices is only a fraud' (pp. 23–4).

Thus the deadly breath of a lungless skeleton, while obviously 'not real', still leaves us with a sense of vulnerability that the dark power underlying the meaning of such an image might be un-

---

[30] Huizinga, *Homo Ludens*, 23.
[31] Bronislaw Malinowski, *Argonauts of the Western Pacific* (1922; repr. Prospect Heights, Ill.: Waveland Press, 1984), 339.

leashed unless we can combat it (Fig. 5). One way to prepare, is to be ready with an image of Death, which, talisman-like, is a sympathetic weapon, understood to allay just such an assault from what allegorically it depicts.[32] By heeding what the image and accompanying words portend, one might just imagine that one keeps Death at bay, for a while, while developing a life-strategy designed to propel oneself, in the end, beyond death.

And yet a tacit level of anxiety accompanies the confrontation of such horrifying figures, whether or not one adheres to the system of beliefs from whence they derive. They conjure up fears one might otherwise not have imagined; and even if one had, those images are rendered more vividly and violently than otherwise might have been considered without such visual prompting. Those who were not raised in a culture that endows such notions with power over one's behaviour and actions, or those who were thus trained but who choose to reject them as irrelevant to their daily life, may see in such images only the patent absurdity of these things ever coming to pass. However one reacts to such figures, though, we need to consider what is transpiring through the interplay of what we believe to be real and what we fear might actually be. We need to consider just how it is that people circumscribe it and contain it, perhaps as an image, perhaps as an experience, perhaps both. We need to consider further how exactly, in the spirit of play, it is to be confronted. As Huizinga noted:

[T]he apparently quite simple question of what play really is, leads us deep into the problem of the nature and origin of religious concepts. . . . When a certain form of religion accepts a sacred identity between two things of a different order, say a human being and an animal, this relationship is not adequately expressed by calling it a 'symbolic correspondence' as *we* conceive this. The identity, the essential oneness of the two goes far deeper than the correspondence between a substance and its symbolic image. It is a mystic unity. The one has *become* the other. In his magic dance the savage *is* a kangaroo. (p. 25)

How are we then to understand the persistent and lingering idea of the magic and power of the image even when it is carefully

[32] James Frazer, *The Golden Bough* (1890; repr. Oxford: Oxford University Press, 1994), 26–7, 285–95, 589.

En lapocalipse est escript que sait iehã vit vng cheual de couleur palle sur le quel seoit la mort ⁊ enfer suyuoit ce cheual. le cheual segnifie le pecheur q̃ a la couleur palle pour sa maladie de peche. ⁊ porte la mort. car peche est la mort de lame. ⁊ enfer le suyt pour lengloutir sil mouroit impenitent.

Sur ce cheual hideux ⁊ palle
La mort suis fierement assise
Il nest beaulte que ie ne halle
Soit vermeille ou blanche ou bise
Mon cheual court cõe la bise
Et en courant mort rue et frappe
Mais ie tue tout cest ma guise
Tout hõme trebuche en ma trappe
Je passe par mons et par vaulx
Sans tenir ne voye ne sente
Je prens par villes ⁊ chasteaulx.
Mon tribut mon sens ⁊ ma rête
Sans donner ne delay nattente
Ne iour ne heure ne demye
Deuant moy fault quon se presente.
A tous viuans iotte la vie

Enfer sait bien quelle tuerie
De gens ie fais car pas a pas
Me suyt et de ma boucherie
Lhũn an fait de gros repas
Quãt ie besoigne il ne dort pas
Par moy attent que proye aura
Daulcun qui ne sen doubte pas
Sen garde qui garder vouldra
Encor me suyt rayson pour quoy
De ceulx que tue de mon dart
Et sont sans nombre croyes moy
Car il en a la plus grant part
Paradis nen a pas le quart
Ne le disme on luy fait tort
Grant si nauoit ou tost ou tart
Lhõme pecheur quãt il est mort   g

Fig. 5. Fierce death rides forth

circumscribed, either literally or in terms of a contained set of conventions ('it is just an allegory')? How are we to understand the transforming power of the symbolic image, especially as it pertains to an Aesthetic of Decline? These are the kinds of questions posed as well by James George Frazer:

> How was it that intelligent men did not sooner detect the fallacy of magic? How could they continue to cherish expectations that were invariably doomed to disappointment? With what heart persist in playing venerable antics that led to nothing, and mumbling solemn balderdash that remained without effect? Why cling to beliefs which were so flatly contradicted by experience? The answer seems to be that the fallacy was far from easy to detect, the failure by no means obvious, since in many, perhaps in most cases the desired event did actually follow, at a longer or shorter interval, the performance of the rite which was designed to bring it about.[33]

Much in the same way as the 'primitives' discussed by Frazer, we moderns (though of course in our own distinctive, culturally and historically bound ways), at times wilfully and at times unconsciously merge and disregard the prevalent categories used for denoting differences between the visible and invisible worlds, between a representation and what it signifies. In part this is explained by the 'play element in culture'; namely, that we like to move from one register of thought to another, from the concrete to the abstract, the material to the spiritual. We enjoy being duped, all the while remaining aware, though perhaps only remotely, that we are being taken in by illusions.[34] Part I takes such a view to task, as a way of looking critically, in Parts II and III, at other sorts of accommodations, through language and history, made during the Renaissance that paid tribute to the double truth of our being, of our going 'from hence, by this to that'.

SHADES OF MEMORY

Through careful scrutiny of the conventions giving life to tragic dramas, to the dictionaries and foreign-language phrase-books,

---

[33] Frazer, *The Golden Bough*, 58.

[34] Jonas Barish, *The Antitheatrical Prejudice* (Berkeley, Los Angeles, and London: University of California Press, 1981), 107.

and to historical writings—and by attending to the mnemonic component associated with each (namely emblems, proverbs, and *exempla* respectively)—this book taps into the internal logic by which the Memory Arts communicate to the spirit what cannot be apprehended by the intellect alone. It thus builds on major claims about visual literacy and aids to memory from benchmark studies of European intellectual history to reveal the extent to which this Art of Memory gave shape to specific dramatic curiosities and formal literary tendencies in the English Renaissance.

Most notably, my book resumes Frances Yates's argument that renewed attention to the classical Memory Arts is a prerequisite for advances in Renaissance scholarship.[35] Her conclusion amounts to a challenge to scholars of early modern culture, a challenge taken up in earnest here: 'The history of the organization of memory touches at vital points on the history of religion and ethics, of philosophy and psychology, of art and literature, of scientific method.'[36] More specifically, with a focus on Renaissance drama and metaphors drawn from drama, this book explores the implications of Yates's contention that: 'The emotionally striking images of classical memory, transformed by the devout Middle Ages into corporal similitudes, in the Renaissance are transformed again into magically powerful images.'[37]

The first two chapters develop a theoretical foundation validating the use of terms like 'magically powerful images', while the final three look critically at how such images returned in other, more self-consciously literary, forms. Throughout, however, my project is concerned with the extent to which the forms being investigated were understood in the Renaissance to carry a trace of their original theurgic power, something beyond mortal efforts alone, to affect change in the world.

But this is not a book about Renaissance magic or about religious controversies. It is rather about how recourse to the classical

---

[35] Frances A. Yates, 'Autobiographical Fragments', in *Ideas and Ideals in the North European Renaissance, Collected Essays III* (London: Routledge & Kegan Paul, 1984), 320.

[36] Frances A. Yates, *The Art of Memory* (1966; repr. Penguin Books, 1978), 374.

[37] Ibid. 161.

Art of Memory enabled Renaissance dramatists and essayists to conjure and evoke commonplace figures of speech and visual conventions, and then, once having set them to work in traditional ways, used them to produce some startlingly original effects. Again I take my lead from Yates: 'Amongst the most characteristic types of Renaissance cultivation of imagery are the emblem and the impresa. These phenomena have never been looked at from the point of view of memory to which they clearly belong. The impresa, in particular, is an attempt to remember a spiritual intention through a similitude.'[38]

With this in mind, my book takes up from Elizabeth Eisenstein's research. She found that, after the advent of printing, 'visual aids multiplied, signs and symbols were codified; different kinds of iconographic and nonphonetic communication were rapidly developed'.[39] Eisenstein, like Walter Ong, takes quite seriously the unprecedented proliferation of memory systems rich in visual allegories during the first century of printing, but, owing to their respective research topics, neither pushes on to investigate it in depth.[40] *Death and Drama*, therefore, takes as its principal concern the different kinds of iconographic and non-phonetic communication that came to be associated, typically, with Renaissance Memory Theatres. And since all such devices were designed to compensate for the limitations of the mind, I look as well at how notions of human frailty and transience were figured into the mix. This book will be concerned with visual aids of the day, especially those touching our mortality, to see to what end they were reproduced and represented; and, in the process, how they came to transform the simple mirror-effect that had been a standard feature of earlier forms of allegory, both in drama and in the telling of history.

And so while the first part of my book relies on the findings of George Kernodle regarding the origin of some dramatic

---

[38] Ibid. 130.

[39] Elizabeth L. Eisenstein, *The Printing Revolution in Early Modern Europe* (1983; repr. Cambridge: Cambridge University Press, 1998), 38.

[40] Ibid. 35–40; and see Walter Ong, *Ramus: Method and the Decay of Dialogue* (1953; repr. Cambridge and London: Harvard University Press, 1983), 83–91, 121.

conventions, it takes a novel turn by looking with a steady and critical eye at the silent staging of death in terms of what I have termed 'fatal perspective'. For, as Kernodle proposed, 'the *tableaux vivants* furnish us with important links between art and theatre. With a knowledge of the habits of mind established in art and pageantry, we can approach afresh the problems of the Renaissance theatre.'[41] *Death and Drama* is the first thorough-going study of these problems as they pertain to representative English tragedies and plays of mourning.[42] But more than this, it is the first attempt ever to look at the 'habits of mind established in art and pageantry' in terms of an affinity between the essentially theatrical way that cultural memory gets organized during the English literary Renaissance and an overriding Aesthetic of Decline.[43]

The term aesthetic, in this study, refers to that branch of philo-sophical inquiry concerned, historically, with perceptions of the beautiful, and which has been extended in recent times to take into account the stunning, the grotesque, and the wondrous.[44] Building on Edgar Wind's premiss that 'disguise is one of the great forces of revelation',[45] my project aims at recovering and situating in their original contexts the formal, though often concealed, mnemonic features of plays and books that happened also to be associated

[41] George R. Kernodle, *From Art to Theatre: Form and Convention in the Renaissance* (Chicago: University of Chicago Press, 1947), 6.

[42] In referring to 'plays of mourning' I have chosen a term that gives coherence to a variety of theatrical events staged during the English Renaissance and delib-erately invokes the work of Walter Benjamin (*Ursprung des deutschen Trauer-spiels*). See Max Pensky, *Melancholy Dialectics: Walter Benjamin and the Play of Mourning* (Amherst: University of Massachusetts Press, 1993), 47.

[43] George Williamson, 'Mutability, Decay, and Jacobean Melancholy', *Seven-teenth Century Contexts* (London: Faber & Faber, 1960); Victor Harris, *All Coherence Gone* (Chicago: University of Chicago Press, 1949); Marjorie Hope Nicolson, *The Breaking of the Circle: Studies on the Effect of the 'New Science' on Seventeenth Century Poetry* (Evanston: Northwestern University Press, 1950); Joseph A. Mazzeo, *Renaissance and Revolution: The Remaking of European Thought* (New York: Pantheon Books, 1965).

[44] Immanuel Kant, *Critique of Judgment*, trans. Werner S. Pluhar (Indianapolis: Hackett Publishing, 1987), 165–70. Cf. Wolfgang Kayser, *The Grotesque in Art and Literature*, trans. Ulrich Weisstein (New York: Columbia University Press, 1981), 31, 186–8; and John Sallis, *Stone* (Bloomington and Indianapolis: Indiana University Press, 1994), 3.

[45] Wind, *Pagan Mysteries*, 16.

with the Renaissance Aesthetic of Decline. For, above all else, this book seeks to help scholars of early modern England become better, more mnemonically attuned, interpreters of scenes by Shakespeare and his contemporaries, and to become better-equipped voyagers in the sea of citations typical of seventeenth-century prose compendia involving universal history; and, in both cases, to become more active participants in locating and working through the cryptic designs often deposited at the core of these cultural, essentially literary, forms of knowledge. In attempting this, I take my lead once more from Wind: 'Aesthetically speaking, there can be no doubt that the presence of unresolved residues of meaning is an obstacle to the enjoyment of art.... In literature, the same sort of embarrassment may be caused by Spenser's, Chapman's, or even Shakespeare's verse in a reader' (pp. 15–16).

And yet *Death and Drama* maintains that the symbols and images associated with Renaissance cultural commonplaces are not as easily 'read' as might generally be assumed. In this regard David Cressy speaks for my project, as well as for his own, when he admonishes his readers about the danger 'in projecting present preoccupations onto the past, and in bringing our opinions to the evidence rather than deriving them from it'.[46] And while I agree with Cressy that 'the margins illuminate the centre, and that the cultural history of early modern England is incomplete without hearing from people on the edge' (p. 7), it is also incomplete without our finding a way to see what is obscured by our contemporary cultural blind-spot. The Art of Memory is the corrective lens that can bring back into view just such aspects of the Renaissance mental life and letters. For my book, unlike Cressy's, is not concerned with a variety of disparate voices of people from the edge, but with the visual metaphors we can recover from the literary remains of dramatists and writers in the thick of things, and yet who were sidetracked by matters that just kept them from acceding to the positions of power and influence to which they aspired.

Specifically, the Introduction looks at Quarles, Wither, and

---

[46] David Cressy, *Travesties and Transgression in Tudor and Stuart England* (Oxford: Oxford University Press, 2000), 114.

Featley; Part I salvages the perspective glasses constructed on
stage by ingenious playwrights like Kyd, Chapman, and Webster,
among others; Part II recovers the easy commerce with Memory
Palaces demonstrated by the extravagant phrase-maker and exu-
berant translator, John Florio; Part III unveils the mirrors of truth
polished by Walter Ralegh and Alexander Ross in their efforts to
write of the world's past and its destiny in a way that provided a
glimpse of the soul of history. Each of these writers, in his own
way, sought to bring under his control what of the world he could,
by contracting it into an emblematic world-in-miniature, using
memory images and mnemonic techniques that were informed by
an Aesthetic of Decline. The Conclusion brings my argument full
circle by looking, in passing, at the origins of religious drama,
'a special act of invention in which impersonation, action, and
dialogue happen to come together',[47] to crystallize how memory
images in the Renaissance came to store and disclose, and to
translate and revive, their symbolic contents and backlog of cultural meanings. We shall then cast a parting glance toward key
translations of classical descriptions concerning those who are beyond meaningful existence in the world, though not yet beyond
the reach of art and language. The main goal of this book, then,
is to recover, in their original contexts, cunning responses to the
ease with which death was figured, and reconfigured, during the
English Renaissance.

  In bringing to light these recessed elements of the literary culture of the period, I remain mindful that 'the past is another country, they do things differently there',[48] and I have sought to attend
to its 'sometimes disorienting affective power'. In this latter respect, although I am more concerned with the history of ideas, my
project bears comparison to that of Albert Tricomi, which 'chal-
lenges the new-historicist habit of offering synchronic readings of
culture while ignoring diachronic ones'.[49] And yet my book has no

---

[47] Hardin Craig, *English Religious Drama of the Middle Ages* (Oxford:
Clarendon Press, 1955), 4, 9.
[48] David Lowenthal, *The Past is a Foreign Country* (1985; repr. Cambridge
University Press, 1995), p. xvi; the citation comes from L. P. Hartley's *The Go-
Between*.
[49] Tricomi, *Reading Tudor-Stuart Texts*, 8, 17.

quarrels with what others have chosen to do to the plays and books that likewise have attracted my scholarly attention. And so, if my book does not give 'readings' of isolated narratives or historical events, and if it does not engage recent trends in 'new critical readings and cultural configurations', like those discussed by Tricomi, it is because I am committed to another course. *Death and Drama* instead offers a mnemonically oriented account of how the predominating form of allegory, based on *mimesis* (that is, imitation; showing one thing in terms of another), was played out, quite literally, during the seventeenth century. In line with this goal, my book presumes that literacy, of whatever sort and no matter what the medium, involves a diverse set of procedures for acting on and thinking about language and images, the world and ourselves.

This larger concern, central to my project, takes off from David Olson's *The World on Paper*, which draws on recent advances in history, anthropology, linguistics, and psychology. Like Olson, I am sceptical of the tendency among some interpreters of literature to treat cultural artefacts as if they were texts whose meanings become transparent once the filter of this critical methodology or that current theory is applied. As a corrective, I take the next step that follows from Olson's argument: 'If literacy is thought of as simply the basic skills of recognizing emblems or of decoding letters to sound or words to meaning, the implications of literacy, while important, are bound to be limited.'[50] Such a limited model of literacy, of reading per se, is one that this book seeks to move beyond, and to favour instead a network of interpretive possibilities grounded in a mnemonic approach to recovering commonplaces of Renaissance life and culture.

My book is able to take such a decisive stand thanks to recent developments in this area of Medieval and Renaissance studies,[51] all of which help to realize Frances Yates's dream of 'a renewed, or

[50] David R. Olson, *The World on Paper: The Conceptual and Cognitive Implications of Writing and Reading* (Cambridge: Cambridge University Press, 1994), 17–18.

[51] See esp. Bruno Roy and Paul Zumthor, *Jeux de Mémoire: Aspects de la mnémotechnie médiévale* (Montréal: Presses de l'Université de Montréal, 1985); and Claire Sherman, *Writing on Hands: Memory and Knowledge in Early Modern Europe* (Madison: University of Wisconsin Press, 2000).

quite new study' of the 'deep-seated movements of the human spirit', reflected in the literature of the seventeenth century.[52] Mary Carruthers, in particular, has explored 'the need for human beings to "see" their thoughts in their minds as organized schemata of images, or "pictures," and then to use these for further thinking.'[53] Further, by building on such work, my project now is able to push beyond my earlier, somewhat cautious, claim about using Memory Theatres to understand how allegorical imagery functioned in the Renaissance. Thus, the methodological approach which I previously termed 'mnemonic criticism', and limited to an interpretive model for works of literature, is seen in *Death and Drama* as a fundamental feature of the organization, not only of memory, but also of knowledge in general, during the early modern period.[54] The use of mnemonics in the seventeenth century, especially when self-consciously employed by the likes of dramatists like Webster and Ford and essayists like Ralegh and Ross, is thus shown to be more than just a *technique* (a tool for thinking and inventing),[55] but also a dominant, if carefully and at times self-consciously deployed, cultural practice with important ramifications for intellectual history, especially as pertains to the Aesthetic of Decline.

This book developed initially as a response to two issues from my previous work on emblems and melancholy. First, although I developed a model for reading the encyclopedic prose of the seventeenth century (mainly Burton and Browne) based on Renaissance notions of the emblem (the combination of image, motto, and commentary), I had not considered the extent to which the

[52] Frances A. Yates, 'Bacon and the Menace of English Literature', review of Brian Vickers, *Francis Bacon and Renaissance Prose*, and Joan Webber, *The Eloquent 'I': Style and Self in Seventeenth-Century Prose*, in *New York Review of Books*, 27 Mar. 1969, repr. in *Collected Essays III*, 67–74, 72.

[53] Mary Carruthers, *The Craft of Thought: Meditation, Rhetoric, and the Making of Images, 400–1200* (Cambridge, 1998), 3.

[54] Mary Carruthers, 'Inventional Mnemonics and the Ornaments of Style: The Case of Etymology', *Connotations*, 2: 2 (1992), 103, a response to my 'Mnemonic Criticism and Renaissance Literature: A Manifesto', *Connotations*, 1 (1991), 12–33.

[55] Carruthers, 'Inventional Mnemonics', 104; see also her *Craft of Thought*, 155–61, and *The Book of Memory* (Cambridge, 1990), 156–88.

metaphor of reading predetermines what, in the end, is able to be discovered.[56] *Death and Drama* is more vigilant about the way some metaphors and figures of speech can be so full of accrued cultural meanings that they predestine what we are able to see in what we read. This applies especially to the metaphor of 'reading' itself. And, even though *Mapping Mortality* demonstrated the extent to which Renaissance cognitive processes and symbol systems were mnemonic in both conception and application, often based on the relation of body and soul,[57] it did not take into account how such structures of thought and related social practices took on what in anthropological circles are referred to as magical properties—namely, totemic elements and talismanic associations.[58] This book redresses these issues.

My argument in *Mapping Mortality* about the transformation of the image of Death in the Renaissance emblematic imagination is mentioned specifically in Michael Neill's *Issues of Death*.[59] Since then I have been rethinking the larger questions raised by this topic, and this book recasts and resolves them, but in a way that differs from Neill's nuanced readings of a host of tragedies with respect to issues of identity. My somewhat more structural treatment of Renaissance plays—some of the same ones discussed by Neill—focuses instead on the essentially mnemonic conventions informing them, as a way to account for their persistent dwelling on representations of death and on what is lost, past, and gone. Also, rather than make drama the principal subject of my

---

[56] William E. Engel, 'Emblems and *Sententiae* in Seventeenth Century Prose: Mystical and Literary Design in Robert Burton and Thomas Browne', Ph.D. thesis, University of California, Berkeley, 1988; Dissertation Abstracts International, 48 (1988), 2193-A.

[57] Engel, *Mapping Mortality*.

[58] I am building on the terminology popularized by Frazer, 'Magic and Religion', in *The Golden Bough*, which is validated by the fieldwork of Bronislaw Malinowski, 'Magic and the Kula' and 'The Power of Words in Magic', in *Argonauts of the Western Pacific*. See also Malinowski, *Coral Gardens and Their Magic* (1935; repr. Bloomington: Indiana University Press, 1965), and Claude Lévi-Strauss, 'The Effectiveness of Symbols', *Structural Anthropology*, trans. Claire Jacobson and Brooke Grunfest Schoepf (New York: Basic Books, 1963).

[59] Cf. Neill, *Issues of Death*, 14, 73, 74, 147; and Engel, *Mapping Mortality*, 72, 74–5, 81–3, 169–88.

inquiry, I have situated it with respect to other literary forms as well, especially foreign-language phrase-books in Part II and historical writing in Part III.

This book thus sets in motion an alternative approach to tragic drama and plays of mourning, by paying special heed to the ways they are reanimated by the Art of Memory. My project shows the extent to which encoded mnemonics, in the form of metaphors and symbols, like any special set of images or commemorative rituals—but especially those touching our mortality—condition how people come to see the world and come to recognize and, subsequently, to narrate and fix, their place in it. I argue that, insofar as what thus ends up being discovered necessarily partakes of the symbolic schemes conceived within (and which, to a certain extent, can be said to characterize) the culture, it comes to function essentially as a memory-picture, as a mnemonic place-holder, set up as a barrier against oblivion.

PART I

Staging Kinetic Emblems of Fatal Destiny

I

'Commonplaces of memory': Visual Regimes and Charmed Spaces

> Show! Show! Show!
> Show his eyes and grieve his heart!
> Come like shadows, so depart!
> (Shakespeare, *Macbeth*, 4.1.123–5)

The epigraph to this chapter comes from lines chanted by those who 'look not like inhabitants o' the earth | And yet are on't'. These words herald the last of the dumb shows that presage the culmination of Macbeth's fatal destiny. The mimed action is conjured up, within the world of the play, using supernatural means. The imagination is thus haunted by an arresting set of memory images involving a pageant of history, revealing to Macbeth a succession of kings that will come in the future, but to the Jacobean audience a succession of kings from the past leading up to the present. The silent procession is ushered in with a charm that calls forth a special space from within the world of the drama, and yet which points beyond it.[1] As such it is framed in a double sense. The pageant of kings involves the staging, and then the narrating, of the newly invoked spectacle, which, within the world of the play is produced by supernatural means, and by theatrical artifice for those of us outside of it.[2] We watch the victim, the

---

[1] On the implications of 'space' as it is used throughout this chapter, see Edward S. Casey, *The Fate of Place: A Philosophical History* (Berkeley: University of California Press, 1997), 134, 167–79.

[2] Arthur F. Kinney, 'Speculating Shakespeare, 1605–1016', in R. B. Parker and S. P. Zitner (eds.), *Elizabethan Theatre: Essays in Honor of S. Schoenbaum* (Newark: University of Delaware Press, 1996), 266.

tragic hero, watch the silent procession, which is then glossed and explained.[3] Like Macbeth, although we resist admitting to ourselves that we have sought to become passive recipients of the images displayed through this conjured perspective glass, we give way to it and let it guide and constrain our inner gaze. The dynamic of its reception, no less than a valid response to such spectacles, is expressed cogently in the line 'Show his eyes and grieve his heart!'

Such emblematic spectacles, especially those portraying images of fatal destiny, are essentially mnemonic in form, content, and character. Moreover, dumb shows and related emblematic scenes in English Renaissance drama reproduce the same principles of design as those underlying the pageant of the kings from *Macbeth*. These principles have both aesthetic and epistemological implications. For example, Guy Debord has analysed the spectacle as being not so much something created to reveal something new, as much as something which conceals its true origins and, in the end, is self-reflexive:

The spectacle is not a collection of images, but a social relation among people, mediated by images. . . . The language of the spectacle consists of signs of the ruling production, which at the same time are the ultimate goal of this production. . . . The concept of 'spectacle' unifies and explains a great diversity of apparent phenomena. . . . Considered in its own terms, the spectacle is affirmation of appearance and affirmation of all human life, namely social life, as mere appearance. But the critique which reaches the truth of the spectacle exposes it as the visible *negation* of life, as a negation of life which *has become visible*. To describe the spectacle, its formation, its functions and the forces which tend to dissolve it, one must artificially distinguish certain inseparable elements. When analyzing the spectacle one speaks, to some extent, the language of the spectacular itself in the sense that one moves through the methodological terrain of the very society which expresses itself in the spectacle. . . . In the spectacle, which is the image of the ruling economy, the goal is nothing, development everything. The spectacle aims at nothing other than itself.[4]

---

[3] Dianne Hunter, 'Doubling, Mythic Difference and the Scapegoating of Female Power in *Macbeth*', *Psychoanalytic Review*, 75: 1 (1988).

[4] Guy Debord, *La Société du spectacle* (1967; trans. and rev. Detroit: Black & Red, 1983), secs. 4–14.

The spectacle, then, is to be understood as a function of a host of variable and often vying cultural forces. This accords well with Aby Warburg's view of art, particularly where symbolic images are involved, as an organ of social memory. More specifically, Warburg maintained that embedded within certain conventional forms of stylized and highly symbolic artifice, like the dumb show, we can detect the seed of some enduring aspect of shared memory, the visible remnants of a kind of cultural residue. We might even say, a shade of memory. It is preserved and transmitted by way of an energy not known to the physical world.[5] Any event effecting living matter leaves a trace, which Warburg, using the terminology of his day, called an 'engram'. Ernst Gombrich has clarified this theory of the symbol as follows:

The potential energy conserved in this 'engram' may, under suitable conditions, be reactivated and discharged—we then say the organism acts in a specific way because it *remembers* the previous event. This goes for the individual no less than for the species. It was this concept of mnemic energy, preserved in 'engrams,' but obeying laws comparable to those of physics which attracted Warburg when he took up theories of his youth on the nature of the symbol and its function in the social organism.

While we need not subscribe in full to this speculative philosophy concerning the symbol to see how it can help us elucidate certain dramatic responses to rhetorically charmed space, the idea of 'engrams' provides an apt point of departure for discussing a peculiar process of theatricality exemplified through dumb shows. Warburg's notion of the mnemonic symbol as part of larger theory concerning specific cultural accretions and their continued circulation and transmission can be applied with instructive results to scenes from Renaissance drama.

For, according to Warburg's theory of social memory, the symbol in the collective mind of a given community or culture corresponds to the engram in the nervous system of the individual. Put differently: symbols are to a culture what engrams are to

---

[5] Richard Semon's theory, expounded in *Die Mneme als erhaltendes Princip im Wechsel des organischen Geschehens*, 2nd edn. (Leipzig, 1908), formed the basis of Warburg's extended ruminations on mnemic energy; see E. H. Gombrich, *Aby Warburg: An Intellectual Biography* (Chicago: University of Chicago Press, 1986), 242.

an individual. Symbols, as cultural creations, are thus charged with individual, engramic, energies waiting to be released or otherwise transferred. Warburg's understanding of engrams, seen in the light of Debord's analysis of the spectacle, gives us a way to characterize and critically assess the aesthetic core of what takes place in the staging of fatal perspective in Renaissance tragedies. And so let us go back to Shakespeare, but consider now another kind of staged event, which, within the frame of the play, likewise sets out to 'show his eyes and grieve his heart!'

THE CUNNING OF THE SCENE

The dumb show preceding the murder of Gonzago is at the heart of *Hamlet*. It is central both with respect to its place in Shakespeare's narrative design, and also to how artifice is set up to work in the world created by the play. It marks off a curious mnemonic space, integral to the forecasting and consummation of the play's dramatic action. Like a vacuole in a cell, complete in and of itself, this space seems to hold the rest of the world of the play temporarily at bay even as it tacitly reinforces the integrity of the disparate parts of the whole. Like a vacuole, it absorbs the shocks caused by the play's fits and starts as it moves inexorably toward its destination. The dumb show heralds the 'mousetrap' designed to 'catch the conscience of the king'. The rationale behind the imputed affective power of such a mimetic event is made clear earlier in the play. After hearing the player recite the death of Priam, Hamlet recalls and does in part believe:

> That guilty creatures sitting at a play
> Have, by the very cunning of the scene,
> Been struck so to the soul that presently
> They have proclaim'd their malefactions.[6]

Hamlet then seeks to appropriate the symbolic power of the spectacle for his own end. It is 'the very cunning of the scene' that is of interest here, as well as the scene itself, for it bespeaks how one

---

[6] Shakespeare, *Hamlet*, ed. Harold Jenkins (London and New York: Methuen, 1982), 2.2.585–8. See also Arthur Brown, 'The Play Within a Play: An Elizabethan Dramatic Device', *Essays and Studies* (1960), 36–48.

comes to respond to being confronted by an affective image resulting in one's being struck to the soul. Is expert acting required or is it the subject-matter alone that can move viewers to see themselves reflected in a mimetic moral mirror? Neither Aristotle's famous dictum about fear and pity nor the modern understanding of catharsis fully accounts for what generates the power by which people in general, and guilty creatures in particular, are jolted out of ordinary existence and made to speak their hearts.[7]

Using Warburg's premiss, though, we can speak of how this comes about in other words: through the represented symbolic actions of the drama, the potential energy conserved in the engram is activated and released. When this happens one can be seen to act on, and in accord with, the remembrance of previous events stirred up by virtue of the cunning of the scene.[8] Thoughts from disparate times and situations are recalled and brought into proximity with one another as a result of the activation of the engram within the individual. Warburg reflected on this process of energy transfer in his notebook: 'The problem of the Renaissance now presents itself as that of the metamorphosis of the energy of the human and individual self-awareness caused by the polarization due to the reinstatement of the memory images of energy-peaks in the classical past—more briefly, "dynamic polarization through restored memory".'[9]

It is with respect to this notion of restored memory that the immemorial theurgic power of drama comes into play and offers itself to our scrutiny. 'Theurgy' derives from the Greek terms signifying 'god' and 'working'. Originally it implied a system of incantations and ceremonies used by Neoplatonists to enlist the aid of spirits to produce miraculous effects. During the Renaissance, largely due to the efforts of Ficino, it indicated that branch of the magical sciences concerned with the production of effects by supernatural, rather than natural, agencies. Viewed less

---

[7] Cf. Hardin Craig, *English Religious Drama*, 4–5.

[8] Jonas Barish, 'Remembering and Forgetting in Shakespeare', in R. B. Parker and S. P. Zitner (eds.), *Elizabethan Theatre: Essays in Honor of S. Schoenbaum* (Newark: University of Delaware Press, 1996), 222; James P. Hammersmith, '*Hamlet* and the Myth of Memory', *English Literary History*, 45 (1978), 598.

[9] Gombrich, *Warburg*, 241–2, n. 3.

historically, as a social phenomenon, theurgic impulses seem to leave their mark anywhere that rituals and rites are practised, whether in a religious context or on stage—or both.

At all events, the key to understanding the 'cunning of the scene' comes from the word 'cunning' itself, which provides a viable way to examine and recover the mnemonic underpinnings of stylized aesthetic devices like dumb shows. Not only does cunning mean skilful or clever, implying deceit or craftiness, but also carried along within the term is the archaic connotation of possessing magical knowledge, including skill in the occult arts.[10] The place where such cunning is exercised—and exorcised—on stage is marked off from within the space of the encompassing spectacle. The root etymology of 'spectacle' can help us see deeper into the way dramas have been said to hold a mirror up to nature: it indicates the process of looking, often through a device, a glass—perhaps a window, mirror, or lens—designed to assist defective, inadequate, or partial sight.

Dumb shows open up, and to some extent are, windows onto another space—one that materially and mimetically remains contained within, but which metaphysically and allegorically reaches beyond, the contours of the main spectacle. They are like miniature mirrors within the larger mirror of the play which conventionally show 'actions that a man might play', to use Hamlet's designation for the outward display of sentiments or intentions. But in the case of dumb shows depicting fatal scenes, like the one in the middle of *Hamlet* that condenses, and allegorically refracts, the play's—and the culture's—crux of kinship and kingship, of cunning and *cyning*,[11] what is it exactly that we are being invited, impelled, and trained to see? What would have been the affective power of such visual commonplaces, given the prevalent regimes of visibility and the accepted codes of legibility?[12]

[10] Cf. 2 *Henry VI* (4.1.34), Suffolk, upon meeting Walter Whitmore says, 'Thy name affrights me, in whose sound is death. | A cunning man did calculate my birth, | And told me that by water I should die.'

[11] The Anglo-Saxon *cyning* means king; *cunnan*, whence is derived our 'cunning', means to know how to do something; *Beowulf*, ed. C. L. Wrenn (London: George G. Harrap, 1958), 240–1.

[12] Clark Hulse, *The Rule of Art: Literature and Painting in the Renaissance* (Chicago: University of Chicago Press, 1990), esp. 151–80; and David Evett,

My approach to these questions steers clear of any answer that relies exclusively on interpreting the images that the spectacle reproduces. The content of such representations is a decisive factor for understanding the events in the world of the play, and yet this is but part of the larger equation. To be sure, though, an informed, 'historicized reading' of the particular images is integral to any reliable recovery of the audience's expectations about what they imagined they were seeing in and by means of the spectacle.[13] And yet, to recall Debord's warning, the spectacle, above all else, as part of its defining character, is bound to reflect its own conditions of artifice. However, if we gaze intently enough at the way the spectacle is said to reflect and carry within itself both the affirmation of its constitutive images and also their negation, then we can begin to twist free from the cycle of reification and mimetic reflection by noting that, when a charmed space is activated in a Renaissance drama, it tends to bring with it some sort of commentary on the conditions of its artificiality. This is especially evident in spectacles involving the emblematic display of fatal perspective. And so, of the many ways we might understand what we are invited, impelled, and trained to see in such spectacles, we will focus on the distinctively mnemonic assumptions informing and animating metatheatrical episodes that also involve death.

While the 'counterfeit presentment' of a corpse or a funeral procession might bring to the stage a moment of stasis, of hushed awe or reverential silence, such episodes, as the plays within which they occur make clear, tend to generate a world of activity around them. This chapter, therefore, addresses the peculiar sense of aesthetics associated with cunning scenes that rhetorically evoke, and then self-consciously stage, fatal perspectives of silent death. The principal aim is to show the extent to which the contours of this cunning fatal perspective in Renaissance drama come into focus when we take into account the overlapping of emblems and the Memory Arts. Moreover, these two traditions, namely the emblem and the Art of Memory, bear comparison to the dual

Literature and the Visual Arts in Tudor England (Athens and London: University of Georgia Press, 1990), esp. 125–54.

[13] Albert Tricomi, *Reading Tudor-Stuart Texts Through Cultural Historicism* (Gainesville: University of Florida Press, 1996), 2, 6.

components of Warburg's psycho-cultural schema of 'symbol' and 'engram': emblems, like symbols, grow out of and reflect larger cultural concerns, collapsing much in little, while the Memory Arts, like engrams, record steps in an individual's journey that point the way toward a larger sphere of involvement with things in the world.

The next section establishes the extent to which dumb shows shared formal and aesthetic affinities with visual emblems. Further, emblems were part of the visual shorthand typically used in Renaissance Memory Theatres. Emblems, like their verbal counterpart, *sententiae*, together with other related mnemonic-ally encoded devices, readily were transferred to the Renaissance stage. Such devices, by virtue of their underlying structural and aesthetic principles, conjured into being a special space from within the dramatic spectacle that enabled them to refer beyond what they were put in place simply to signify. In the world of the play they create a cunning kind of double perspective, thus making it possible for 'point of view' to become tacitly equated with the achievement of some sort of moral perspective.[14] But, as my analysis of scenes depicting silent death in *The Revenger's Tragedy* and *The Spanish Tragedy* indicates, this is not to say that it was concerned with gaining higher moral ground. Rather what we find is an amoral 'no man's land' that takes shape in the theatre of our mind as a process of thought,[15] thus making it possible to scan beyond the limits of what the material staging of such per-spectives ostensibly allowed. This opens the way for us to ask more pointedly about the theurgic power of the artifice, effects, and machines accounting for the 'stage magic' that facilitates the cunning of the scene. In particular: what was the Renaissance audience invited, impelled, and trained to see in such spectacles of silent death? And so, after establishing several fundamental points about the visual regimes operating during the period, the next chapter will consider emblematic trigger points in Webster's *The White Devil*, Chapman's *Bussy D'Ambois*, and Ford's *The Broken Heart*.

[14] Michael Neill, 'The Moral Artifice of *The Lovers Melancholy*', *English Literary Renaissance*, 8 (1978), 85–106.

[15] Tricomi, *Reading Tudor-Stuart Texts*, 8.

In Renaissance tragedies the audience's knowledge of how the illusion was set up, and cognizance of how the on-stage mirrors presented and refracted images from within the larger spectacle, did not diminish the power of the overall dramatic affect.[16] In fact, as was mentioned in the Introduction, in plays of mourning that used scenes that rhetorically conjured fatal perspectives, one's awareness of how elements of the spectacle were activated and internalized serve as an index to one's enjoyment of the aesthetic experience, gruesome though it may seem. Still, though, this space of rationalization, which acts as a buffer between the viewer and his or her confrontation with the violence depicted through the spectacle, is far from a safe space. For, above all else, the consummate dramatist is concerned with setting up the conditions for a response so that viewers will believe they have recourse to just such a safe harbour of the mind, only to realize in time that this illusion is just that—an illusion. If we have allowed ourselves to be thus taken in by this affective double reverse made possible through the staging of fatal perspective, then we are left vulnerable to a sense of abjection.[17] Identifying the decorum and regulations associated with visual regimes and charmed spaces during the period shows how this truth of the spectacle, as aiming at nothing other than itself, came to be the case—as can be seen in some exemplary scenes from English Renaissance tragedies that evoked images of fatal destiny.

Both in the Renaissance and now, the word 'emblem' can be used to refer to symbolic pictures. But 'it is more helpful to regard the commonest form of the emblem as an interdependent combination of symbolic picture (*pictura*), pithy motto or title (*inscriptio*), and a passage of prose or verse (*subscriptio*)'.[18] Both verbal and visual elements are necessary. What passed as a fairly typical definition of the emblem in the seventeenth century is recorded,

---

[16] A. R. Braunmuller, 'The Arts of the Dramatist', in A. R. Braunmuller and Michael Hattaway (eds.), *The Cambridge Companion to English Renaissance Drama* (Cambridge: Cambridge University Press, 1990), 88.

[17] Julia Kristeva, *Powers of Horror*, trans. Leon S. Roudiez (New York: Columbia University Press, 1982), 3, 16.

[18] Charles Moseley, *A Century of Emblems: An Introductory Anthology* (Aldershot: Scolar Press, 1989), 2.

among other places, by Francis Pastorius: 'Emblems signify mottos or devices, which point at a mystical or hidden sense of certain pictures. Emblems are speaking pictures, containing general documents, instructions, and morals.'[19] Emblems thus brought together word and picture in a way that invited commentary, ranging from the most dully commonplace to the most sparklingly ingenious. Emblems were used in nearly every art form of the period.[20] They figured prominently in dramas and also in the design and adornment of playhouses.[21]

An emblematic device, whether used as a passing allusion or as a main part of the play, did not stretch the imagination of a Tudor or Stuart audience.[22] It might take the form of a pageant involving heraldic displays (*Pericles*, 2.2), involve puns on *imprese* (Marlowe's *Edward II*, 2.2), make a point through the commentary (Kyd's *Spanish Tragedy*, 1.4), or simply allude to an emblem from the stock repertory (Marston's *Antonio and Melida*, 5.2). The well-established tripartite components of the traditional emblem—image, motto, and commentary—gave the dramatist an ideal outlet for displaying his ingenuity.[23] For example, in Webster's *The White Devil* (2.2) an emblem is thrown through the window for Camillo.[24] The image, we are told, is a stag weeping for the loss of its horns; the motto is 'Inopem me copia fecit', which Monticelso translates 'Plenty of horns hath made him poor of horns'. Finally, serving as the commentary to the device, which wraps up this bit of stage-business, he explains the reference to

[19] Francis Pastorius, 'Emblematical Recreations', Newberry Library, Chicago, MS W1025, p. 176. On the first leaf is written: *Brevitas amica Memoriae*.

[20] See Michael Bath, *Speaking Pictures: English Emblem Books and Renaissance Culture* (London: Longman, 1994), and Peter M. Daly, 'The Cultural Context of English Emblem Books', in Peter M. Daly (ed.), *The English Emblem and the Continental Tradition* (New York: AMS Press, 1988), 1–60.

[21] Frances A. Yates, *Theatre of the World* (Chicago: University of Chicago Press, 1969), 136–68.

[22] Peter M. Daly, *Literature in the Light of the Emblem: Structural Parallels between the Emblem and Literature in the Sixteenth and Seventeenth Centuries* (Toronto: Toronto University Press, 1973), 153.

[23] A. Robin Bowers, 'Emblem and Rape in Shakespeare's *Lucrece* and *Titus Andronicus*', *Studies in Iconography*, 10 (1985), 90.

[24] *The White Devil*, ed. John Russell Brown (Manchester: Manchester University Press, 1979).

cuckoldry as it applies to the play's action.[25] The audience thus receives the message in three different forms, and, moreover, carries with it the moralized memory-picture of the weeping stag. And so neither the time-out from the dramatic action to puzzle out an emblem nor the stage effect are arbitrary, but are designed to imprint a key issue upon the audience's memory.[26]

Further, the function of the emblem (and the same holds for the pageant or dumb show) is at once interpretation and representation; what is depicted means more than it portrays.[27] The emblem, like a dumb show, contracts recognizable icons into a single frame and imparts a message through multiple means. Thus a kind of double perspective is set up for the audience to marvel at and to ponder.[28] Accordingly, Rosemary Freeman argued that 'the dumb show of the stage is in both form and function only a much more elaborate version of the pictures in an emblem book'.[29] In the same way that the tableaux of civic pageants may be said to be animated emblems,[30] dumb shows in dramas are like pages in a kinetic emblem book.[31]

[25] Michael Bath, 'Weeping Stages and Melancholy Lovers: The Iconography of *As You Like It*, II.i', *Emblematica*, 1 (1986), 13–52; and also, on word-emblems and the ways emblems appeared in Renaissance dramas, see Daly, *Literature in the Light of the Emblem*, 134–67.

[26] Cf. Michael Neill, 'Exeunt with a Dead March': Funeral Pageantry on the Shakespearean Stage', *Pageantry in the Shakespearean Theatre*, ed. David M. Bergeron (Athens: University of Georgia Press, 1985), 168.

[27] Albrecht Schöne, *Emblematik und Drama im Zeitalter des Barock* (Munich: Beck, 1968), 22; and cf. Peter M. Daly, *Emblem Theory: Recent German Contributions to the Characterization of the Emblem Genre* (Nendeln: KTO Press, 1979), 22–5, and Bath, *Speaking Pictures*, 4–5.

[28] Cf. Robert Klein, 'Théorie de l'expression figurée dans les traités italiens sur les *imprese*, 1555–1612', *Bibliothèque d'Humanisme et Renaissance*, 19 (1957), 320–41; and John Greenwood, *Shifting Perspectives and the Stylish Style: Mannerism in Shakespeare and his Jacobean Contemporaries* (Toronto: University of Toronto Press, 1988).

[29] Rosemary Freeman, *English Emblem Books* (1948; repr. New York: Octagon Press, 1978), 15. See also Dieter Mehl, *The Elizabethan Dumb Show: The History of a Dramatic Convention* (London: Methuen, 1965), 14.

[30] David M. Bergeron, *English Civic Pageantry, 1558–1642* (Columbia: University of South Carolina Press, 1971), 275.

[31] See Henry Green's *Shakespeare and the Emblem Writers: An Exposition of their Similarities of Thought and Expression* (London: Trübner & Co., 1870); and John Doebler, *Shakespeare's Speaking Pictures: Studies in Iconic Imagery* (Albuquerque: University of New Mexico Press, 1974).

Dumb shows in early dramas like *Gorboduc* (1562) and *Jocasta* (1566) tended to mime the action and precede the scene.[32] As Ophelia observed more correctly than she could have realized, the dumb show 'imports the argument of the play' (*Hamlet*, 3.2.136). Judging from expense records, however, some mute pageants were little more than an excuse for spectacular displays of pomp and gorgeous apparel.[33] But by the time of *Hamlet* dumb shows were, according to Andrew Gurr, 'laughably archaic' and were used 'deliberately as old-fashioned devices'.[34] Harold Jenkins has noted the 'usual dumb show either presented things that could not be conveniently given in dialogue, or alternatively, if it foreshadowed things which *would* be given in dialogue later, it did so emblematically'.[35] Insofar as dumb shows can be said to have figured forth mimetic vignettes emblematically, they are a viable and reliable index to the staging of practical aspects of the Renaissance Memory Arts.[36] The tradition of the *ars memorativa* was as much a part of humanist training as it was a fixture in early modern English popular culture.[37]

From the time of Cicero until well into the seventeenth century mnemonic programmes gave ready access to vast catalogues of inventions and arguments that were grounded in pithy words and exemplary deeds. Although the Roman teacher of rhetoric Quintilian was somewhat reserved in his praise for the claims one could make about mnemonics, he was often cited in the Renaissance as a place to begin.[38] In its most rudimentary form, an artificial memory began with a recognizable structure—such as animal, man, wall, room, house, theatre, or even city—onto

---

[32] Mehl, *Elizabethan Dumb Show*, 173–99, gives a complete list of those plays containing the conventional elements which came to be associated with the dumb show.

[33] Some, for example, involved pageant funerals like that in *Jocasta*, calling for two coffins and sixteen mourners; see Neill, 'Funeral Pageantry', 182, n. 3.

[34] Andrew Gurr, *The Shakespearean Stage, 1574–1642*, 2nd edn. (Cambridge, 1980), 174.

[35] *Hamlet*, ed. Harold Jenkins, 501.

[36] Cf. Edward Pechter, 'Remembering *Hamlet*: Or, How It Feels To Go Like a Crab Backwards', *Shakespeare Survey*, 39 (1987), n. 13.

[37] Carrol Camden, 'Memory, The Warder of the Brain', *Philological Quarterly*, 18: 1 (Jan. 1939), 52–72.

[38] Quintilian, *Institutio Oratoria*, XI. ii. 18–21.

which were superimposed a series of striking, memorable symbols or images capable of being easily retrieved.[39] Such schemes in the Renaissance were useful in the effort to remember the contents of personal notebooks. For example, Leporeus advised his students to imagine their bedroom wall divided into eight segments in which were noted the facts they wished to remember; as they passed from one segment to the next, the information noted there would reappear.[40] He is also known for his House of Memory (*Domus locorum*): the first place, appropriately, is an entry arch; one moved through the house, retrieving symbolic contents from their remaining places (Fig. 6).[41]

Explicit references and allusions to the Memory Arts show up time and again in Renaissance dramas. For example, in Webster's Induction to Marston's *The Malcontent*, Will Sly, while playing himself, jests about the artificial memory technique of placing items in a sequence of shop-stalls, as if at a market, namely Goldsmith's Row in Cheapside. In Jonson's *The Case is Altered* (2.4.39–43), Francisco says to Phoenixella: 'I will be silent, yet that I may serue | But as a *Decade* in the art of memory | To put you stil in mind of your owne vertues.'[42] Beaumont and Fletcher's *The Lovers' Progress* (2.2) has Malfort ironically remark that he would 'learn the art of memory from your table book'.[43] The currency of this theme, and of the *ars memorativa* in general, is echoed in *Hamlet* regarding the 'table of memory' (1.5.98), and, regarding Osric's hyperbolic praise of Laertes' virtues, to which Hamlet replies: 'to divide him inventorially would dozy th'arithmetic of

---

[39] On classical 'place-system', see *Rhetorica ad Herennium*, III. xvii–xx. For a good, compact survey of this aspect of *artes memorativae*, see Mary Carruthers, *The Book of Memory: A Study of Memory in Medieval Culture* (Cambridge, 1990), 122–55.

[40] R. R. Bolgar, *The Classical Heritage and its Beneficiaries* (1954; repr. Cambridge, 1958), 274.

[41] Guilelmus Leporeus, *Ars memorativa* (Paris, 1520); cf. Ludwig Volkmann, *Ars Memorativa* (Vienna: Anton Schroll, 1929), 163–5, and Claire Richter Sherman, *Writing on Hands: Memory and Knowledge in Early Modern Europe* (Seattle: University of Washington Press, 2000), 13, 15.

[42] Ben Jonson, *The Complete Works*, ed. C. H. Hereford, Percy Simpson, and Evelyn Simpson (Oxford: Oxford University Press, 1927), iii. 131.

[43] Beaumont and Fletcher, *Works*, ed. Alexander Dyce (London: Edward Moxon, 1846), xi. 50.

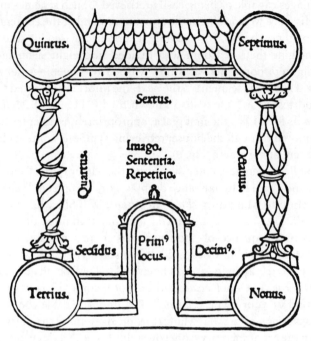

Domus Locorum Decem.

Quintus. Septimus.

Sextus.

Imago.
Sentenria.
Repetitio.

Quartus. Octauus.

Prim⁹ locus.

Secūdus Decim⁹.

Tertius. Nonus.

Fig. 6. House of Memory

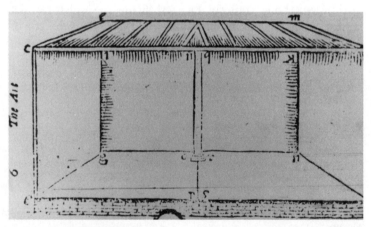

The Air

Fig. 7. Basic Memory Theatre

memory' (5.2.113–14); while in *1 Henry VI* Richard Plantagenet says to Somerset: 'I'll note you in my book of memory | To scourge you for this apprehension' (2.4.101–2).

Dramatists, in addition to inventing their own images and keeping them handy in their 'table books',[44] like Renaissance readers in general, could cull them from source-books conveniently suited to this end.[45] Collections of commonplaces circulated widely, whether Erasmus' *Adages* or Meres's popular *Wits Treasury*, as did digests of classical texts.[46] Accordingly, John Willis argued that such books were suitable repositories of mnemonic places.[47] He was convinced of the emblem's capacity to collapse complex ideas into easily recognized images. Francis Bacon too maintained that the emblem's efficacy resided in its ability to reduce 'conceits intellectual to images sensible, which strike the memory more'.[48] Such views, while grounded in an ideal of intellectual reformation and the early modern belief in the viability of progress,[49] are put forward with full cognizance of the way that decline ineluctably characterizes the life-course of every individual. The Art of Memory, however, was seen by many Renaissance intellectuals, and by Bacon in particular, as part of the New Science that was capable of stemming the tide of oblivion and even, it was to be hoped, bringing an upward turn to the course of history.[50]

[44] R. W. Dent, John *Webster's Borrowing* (Berkeley and Los Angeles: University of California Press, 1960); see also Engel, *Mapping Mortality*, 48–54, 100–8.

[45] Daniel Russell, *Emblematic Structures in Renaissance French Culture* (Toronto: University of Toronto Press, 1995), 236.

[46] William E. Engel, 'Mnemonic Emblems and the Humanist Discourses of Knowledge', in Peter M. Daly and John Manning (eds.), *Aspects of Renaissance and Baroque Symbol Theory, 1500–1700* (New York: AMS Press, 1999), 129.

[47] John Willis, *Mnemonica; or the Art of Memory* was first printed in Latin in 1618 and then expanded and 'Englished' in 1621; it was revived and augmented in 1661 by William Sowersby.

[48] *The Works of Francis Bacon*, ed. James Spedding, Robert Leslie Ellis, and Douglas Denon Heath (Boston: Brown and Taggard, 1861–5), vi. 282. See also *Advancement of Learning* (1605), II. xv. 3, ed. Arthur Johnson (Oxford: Oxford University Press, 1980), 130.

[49] J. B. Bury, *The Idea of Progress* (London: Macmillan, 1920); Samuel Lilley, 'Robert Recorde and the Idea of Progress: A Hypothesis and Verification', *Renaissance and Modern Studies*, 2 (1957).

[50] Lisa Jardine, *Francis Bacon: Discovery and the Art of Discourse* (Cambridge: Cambridge University Press, 1975).

Emblems figured prominently in the Memory Arts. Indeed, the emblematic quality of memory images, and the mnemonic quality of emblems would have been taken for granted in Shakespeare's day.[51] For example, the commonplace assumptions about the emblem's mnemonic efficacy, and the decorous use of such images to stimulate the imaginative faculty, are rehearsed by, among others, Philip Sidney: 'For as the image of each action stirreth and instructeth the mind, so the lofty image of such worthies most inflameth the mind with the desire to be worthy, and informs with counsel how to be worthy. Only let Aeneas be worn in the tablet of your memory.'[52] Likewise, Willis advocated that all kinds of '*Hyeroglyphicks*, and innumerable sentences' be situated in 'an imaginary house or building,' namely 'Emblemes, written by *Beza, Alciat, Peacham* . . . [f]or in all Emblemes, the picture occupying the vpper part of the table, is a relative Idea; and that which is written vnderneath, a Scriptile'; further, he approved of making use of things 'expressed in action upon the stage', like an 'armed Knight bearing his Scutcheon and imprese written therein'.[53]

While any background structure could serve as an artificial memory site, the theatre above all was ideally suited to house and display, and to stage, such dynamically disposed emblems.[54] Theatres, after all, were places where people expected to hear impressive words emphatically repeated and to see memorable deeds ingeniously performed. Willis was quite specific about how one should go about building, and appointing, such mental constructions.[55] He included a diagram for readers to fill in according

[51] Yates, *Art of Memory*, 130.

[52] Philip Sidney, *Apology for Poetry*, ed. Geoffrey Shepherd (1965; repr. Manchester: Manchester University Press, 1973), 119; moreover, Sidney remarked 'even they that have taught the art of memory have shown nothing so apt for it as a certain room divided into many places well and thoroughly known' (p. 122). See also Shepherd's note on this passage (pp. 196–7), and Jan van Dorsten, 'Arts of Memory and Poetry', *English Studies*, 48 (1967), 424.

[53] Willis, *Art of Memory*, 47. The same principles of distillation applied as well to Willis's method of 'compendious writing', in his *Art of Stenographie, or Short Writing by Spelling Characters* (London, 1602); by mid-century it was in its 14th edition, had been translated into Latin, and generated a companion text, *The school-maister to the art of stenography* (1622, 1628, and 1647).

[54] Most notably, Guilio Camillo, *L'Idea del Theatro* (Florence, 1550).

[55] Willis, *Mnemonica* (London, 1661), 52–6.

to their needs and wit (Fig. 7).[56] Within such a theatre various arresting and memorable images, in the form of mnemonic emblems or trigger symbols, were supposed to be placed so that one could recover the reposited images with ease. Such mnemonic *loci*, when retrieved in sequence, made it possible to recall and recite a set speech, or even to reconstruct an entire play scene by scene, speech by speech.

The immemorial affinity among intense visualization techniques, poetic devices, and mnemonic images took on a renewed life in the early modern period.[57] For example, Willis's almost ludicrous attention to detail in devising a Memory Theatre reminds us that part of its effectiveness comes from the artifice appearing as 'natural' as possible. Still, the images have to remain distinct; in fact, the more striking—or as we shall see, the more curious and quaint—the mnemonic cue, the better. William Fulwood stressed that 'in placing or setting of the images or figures in their places the thing is alwaies to be placed with mery, a merueilous or cruel act, or some other unaccustomed maner: for mery, cruell, iniurious, merueilous, excellently faire, or excedingly foule things do change and moue ye senses, & better styre up the Memorie, when the minde is much occupied about such things'.[58]

Thus the staging of fatal dumb shows brings together the practical applications of the Memory Arts and the vast repository of images charged with emblematic significance. English tragic dramas evoked, and themselves became, melancholy Memory Theatres. For example, in plays of blood-revenge like *The Revenger's Tragedy*, and *The Spanish Tragedy*, discussed in the next section, we find the exemplary juxtaposing of merry, cruel, injurious, and marvellous acts; the excellently fair and excellently foul overlap and bleed one into the other once the charmed space has been invoked. The viewer's memory is stirred up indeed by

---

[56] Yates, *Art of Memory*, 325.

[57] Ibid. 43.

[58] William Fulwood, *The Castel of Memorie* (London, 1562), sig. H6. For the most part, this is a translation of Guglielmo Gratarolis's guide to health and the memory arts, *De Memoria* (Zurich, 1553), dedicated to Edward VI of England. And so by the time of Fulwood's English version, dedicated to Robert Dudley, Earl of Leicester, continental ideas about Memory Theatres and place system mnemonics had been in circulation for some time.

such images, not only because of the stunningly rare sights or grisly actions leading to bloody displays, but also because of the opposing extremes that are evoked simultaneously from one and the same staged event. This is especially the case when the charm is wound up to its most forceful pitch through words—words which seem to partake of the same kind of theurgic magic they seek ceremoniously to depict.

TABLEAUX VIVANTS AND TELLING SCENES

When dumb shows function as part of the dramatic action, they often involve a cruel act at once fair in design and foul in what is shown. English tragic dramas also include tableaux in which a single, apparently static image heralds, epitomizes, and propels the play's lamentable action. For example in Webster's *The Duchess of Malfi*, when Ferdinand seeks to 'plague' his sister 'in art', Bosola reveals to her, 'behind a traverse', wax figures said to be her dead husband and children (4.1.55).[59]

This same framing technique of portioning off a space within which to present a fatally reflective allegorical perspective-glass of death is used as well in *The Revenger's Tragedy* (1.4). Antonio, whose wife has been raped by Spurio, 'discovers the body of her dead to certain Lords and Hippolito'.[60] While similar in kind to the macabre tableau in *The Duchess of Malfi*, this one is different both with respect to its explicit self-referential description of theatricality and also the final end to which the emblematic artifice is used.

> ANTONIO: Draw nearer, lords, and be sad witnesses
> Of a fair comely building newly fall'n,
> Being falsely undermined: violent rape
> Has play'd a glorious act. Behold, my lords,

[59] On this scene as it relates to the *ars moriendi* tradition, see Charles R. Forker, *The Skull Beneath the Skin: The Achievement of John Webster* (Carbondale and Edwardsville: Southern Illinois University Press, 1986), 339. On perspective stage curtains, 'discovery', and *tableaux vivants*, see George R. Kernodle, *From Art to Theatre: Form and Convention in the Renaissance* (1943; repr. Chicago: University of Chicago Press, 1947), 10–12, 214–15.

[60] Cyril Tourneur, *The Revenger's Tragedy*, ed. Lawrence J. Ross (Lincoln: University of Nebraska Press, 1966).

A sight that strikes man out of me.
PIERO: That virtuous lady!
ANTONIO: Precedent for wives!

(1.4.1–7)

This *tableau vivant*, which obviously evokes Lucrece,[61] is offered as a mirror of and for virtuous wives.[62] The peculiar way this particular case is staged for our consideration urges us not to rest easily with a simple emblematic 'reading'. The frisson elicited by this scene and the apparent incongruity of the ensuing speeches have not gone unrecognized by readers, especially those interested in the intersection of death and the erotic in English tragedy.[63] Furthermore, there is an unmistakable mnemonic quality of the scene highlighted by the moralization of the staged emblem; it directs attention to the image itself through the motto 'Better to die in virtue than to live through dishonor' (1.4.17).

> ANTONIO: Dead!
> Her honor first drunk poison, and her life,
> Being fellows in one house, did pledge her honor.
> PIERO: O grief of many!
> ANTONIO: I mark'd not this before:
> A prayer book the pillow to her cheek.
> This was her rich confection; and another
> Plac'd in her right hand, with a leaf tuck'd up,
> Pointing to these words:
> *Melius virtute mori, quam per dedecus vivere.*
> True and effectual it is indeed.

The dramatic tension in this episode is relieved and resolved through the initially unseen textual clue, the Senecan-sounding *sententia*. Antonio fixes the tableau in terms of its being an emblem, complete with image, motto, and commentary. Evoking a rhetorically charmed space through these words spoken as if from beyond the grave, the motto of her life reaches out to the

---

[61] Bowers, 'Emblems and Rape', 79.

[62] On the English tendency to adapt the conventionalized façades of the *tableaux vivants*, see Kernodle, *From Art to Theatre*, 219.

[63] e.g. Karin S. Coddon, ' "For Show or Useless Property": Necrophilia and *The Revenger's Tragedy*', *English Literary History*, 61 (1994), 71, 81.

lords and, by extension, to the audience through what appear to be written words. When these words echo on stage they herald the approach of blood-revenge. This image of a woman's heroic body shown in death provides a moment of arrested stage movement and an occasion to reflect. Along with its Latin *sententia*, this image functions as a virtual placeholder, both visually on stage and also emblematically within the narrative tug of the drama. In this way the moment of death is framed within the already special space of the stage provided by the tableau to create a mnemonic point of reference set off from the play's dialogic flow and from its main mimetic design. It calls forth a living *exemplum*, or rather the image of a dead one, that momentarily monumentalizes the event. It is from within the space of this reflective pause that the outraged courtiers link their destinies and vow to avenge her rape and death. Although Vindice has reasons of his own to murder the duke (involving another rape and death—that of his beloved Gloriana),[64] still he later refers to this incident as the rationale for his part in the conspiracy: 'The rape of your good lady has been 'quitted, | With death on death' (5.3.88–9). Finally then, the image and motto encapsulating, summing up, and commenting on her life—as well as on the tableau of fatal destiny within the play—is 'true and effectual'.

These parting words of the commentary address the emblematically staged event no less than the play's own overt theatricality. For, according to Walter Benjamin, one of the characteristic traits of the dramatist, as a self-conscious allegorist, was that he did not conceal the fact that his activity was one of arranging, 'since it was not so much the mere whole as its obviously constructed quality that was the principal impression which was aimed at'.[65] Moreover, for the dramatist who borrowed freely from the available store of commonplace and mnemonic images, allegory is not to be understood as a convention of expression, but rather as the expression of convention.[66]

Another example of a cunning memory image used to encapsu-

---

[64] Cf. Neill, *Issues of Death*, 138.

[65] Walter Benjamin, *The Origin of German Tragic Drama*, trans. John Osborne (London: New Left Books, 1977), 179.

[66] Ibid. 175.

late the main themes, and which emblematizes the fatal ethos of a play, is the dumb show in Kyd's *Spanish Tragedy*. It highlights for us the theurgic power activated by the doubled perspective of silent depictions of fatal tableaux and pageants situated within the encompassing spectacle of blood-revenge. Understandably so, for the entire drama relies on, and is concerned with, emblems of remembrance.[67] The Ghost of Andrea, who earlier had chided Revenge for sleeping on the job, is puzzled by a silent procession. Revenge recalls that Hieronimo, father of Andrea's friend Horatio (who was murdered by a clique including Don Balthazar, Andrea's killer), has not forgotten his son—and neither has the audience, especially after such a reminder. Both in response to Andrea, and as a consummate metatheatrical gesture which introduces the dumb show, Revenge utters words that serve as a moral to this scene, and can be applied as well to the entire tragic drama:

> Nor dies Revenge although he sleep awhile,
> For in unquiet, quietness is feigned,
> And slumbering is a common worldly wile.
> Behold, Andrea, for an instance how
> Revenge hath slept, and then imagine thou
> What 'tis to be subject to destiny.[68]

By the play's end we have watched Andrea watch all of his enemies (as well as his beloved Bel-Imperia, among others) meet their deaths. Andrea sues for, and is granted, the right to 'judge, and doom' his enemies 'to unrest' by putting them in the places of torment from the classical underworld (4.5.30ff.). The ambitious Balthazar, betrothed to Bel-Imperia, is to be hung about Chimaera's neck; Don Lorenzo, the play's main Machiavel, takes Ixion's place on the wheel, and so on. His friends are placed 'in ease, the rest in woes' and the cycle of revenge comes full circle with Andrea being able to rest, duly avenged. But all of this hinges on the mnemonic placeholder, in the form of an emblematic procession at the end of Act 3. Like Warburg's notion of an engram,

---

[67] Cf. John Kerrigan, 'Hieronimo, Hamlet, and Remembrance', *Essays in Criticism*, 31: 2 (Apr. 1981), 107.

[68] Thomas Kyd, *The Spanish Tragedy*, ed. J. R. Mulryne (1970; repr. New York: Norton, 1985), 3.15.24–9.

the procession calls upon and activates further a series of key, remembered images. As the mummers exit, Andrea urges Revenge to wake up and reveal the meaning of 'this mystery'. Revenge explicates, or 'moralizes', the emblematic pageant:

> REVENGE: The two first, the nuptial torches bore,
>   As brightly burning as the mid-day's sun;
>   But after them doth Hymen hie as fast,
>   Clothed in sable, and a saffron robe,
>   And blows them out, and quencheth them with blood,
>   As discontent that things continue so.
> ANDREA: Sufficeth me; thy meaning's understood,
>   And thanks to thee and those infernal powers
>   That will not tolerate a lover's woe.
>
>   (3.15.30–8)

The proposed wedding of Bel-Imperia (Andrea's secret lover) to Don Balthazar is presaged as being doomed, and so is the prospective union of the Spanish and Portuguese houses (the attempted marital solution to the play's main conflict). Andrea was killed in Spain's war against the Portuguese who had refused to pay tribute (the attempted martial solution to the conflict). Despite his death and that of his beloved, because he is avenged, from Andrea's perspective, he has neither loved nor died in vain. And yet the reason why is, on the surface, astonishingly arbitrary. Upon arriving in the underworld, the ultimate destination of this lover and warrior is disputed by the judges, Minos and Aecus. Because they are deadlocked, Radamanth sends the case to a higher court. The reason the infernal powers would 'not tolerate a lover's woe' is that Proserpine, for reasons of her own, interceded and begged Pluto to let her rule on Andrea's fate (1.1.79).[69] Pluto approves of her plan and, in a gesture charged with both erotic and thanatopic overtones, with theurgic if destructive energies that continue to reverberate thematically throughout the play, 'sealed it with a kiss'.[70] From the outset of the play then, a memory image is

---

[69] Cf. Kerrigan, 'Hieronimo', 108.

[70] See Robert N. Watson, 'Tragedy', in A. R. Braunmuller and Michael Hattaway (eds.), *The Cambridge Companion to English Renaissance Drama* (Cambridge: Cambridge University Press, 1990), 322, which describes this being a

activated that betokens the kiss of death.[71] Although relying on
the mimetically driven tropes of verisimilitude to convey this
allegorical message, it is by virtue of the mythopoetic content of
the symbolic action linked to the implied future violence that this
scene fixes a lasting impression—as an engram—in the mind's eye
of the audience.[72] Further, other kinds of theatrical operations
challenged the audience to dis-invest itself of the effects of the
spectacle, irrespective of the degree to which it is represented in
terms of allegory or verisimilitude.

For example, the dumb show in Act 3 symbolically mirrors and
dramatically anticipates the fatal wedding masque (a convoluted
polyglot court-entertainment devised by Hieronimo to avenge
Horatio's death). The play within the play, like a portentous and
confused dream that washes over and inundates us, emblematically foreshadows and allegorically enacts the play's end. Implied
in my use of 'end' here are both the inexorable narrative destination of the author's dramatic design and also the self-reflective
aesthetic aim of the spectacle. As with the *tableau vivant* in *The
Revenger's Tragedy*, this dumb show in *The Spanish Tragedy* is a
mnemonic placeholder, invested with and capable of generating
theurgic energies which, in both form and function, recall
Warburg's notion of engrammic discharge. An attentive viewer,
especially one who heeded the verbal instructions of the on-stage
commentator, Revenge, could reconstruct the main action of the
play, moving either forward or backward, using it as a mental
magnet to pick up related scenes and themes along the way. But
the viewer is not left with a clear-cut sense of the moral, which one
would expect to get from a traditional emblem. Still, such

'spiritual tightrope between a sort of hell and a sort of heaven, overseen by the
discordia concors of Pluto and Proserpine, who represent the primal oppositions
evoked by those seventeen lines [which open the play]: war and love, death and
life, winter and summer.'

[71] There is a long tradition in the Renaissance of simplifying images of Pluto
and Proserpine, though leaving no doubt as to the message the artist, or, in this
case, the dramatist, wished to convey. See e.g. Jean Seznec, *The Survival of the
Pagan Gods: The Mythological Tradition and Its Place in Renaissance Humanism
and Art*, trans. Barbara F. Sessions (1953; repr. Princeton University Press, 1961),
195–6.

[72] Braunmuller, 'The Arts of the Dramatist', 88.

ambiguities were fundamental to the more ingenious type of device, which called on the viewer to make sense of the image and text, and then to determine what meaning, in this instance, was being imported.[73]

To provide further theoretical bearings for understanding the aesthetic assumptions and to investigate further the theurgic effect of such dumb shows, let us turn to a scene from modern cinema. As we do so, let us keep in mind the memory image of Hymen's blood-interrupted procession, and also Andrea's inserting his enemies into *loci* of classical torture, and look now at an example that will provide stunning insight into 'the very cunning of the scene'. It does so owing to its subtle encoding and depiction of the aestheticization of violence. This episode, like each of the Renaissance examples used in this chapter, conjures up a double perspective where moral consciousness is ordained, and eclipsed, by aesthetic consciousness.[74]

Pier Paolo Pasolini's film *Salo* (1975) moves the Marquis de Sade's chateau of the *120 Days of Sodom* to a Fascist enclave at the end of World War II. Within such isolated and self-contained locations, and according to rigid schemes of political and social organization, the will to power is expressed clearly and unmistakably in terms of violence—and especially in terms of aberrantly violent acts.[75] This applies as well to the debauches, excesses, and intrigues of the courts in *The Revenger's Tragedy* and *The Spanish Tragedy*, as it does to the outrageous acts carried out in the villa of Pasolini's *Salo*. Attuned to the powerful possibilities of traditional dumb shows, especially those depicting aberrantly violent acts, Pasolini arranges for the systematic torture of the victims to take place without the interference of spoken words, without sounds of agony, without language that comes out of or comments on the gruesome situation. Instead ceremonial music fills the soundtrack, just as stately music typically would accompany *tableaux vivants* or processions in the Renaissance.

[73] Engel, *Mapping Mortality*, 1, 13, 131.

[74] Leo Bersani and Ulysse Dutoit, 'Merde Alors', *October*, 13 (1980), 31.

[75] Pierre Klossowski, *Sade: My Neighbor*, trans. Alphonso Lingis (Evanston: Northwestern University Press, 1991), 40.

The dumb show effect is presented cinematically in *Salo* through the projection of a border frame that makes it appear as if the audience is looking at the melee through binoculars, thus seeing it through the eyes of one of the powerful perpetrators. And so the viewers, like the libertines who have chosen not to take an active part in the massacre, witness the bloodletting from a distance. We are brought closer to the spectacle of violence by means of modern 'magic' spectacles. In the activation of this cinematic trope simulating the achievement of a privileged, if painful, perspective, the conditions of its artifice, as an aid to vision, momentarily are subsumed in the presentation of the fatal spectacle. By losing ourselves in the spectacle, we allow ourselves to be blind to the way this cinematic device, like the staging of fatal perspective in dumb shows, doubles back on itself.[76] In devising cinematic means to compel the viewer to see himself as being both victim and torturer (and thus, to some extent, to see the world from these various points of view simultaneously), Pasolini conjures up a mode of consciousness that remains true to Sade's more subtle literary craft,[77] and which can be seen to be reflected in similar scenes of Renaissance tragedies.

And yet, the manipulation of the viewer's perspective in the way advocated by Sade and replicated by Pasolini is misdirected, according to Brecht's ideas about theatre's capacity to reveal the truth of both its operations and our lives. Brecht rejected any form of audience identification with the subjects in the spectacle. To combat the tendency to waver between objective detachment from and subjective absorption into the spectacle, he proposed the staging of alienation effects. He wanted to foster judgement rather than self-abandon or emotional participation, and to this end he sought to interrupt 'the current of sympathy' whenever it

[76] Jean-Louis Baudry, 'Cinema: effets idéologiques produits par l'appareil de base', *Cinéthique*, 7/8 (1970).

[77] Cf. Georges Bataille, 'The Use Value of D. A. F. de Sade', in Allan Stoekl (ed.), *Visions of Excess, Selected Writings, 1927–1939*, trans. Allan Stoekl, Carl R. Lovitt, and Donald M. Leslie, Jr. (Minneapolis: University of Minnesota, 1985), 101; and Annie Le Brun, 'Sade and the Theatre', in Deepak Narang Sawhney (ed.), *The Divine Sade*, trans. Justin Barton (University of Warwick: PLI, 1994), 42.

threatened 'to flow too strongly between stage and onlookers'.[78] He wanted to encourage reflective and critical engagement with the spectacle and, by extension, with what one encountered in the world. Recognizing the theurgic power of the spectacle, and thus in an effort to mitigate it, Brecht insisted that the actor 'discard whatever means he has learnt of getting the audience to identify itself with the characters which he plays. Aiming not to put his audience in a trance, he must not go into a trance himself.'[79]

In the very cunning of the scene, though, in its mode of presentation no less than the mimetic actions it sets out to depict, we are impelled to waver between immersion and critical detachment. Once a violent spectacle has been viewed (like Kyd's polyglot play within a play written by the vengeful Hieronimo, and like Pasolini's circus of blood orchestrated by the fascist libertines), we cannot easily erase the images from our mind's eye. Although we can retrieve the symbolic and social meanings deposited in such kinetic emblems, in this act of recovery we necessarily translate them with an eye toward seeing how they speak to us. In doing so we *re-cover* the meaning. We take it from its resting-place in the spectacle—we might even say exhume it—only to replace it, to bury it again somewhere else. As such, the process of recovery becomes a part of our experience as well, whether or not we are aware of our role in translating these symbols and thus in transferring engrammic energy. We have something to show for our efforts though: before we realize it, we have allowed ourselves to be subjected to the spectacle and to become passive victims of the violence it depicts. We are subjected to it even as we have recovered the symbolic meanings presented, much in the same way that the hapless victims of stage violence are themselves constrained and tormented. They learn their fate even as it transpires, and by then it is too late. The same may said of the audience of such melancholy Memory Theatres as well. We are left wondering: what is being reflected here, if not the motivating process of thought that animates, and which enables, the staging of fatal perspective?

In *The Spanish Tragedy* onlookers are invited to envision

[78] Barish, *The Antitheatrical Prejudice*, 456.
[79] Bertolt Brecht, *Brecht on Theatre: The Development of an Aesthetic*, trans. John Willet (New York: Hill and Wang, 1974), 193.

images of the characters placed in positions of torment according to Andrea's dictates. The conspirator Serberine takes Sisyphus' place rolling the stone, and his sometime-friend and murderer Pedringano is made to be 'dragged through boiling Acheron, | And there live, dying still in endless flames, | Blaspheming gods and all their holy names' (4.5.42 ff.). And so it is with the other characters created by Kyd along with those taken from the classical tradition, who, like us, are called on to participate in Andrea's revenge. Each member of the audience thus actuates the terrible revenge in conjunction with hearing it, all the more so because it is inflected and proposed subjunctively:

> Then, sweet Revenge, do this at my request;
> Let me be judge, and doom them to unrest:
> Let loose poor Tityus from the vulture's gripe,
> And let Don Cyprian supply his room.
>
> (4.5.29–32)

In scenes from English Renaissance tragedy like this one, our reward for complicity, for tacitly entertaining the eternal torment of Andrea's enemies, is whatever vicarious pleasure there is to be derived from taking part in a fairly typical, if grandiosely played out, wish-fulfillment fantasy; namely, of being empowered as both judge and executioner of those over whom, by the light of day, you exercise little if any power.[80] Using the familiar Virgilian scenes of infernal judgements, like those typical of artificial memory schemes,[81] we extend Kyd's drama. We become the co-authors of Andrea's proposed script when we stage, and can imagine that we hear, the torment of his victims in the theatres of our minds. It is in this respect that we become its victims, all the more so because we believe we are in control of the images in our mind's eye.

Looking critically at several other representative, though more perspectivally complicated, scenes from tragic drama provides us with the grounding we need to glimpse what Renaissance English audiences were able to see through, and see past, when confronted with seemingly trite, 'laughably archaic' devices and static emblematic images. The questions before us, therefore, will

[80] Cf. Watson, 'Tragedy', 333–4.   [81] See Yates, *Art of Memory*, 102–5.

concern the nature of the aesthetic responses associated with being confronted by the generation of on-stage charmed spectacles that herald death. The dramatist recognized that something had to be done to evoke the desired mnemonic responses and regulate the theurgic response, while never ceasing to entertain the audience. And so, the form and function of the projected spectacle had to be carefully defined, narrated, and explained with respect to the conditions of artifice operating within the world of the play. Only in this way was both wonder and suspense sustained in such a way that victims of fatal destiny could communicate beyond the grave—and the stage—something that also went beyond the lessons mirrored in their brief lives.

2

'But yet each circumstance
I taste not fully':
Spectacles of Ruin

> . . . Learn by me
> To know your foes. In this belief I die:
> .   .   .   .
> Pride, greatness, honours, beauty, youth, ambition,
> You must all down together; there's no help for 't.
> Yet this my gladness is, that I remove,
> Tasting the same death in a cup of love. [*Dies.*]
> (Middleton, *Women Beware Women*, 5.2. 213 ff.)

These lines, spoken by Bianca, the factor's wife, after she has
seized the poisoned cup and drunk from it—the last in a series of
many deaths depicted on stage—invite the audience to see her
death as an object lesson. But we are asked to learn by her fate, not
how to live more moral or chaste or well-ordered lives, but how to
recognize our foes. As we saw in the previous chapter, the slump-
ing into death calls forth a moment of reflection, during which
time we can frame up, in the theatre of our minds, the image
evoked through the presentation of fatal destiny. This passage also
comments on the toppling of mortal strivings and attributes, and
the contentment this can bring. Wresting something from this de-
feat, to the point of greeting death with gladness—even smiling—
is something this chapter seeks to examine more closely with
respect to the Aesthetic of Decline. Also the verb 'tasting' is something that will recur in dramatic exhibitions of quaint devices
associated with the coming of death. This brief passage will have

served its purpose if these several themes are recalled as we pro-
ceed; and so, Bianca, adieu.

Such kinetic emblems, like dumb shows and *tableaux vivants*,
drew on principles of the Renaissance Memory Arts—especially
where sorrow and lamentation, loss and decline, are involved. The
extent to which they overlapped with theurgic concerns, through
the projected doubling of fatal perspectives on stage, comes further into focus through a cunning pair of spectacles. The word
'spectacles' here is to be taken in a double sense. First, quite literally, meaning a pair of magic glasses; a convenient stage prop in
Webster's *White Devil*, reminiscent of Pasolini's binoculars. And
second, 'two spectacles' implies as well a larger, more complicated, staged event, involving the conjuring of a perspective glass,
or magic mirror, within the already charmed frame of the play. By
virtue of the mnemonic principles brought into play, in conjunc-
tion with the individual 'engrammic energy' that is thus aroused,
the memory-picture evoked and represented through such stage
artifice is both easy to recover and difficult to forget. While the
effect of such scenes mirroring fatal destiny are enduring and pro-
found, what, finally, is the end of such melancholy stagecraft, and
how is it to be assessed? This chapter takes up just such a line of
questioning, and does so with respect to the principles associated
with the Renaissance Aesthetic of Decline.

PERSPECTIVE GLASSES AND PROJECTIONS OF DEATH

Webster's *The White Devil* (2.2) presents an exemplary staging of
double perspective which, by modern standards, is comparable to
a concealed closed-circuit television camera. Given the theurgic
elements evoked and represented in this episode, it is most fitting
that a conjurer sets up, verbally designates, and thus context-
ualizes this plot of charmed stage-space. Mimicking the role of a
playwright, the conjurer seeks to convince the on-stage viewer,
like the audience, to attend to the subtle device. Bracciano's gaze
is directed first to one far-removed place and then to another. This
charmed, privileged vision reveals what amounts to 'off-stage'
action that is central to the drama's main plot. It has the effect of
emblematically collapsing time and space by virtue of esoteric

artifice. These mimed images are therefore all the more memorable because they are accorded a separate (and, as it were, impossible) space within which to transpire. To account for this staging of doubled vision, Webster calls attention to the correspondence between the place of dumb shows and that of dreams by using the stage-property of a magical nightcap.[1]

> . . . pray sit down.
> Put on this night-cap sir, 'tis charmed,—and now
> I'll show you by my strong-commanding art
> The circumstance that breaks your duchess' heart.
>
> (2.2.20–3)

This device both embodies and emblematizes an extraordinary form of specular artifice which is contextualized as transgressing what is considered lawful or 'natural'. In this sense, both the device used and the fatal double perspective presented are explained and excused as the result of supernatural cunning. With his nightcap secure on his head, Bracciano sits comfortably before a charmed perspective space to watch henchmen set up the artifice that will kill his wife, the duchess; they are wearing protective 'spectacles of glass'.[2] A description of the mimed action follows and, as with an emblem, the matter depicted through the kinetic memory images is clarified through commentary:

Enter suspiciously, JULIO *and another, they draw a curtain where Bracciano's picture is, they put on spectacles of glass, which cover their eyes and noses, and then burn perfumes afore the picture, and wash the lips of the picture, that done, quenching the fire, and putting off their*

---

[1] The overlapping of reported dreams and on-stage emblematic commentary, contextualized as the projection of a fatal perspective, inaugurates the main course of bloody action in *The White Devil* (1.2.229–68). Further, a kind of mnemonic echo is set up from within the linguistic world of the play regarding 'night-cap', which thereby creates an associative link between impending death and marital deception: 'Come you know not where my night-cap wrings me' (1.2.87).

[2] Cf. Flamineo's extended conceit about the 'spectacles fashion'd with such perspective art' so that one image appears to be multiplied many times over (1.2.99–107). This is another case where the rhetorical register of the play sets up associative, mnemonic traps for the audience, in the form of resonant verbal cues, for the future appearance of images that will play off and extend the meaning of the quaint devices the playwright so meticulously puts in place.

spectacles they depart laughing. Enter ISABELLA *in her nightgown as to bed-ward, with lights after her, Count* LODOVICO, GIOVANNI, *and others waiting on her, she kneels down as to prayers, then draws the curtain of the picture, does three reverences to it, and kisses it thrice, she faints and will not suffer them to come near it, dies, sorrow express'd in* GIOVANNI *and in Count* LODOVICO; *she's convey'd out solemnly.*

BRACCIANO: Excellent, then she's dead,—
CONJURER: She's poisoned,
By the fum'd picture,—'twas her custom nightly,
Before she went to bed, to go and visit
Your picture, and to feed her eyes and lips
On the dead shadow,—Doctor Julio
Observing this, infects it with an oil
And other poison'd stuff, which presently
Did suffocate her spirits . . .

         .   .   .   .

                              —now turn another way,
And view Camillo's far more politic fate,—
Strike louder music from this charmed ground,
To yield, as fits the act, a tragic sound.

(2.2.24–37)

The second dumb show and execution, following the specular and rhetorical pattern established by the first, likewise is conveyed doubly through image and motto—thus fixing it in the charmed ground upon which our own Memory Theatre can be constructed.

Enter FLAMINEO, MARCELLO, CAMILLO, *with four more as Captains, they drink healths and dance; a vaulting-horse is brought into the room;* MARCELLO *and two more whisper'd out of the room while* FLAMINEO *and* CAMILLO *strip themselves into their shirts, as to vault; compliment who shall begin; as* CAMILLO *is about to vault,* FLAMINEO *pitcheth him upon his neck, and with the help of the rest, writhes his neck about, seems to see if it be broken, and lays him folded double as 'twere under the horse, makes shows to call for help;* MARCELLO *comes in, laments, sends for the Cardinal [*MONTICELSO*] and Duke [*FRANCISCO*], who comes forth with armed men; wonder at the act; [*FRANCISCO*] commands the body to be carried home, apprehends* FLAMINEO, MARCELLO, *and the rest, and [all] go as 'twere to apprehend* VITTORIA.

BRACCIANO: 'Twas quaintly done . . .

Instead of a moral tag to sum the event, Bracciano comments on the manner and not the matter of the execution. Attention thus is redirected to the quaintness of the device. He continues: 'but yet each circumstance | I taste not fully' (2.2.37–8).[3] Through additional narration Bracciano is allowed to 'taste' them again, and so too are we made to revisit in another way these simulated violations of life, and like Francisco to 'wonder at the act'. Above all else this double take enables us to marvel as well at Webster's highly developed theatrical sense of how to get the most out of a cunningly ingenious fatal design. The narration leaves no doubt about the events being mimed. The conjurer again plays the role of the chorus; an instrument of the design, he doubles now as the commentary to this page from a kinetic emblem book.

> CONJURER: O 'twas most apparent,
> You saw them enter charged with their deep healths
> To their boon voyage, and to second that,
> Flamineo calls to have a vaulting horse
> Maintain their sport. The virtuous Marcello
> Is innocently plotted forth the room,
> Whilst your eye saw the rest, and can inform you
> The engine of all.
>
> (2.2.39–46)

A threefold function is served by rhetorically recalling the 'engine of all', which, with the elimination of Isabella and Camillo, sets in motion Bracciano's scheme to consolidate power and make Vittoria his wife. First, it fixes the double frames of the executions in the viewer's mind's eye. Second, it underscores Bracciano's amoral aims. And third, it allows us to marvel again at the quaint device. The magic nightcap and prophylactic spectacles are central both in evoking and effectuating the staging of such enframed fatal perspectives which, as we have seen before, function as mnemonic placeholders in the drama and wind up the charm conducing to the theurgic charge of the overall spectacle.

---

[3] Cf. *The Revenger's Tragedy* (1.4.19–21), when Hippolito says to Antonio about the details of the virtuous lady's ceremonial suicide, thus evoking a kind of macabre savouring of the event: 'My lord, since you invite us to your sorrows, | Let's truly taste 'em with equal comfort, | As to ourselves, we may relieve your wrongs.'

Marvelous, macabre, and at times grotesque moments like these were part and parcel of both Memory Theatres and Renaissance English tragic dramas.[4] They bring into view the underlying tension between old and emerging dramatic conventions, and also the tension between the world of the drama and the reality it both mocks and laments. How exactly, though, this comes about can be discovered in the double nature of silent fatal spectacles which project and presume several things at once.[5] For example, George Chapman's *Bussy D'Ambois* presents a more complex version of this coincidence of death, dumb shows, and the staging of double perspective. In it we find laid bare the workings of the Aesthetic of Decline, which to a large extent characterize this tragedy's peculiar use of mnemonic frames of reference and theurgic incantations to body forth evanescent images of ruin.

The friar in *Bussy D'Ambois* uses obscure incantations and fustian Latin, rather than a magic nightcap, to conjure up forbidden images. The words themselves are said to have the theurgic power to raise a spirit, just as stage-rhetoric can call to mind the locale of a battle, as with the chorus of Shakespeare's *Henry V*. But something else is called up when the stage-rhetoric mimics the conjuring of spirits, not places. And so let us consider another display of stage-conjuring that, on the surface, appears to be a more overt use of words of power to accomplish a comparable, long-lasting mnemonic effect. Specifically, in Marlowe's *Doctor Faustus* the invocatory spell is not the primary cause leading to the appearance of Mephistophilis. Rather, this demon, while travelling through the world, happened to hear someone abjure the Trinity, which, according to the demon, put the blasphemer's soul at risk. Although in and of themselves the words are important in *Doctor Faustus*, they are not what raise the spirit. While there seems to be a more direct correspondence to words and theurgic activity in the world of Chapman's play, the issues of salvation and

---

[4] It is appropriate here to recall Fulwood's *Castel of Memorie* on the decorum of appointing artificial Memory Theatres with 'mery, cruell, iniurious, merueilous, excellently faire, or excedingly foule things' that 'better styre up the Memorie'.

[5] Cf. Neill, 'Funeral Pageantry', 189, n. 34; and Phoebe S. Spinrad, 'Ceremonies of Complement: The Symbolic Marriage in Ford's *The Broken Heart*', *Philological Quarterly*, 65: 1 (Winter 1986), 34.

damnation and of moral bearings in general are not at all self-evident here.

So too, despite generations of moralized and moralistic readings of Marlowe's *Tragicall History of the Life and Death of Doctor Faustus* (for we need to keep in mind the publisher's evocation of certain theatrical expectations associated with the biographical allegory presented through the play), the aim of the spectacle, as the Prologue announces, is to 'perform the form of Faustus' fortunes good or bad'.[6] The Latin root of 'form' means shape or physical manifestation. Therefore, to 'perform the form' of one's fortunes is, mimetically and allegorically, to body forth the shape that those fortunes can be said to have taken in the world howsoever we subsequently judge them to be. What is more, this issue, which merges theurgic and aesthetic concerns, is commented on at a key juncture in Faustus's changing fortunes.

The form that the spirit takes is too terrible for Faustus to look upon, and so he orders him to 'change thy shape . . . | Go, and return an old Franciscan friar; | That holy shape becomes a devil best' (1.3.23–6). It is not, as we later learn, his command that impels Mephistophilis to take on the outward show of a friar. Rather, reminiscent of Hamlet's attempt to appeal to the power of the spectacle to cause the malefactor to be struck to his soul, Mephistophilis is out to get a soul. The only way to do this, though, is to cause someone, of his own free will as it were, to give himself over to the joys of spectacles. One way of bringing this about, as the tricks and visual deceits presented in *Faustus* bear out (especially the episode with the sham Helen of Troy), is to cause the viewer, who thinks he is in control, to be distracted and delighted with the rapture made possible through conjured images—namely, through the cunning of the scene.[7] In this case the scene was cunningly played, but the viewer, Faustus, was not cunning enough to see through the illusion. Either that, or he did not want to believe what he knew the truth to be regarding what he was seeing, and thus allowed himself (and ultimately, his soul) to be carried away by what he saw. As we have seen, 'cunning' in the

[6] Christopher Marlowe, *The Complete Plays*, ed. Irving Ribner (Indianapolis and New York: Bobbs-Merrill, 1963), 358.

[7] Cf. Watson, 'Tragedy', 336.

Renaissance carried with it a backlog of meanings relating variously to stage plays, deceitfulness, and supernatural craft—all
three of which apply to the cases of Faustus and to Bussy. Both
plays, through the content portrayed as well as through the forms
of artifice staged, partake of and reflect an overriding Aesthetic of
Decline. Both tragic heroes ride the wheel of Fortune and both are
cast down, declining ever further, toward death—and beyond even
this.[8] The forms of their fortunes, however, once they leave the
world, are spoken of in quite different terms: Faust descends to
burn in Lucifer's realm, and Bussy rises to join with a flaming star,
as part of the empyrean.[9] And yet both, in their fiery, fleeting
evanescence, are exemplary emblems of the Spirit of Decline, so
much a part of the Renaissance view of the destiny of mankind
and human history.

In line with this, and given the appearance of an actor disguised
as a friar understood to be a devil throughout *Faustus*, it is wholly
in keeping with a certain dramatic and emblematic spirit of the
age that in *Bussy* it is a friar, acting as a conjurer, who raises
and commands demons. The Friar in *Bussy* does this by virtue of
knowing—and chanting—the correct words of power. Behemoth
comes from the world of darkness, which is comparable to the
uncanny dream-space that lent emblematic lustre to Kyd's parable
of 'sweet Revenge' in *The Spanish Tragedy*, and to the conjurer's
cunning art that brings about the quaint deaths in Webster's
dramatic web of intrigue and counter-plots in *The White Devil*.

The Friar in *Bussy* orders a lesser spirit to retrieve a letter that
implicates Bussy's beloved Tamyra, which leads ultimately to her
being beaten and put on the rack by her husband. Bearing in mind
the importance of letters in this drama, whether those said to be
written in ink or in blood, it is both appropriate and chillingly
ironic that this spirit is named Cartophylax, 'Keeper of Papers'.
The friar entreats: 'Show us all their persons, | And represent the
place, with all their actions' (4.2.88–9). This part of the conjuring
goes as expected, but the mission ultimately is frustrated because

---

[8] Cf. Frederick Kiefer, *Fortune and Elizabethan Tragedy* (San Marino:
Huntington Library Press, 1983), 286.
[9] Alastair Fowler, *Time's Purpled Masquers: Stars and the Afterlife in
Renaissance English Literature* (Oxford: Clarendon Press, 1996).

another, more powerful spirit already has been raised to guard the paper. Though we do not see this greater spirit being conjured, its imputed presence is an acceptable, if facile, explanation for why the design is thwarted. It also indicates that certain cosmic principles govern the world of the play, which pertain both to the natural and supernatural realms depicted within it, and that there is a definitive hierarchy of powers, rules, and rituals that must strictly be obeyed even though they may not be discernable from a mortal (and conventionally moral) point of view. Some other order of perspective must be enlisted, by means of which the audience must be trained to see what the spectacle portends. But uncovering it is not self-evident.

The *tableau vivant*, instead of being transparent and immediately accessible, thwarts protocols of expected legibility. Bussy's enemies silently are shown examining the fatal letter. Bussy asks, 'May we not hear them?' The Friar instructs him in the rules of this spectacle: 'No, be still and see' (4.2.99). Bussy has been taken in by the illusion, and like the naïve but well-meaning bumpkin who jumps on-stage to save the play-heroine, resolves: 'I will go fetch the paper.' The Friar, who has been his intermediary from the start, patiently defines the limits of these supernatural powers to Bussy, and also reminds the audience of the rules and boundaries of the charmed perspective: 'Do not stir. | There's too much distance and too many locks | 'Twixt you and them, how near soe'er they seem, | For any man to interrupt their secrets' (4.2.100–3).

Similar fatal spectacles and accompanying commentary on the charmed space of such multiple perspectives—also generated by a theurgically adept friar—occur, among other places, in the sixth scene of Greene's *Friar Bacon and Friar Bungay*. Upon being admonished by Friar Bacon to hold his hands back from stabbing the images he beholds in the glass, Edward admits: 'Choler to see the traitors 'gree so well | Made me think the shadows substances'; Bacon replies to Edward: ' 'Twere a long poniard, my lord, to reach between | Oxford and Fressingfield. But sit still and see more.'[10]

---

[10] Robert Greene, *Friar Bacon and Friar Bungay*, ed. Daniel Seltzer (Lincoln: University of Nebraska Press, 1963), scene vi, ll. 129–32.

More poignant still is the scene when Bacon destroys his magic mirror after it has led two sons to fight with and kill one another once they see, in the charmed glass, their fathers fighting (13, 20–84). The same applies to Bussy, who, like Greene's Edward and like the audience, must be still and watch the tragic action unfold. Bussy is shown sights that cause him grief and distress, and what aggravates him all the more is that he sees things that call for action and yet he cannot act. He is helpless to do anything to stop the conspirators from reading the fatal letter in silence. The power of these silent 'characters' (in both senses of the term) to condemn her is recognized fully by Tamyra (4.1.204–5): 'Papers hold | Oft times the forms and copies of our souls'; and further, her written words are figured as 'a glass of ink where you may see | how to make ready black-fac'd Tragedy' (4.2.109–10). It is in and through this metaphorical mirror of ink that Montsurrey reads and sees himself as a cuckold, which leads to the bloody and 'black fac'd' tragic conclusion of Tamyra, of the friar, of Bussy, and of the play bearing his name.

From the outset, Bussy has advocated, and ends up being an emblem of, plain speaking and plain dealing. The audience is made to see in him the traits and ideals of a previous era; he is a man 'out of time', both in the sense of honouring bygone virtues and of having reached the end of what he can accomplish with his life. The opening scene characterizes him as being out of favour with the existing order, out of step with 'Occasion'. Bussy's first soliloquy is a fairly commonplace invective against fortune.[11] And yet some of his words, which are resonantly proverbial, take on deeper resonance with respect to the theurgic undercurrent of the play: 'Man is a torch borne in the wind, a dream | But a shadow, summ'd with all his substance' (1.1.18–19). This sententious formulation of an old motif, which parallels the visual confusion of shadow and substance in the magic mirror of Friar Bacon, is given voice by a character (Bussy), whose own life (his substance) is summed up, chorus-like, by the ghost (the shadow or shade) of the Friar, Bussy's friend, teacher, and procurer: 'Farewell, brave relics of a complete man' (5.4.146). The literal and figurative decline

---

[11] Cf. John Huntington, *Ambition, Rank, and Poetry in 1590s England* (Urbana and Chicago: University of Illinois Press, 2001), 83.

and fall of Bussy coalesce in the moment when, mortally wounded, he chooses to prop himself up with, and then to fall on, his own sword. More an antique Roman than a Frenchman ('I am up | Here like a Roman statue! I will stand | Till death hath made me marble' (5.4.95–6)), Bussy exemplifies and exhausts a lost standard of heroic virtue. In the end the play's hero, displayed as a corpse, is apostrophized as a relic. It is then said of him that his 'spirit made a star' joins 'flames with Hercules' (5.4.147).[12]

This is not, strictly speaking, a dramatic apotheosis; neither is it a simple encomium.[13] Closer scrutiny of this passage reveals that Bussy is linked to Hercules. Like Bussy, Hercules' passion leads to the death of his beloved, and both are given a heroic life beyond their mortal span.[14] In the Renaissance Hercules was a symbol not only of physical strength but also of earthly glory; and he was often depicted 'at the crossroads' of the easy road of pleasure and the more arduous road of virtue and honour—he chooses the latter.[15] Further, Bussy's remains are linked to the disparate stars making up the constellation 'Hercules', which is itself a mnemonic map in the heavens that calls to mind the shape of this hero and, along with it, the form of his fortunes. As such it provides a key to recognizing the new and involved kind of allegory being projected onto the backdrop of the personal Memory Theatre of someone watching this spectacle. It anticipates the dissolution of the very image which is being projected. As such, it portends and conveys an allegory of fatal passage. Bussy's flesh is metaphorized as being the relics of what was once a complete man; his spirit, a fireball in the heavens. Both flesh and spirit are figured, each after its own realm, as disintegrating. Furthermore, the emblem that is presented through the passing away of Bussy is a mnemonic placeholder that urges us to look from multiple, and in this case appositive but complementary, points of view.

[12] Cf. the poetic commentary to Fig. 4: 'Death puft this light: and his earth-banisht Flame | Flew up to heav'n, and so a starre became.'

[13] Cf. Neill, *Issues of Death*, 37.

[14] Ovid, *Metamorphoses*, ix. 240–73, treats the apotheosis of Hercules, when he is borne aloft in divine chariot and weds Hebe, goddess of youth—the first mortal to be thus honoured with deification.

[15] Erwin Panofsky, 'Hercules am Scheidewege', *Studien der Biblothek Warburg* (Leipzig, 1930).

Thus, with the passing of Chapman's Bussy, we are presented with an image of the passing away of an entire order: his spirit 'made a star' and joined 'flames with Hercules', whose new lustre will 'cheer with new sparks of old humanity'. In the end, the moralized spectacle of his bloody corpse turns the dramatic moment into a stylized and complicated emblem of transience, not only of man but also of the principles governing the aesthetic through which such meanings emblematically were conveyed. It is with this fallen temple of a man, this ruin, figured as 'brave relics', that we reach for an end, not only of this play, but also of the mimetic viability of the staging of such allegorical figures in a English Renaissance drama.

Appropriately then, this judgement concerning the death of Bussy (like the Ghost in *The Spanish Tragedy*) is passed by one who is himself already dead. The Friar is referred to as 'Umbra', meaning shadow or shade.[16] Indeed, he is a 'shade of memory', to call on one of the plays of meaning implicit in the subtitle of this book. He portrays, and can be said to stand for, a man's shadow— a cunning double reverse of the commonplace theme that actors were said to be shadows of things in the world.[17] It is in this light that I would have us review Bussy's proclamation that 'Man is a torch borne in the wind, a dream | But a shadow, summ'd with all his substance' (1.1.18 f.). For in the shadow, the simulacrum, taking on a theatrical life of its own through the character of the Friar, we can glimpse the darker purpose of Chapman's use of it at the conclusion of his drama. The words of final benediction pronounced over the body, over the ruins of Bussy, over the emblem of the fall of antique manly virtue (and, by extension, over the artifice it uses and the Aesthetic of Decline it thus enshrines), would

---

[16] R. H., *Of Ghosts and Spirites* (London, 1596), sig. A11ᵛ: 'Servius writeth, that *Vmbrae* were called *Laruae* and they call dead mens souls by the name of *Vmbrae*.'

[17] Cf. Puck's commonplace reference to actors being shadows that but body forth actions people might play in life (*A Midsummer Night's Dream*, 5.1.423–6). On the philosophical framework for the debate over art being a shadow of the sensory world, with special reference to forms of imitation, see Barish, *The Antitheatrical Prejudice*, 5–37; and on the currency, and implications, of such tropes concerning shadows in the Renaissance, see Engel, *Mapping Mortality*, 203–9; see also Shakespeare, 'Sonnet 43'.

have been uttered by a chapel boy who was a 'counterfeit present-ment' of a friar's shade or shadow, thus collapsing three frames of reference, where he stood, into one voice.

For it is from within the magic circle of the stage that such char-acters speak about the troubling status of others who are made to speak their own parts in a more encompassing allegorical spec-tacle.[18] The shadow of the Friar, with all of its moralizing fervour, thus speaks about the status of a figure of ruin. At the vertiginous bottom of this dark conceit is the message that whenever allegory speak about itself, it does so from beyond the grave, as it were, and can do so best when commenting on death itself. This bears comparison to the brave fall of Antonio's wife in *The Revenger's Tragedy*. She is declared to have embodied, and died in the name of, virtues of an older order, virtues that are out of step with and different from those prevalent in the existing court. As a drama-tized version of an emblem of heroic death, she sends her message from beyond the grave, both to those on and those beyond the stage.[19] The ramifications of Bussy's allegorical fall, and the fall of allegory in the play commented on by the shade of memory, by 'Umbra', can be discussed in terms of Walter Benjamin's sugges-tion that history does not assume the form of the process of an eternal life so much as that of irresistible decay. Though ruined, Bussy is said to become one with a shooting star whose force and movement will, it is projected, 'Make the vast crystal crack with thy receipt' (5.4.150). And by extension, in the tragic drama of this period, allegory, by virtue of the decay it signals and embodies, can be said to cling to, and mimic, and declare itself to be beyond earthly beauty.

BEYOND CONJURING ART

Having seen, and 'tasted', the effect of a pair of lamentable spec-tacles of death in *The White Devil* and *Bussy D'Ambois*, and with the fates and fortunes of the heroic victims thus emblazoned in the

[18] *Antony and Cleopatra*, 5.2.218–22.
[19] This presents a subtle twist to the similar display of mute action in *The Revenger's Tragedy*, with respect to Antonio's wife, discussed in the previous chapter.

Theatre of Memory, let us consider a final scene from English tragic drama with respect to the analogy that allegories are in the realm of thoughts what ruins are in the realm of things.[20] In what may well be the most conspicuously self-referential allegorical English play of lamentation, John Ford's *The Broken Heart*, the characters' names signify their states of being, which evolve from, and are revealed by, the play's main action.[21] This is similar in kind though different in degree from the reductive use of attributes, virtues or vices, or states of mind to designate characters in earlier morality plays like *Everyman* or in political satires like Skelton's *Magnyfycence*; the same goes for 'humour plays', like those championed by Jonson, where names correspond to animals or attitudes or stock character-types.[22] In Ford's play, though, the characters themselves, no less than what they are said to stand for, mediate a process of thought rather than the thought itself.[23]

It is this emphasis on the process of the unfolding of signification that recalls one's engagement with discovering the marvellous that attends the mental piecing together of an ingeniously devised emblem. Accordingly, Penthea conveys and displays the range of lament that her name implies. Orgilus, because of ancient family enmities is, as his name connotes, a hyper-kinetic memory image of pride. Likewise, owing to the putative internal development of Ithocles, his character displays and projects the honouring of loveliness; and his beloved Calantha, a beautiful flower too fragile and delicate to live long or well in the inhospitable clime of the court.[24] Each of these characters' characters, thus personified, can be apprehended as coming across (from the allegorical space of the play to the theatrical space animated by the presence of an audience) in terms of conventional emblems. Their names are like the word or motto, and the image or picture is captured in their actions—especially those performed as if from

---

[20] Benjamin, *Origin of German Tragic Drama*, 178.

[21] Thelma N. Greenfield, 'The Language of Process in Ford's *The Broken Heart*', *PMLA* (1987), 398.

[22] Hardin Craig, *English Religious Drama*, 341–53, 382–9.

[23] William Morris's introduction to Algernon Swinburne, *Essays and Studies* (London: Chatto and Windus, 1875), p. xxviii, as discussed by Greenfield, 'Language of Process', 397.

[24] Cf. Spinrad, 'Ceremonies of Complement', 25.

within the frame of a highly stylized vignette, like the preparations for the opening of Ithocles' veins or like Calantha's ceremonial marriage to a corpse. The third component of the emblem, the commentary, comes from the choric pronouncements which, more often than not in *The Broken Heart*, rhyme and are set to music. With Ford's characters thus functioning like separate pages making up a larger, thematically consistent, kinetic emblem book, we are left wondering not only at the strangeness of some of the memorably vivid images, but also at what, if anything, might be the unifying theme or character of this collection as a whole.

No single character stands out as a hero (in the conventional sense of the term), and none is worthy of our unconditional sympathy or antipathy, thus making the dramatic plan of this play an early modern precursor of what Brecht called 'Alienation-effects': 'Stories have to be narrated in various ways . . . the Englishmen of the Elizabethan age with the self-awareness of the new individual personality which was then uncontrollably bursting out. [. . .]The old Alienation-effects quite remove the object represented from the spectator's grasp, turning it into something that cannot be altered.'[25] The conditions of artifice are so pronounced in Ford's spectacle that they become like a character in their own right, whose movements, and whose steady and unswerving decline, characterize the ethos of this play of mourning. As such the drive toward allegorization functions here like a kind of supernal demiurge, overseeing and invisibly taking part in, and, to some extent, guiding, the action. The theurgic energy can be detected through its effects—effects that in the dynamics of their reception might well have been considered alien and alienating to some members of the Caroline audience, whether because of uncanny parallels with aspects of High Church ritual or because of the elements of archaic stage artifice.

But, irrespective of changing attitudes toward the reformation or counter-reformation of religious rites during Ford's day, we have here, in *The Broken Heart*, a remarkable iteration of the way sheer aestheticism can supercharge actions on stage—actions involving decline, death, and passage—and endow them with a

[25] Brecht, *Brecht on Theatre*, 180, 182, 192.

kind of emblematic theurgic power that is difficult to name. Still, the highly ritualized expressions of the artifice are never fully concealed in the world of the play. Those in the audience who become so absorbed in what is being represented, and forget to attend to how it is being rendered, however, will lose sight of them temporarily; and yet, they do so at their own peril. Such spectators are punished, not so much for *mis*reading the play as for believing that it is something they can read at all using everyday eyes. The evocation of theurgic power through the apparently static, ritual actions on the stage, within the closed circuit of charmed theatrical space, complicates any simple, narrative-oriented reading of the drama or of the emblems depicted.

For example, the complex machinations of the play's many plots culminate in a double ceremony of abdication and marriage. The symbolic quality of the deteriorating political and social issues, as the spectacle unfolds death upon death, is revealed more through the reflection of the conditions of artifice that effectuate the staging of certain emblems rather than through the words or images alone.[26] Prior to the double ceremony, Penthea dies by her own hand; and, even more dramatically, Orgilus drains his blood by a slow, ritual suicide (5.2.97–160). The effect is that, while his life is being drained from his body (this shadow of a man, this actor, becoming, in the world of the play, a shadow or shade of a man), his capacity to signify meaningfully in the world, in and through this extreme act, instead of being depleted of signifying content, is consummated and realized. It is with this in mind that the audience is invited, impelled, and trained to see the final scene, which, although not a framed spectacle properly speaking, is a highly charged, extravagant allegory of the staging of fatal perspective.

The last minutes of this play bring together the artifice of the dumb show and death, and, in a more stylized presentation than the cases discussed so far in Part I, it thereby creates a double perspective in which the staged action elides, and eventually gives way to, ceremonial, though nearly static, stagecraft. We are like pro-

---

[26] John Ford, *The Broken Heart*, ed. Brian Morris (New York: Hill & Wang, 1966), p. xxv.

fane interlopers in a world of high ritual where awesome mysteries are unfolding before our eyes.

An altar covered with white; two lights of virgin wax, during which
music of recorders; enter four bearing ITHOCLES *on a hearse, or in a*
chair, in a rich robe, and a crown on his head; place him on one side of the
altar. After him enter CALANTHA, *in a white robe, and crowned;*
EUPHRANEA, PHILEMA, CHRISTALLA, *in white;* NEARCHUS, ARMOSTES,
CROTOLON, PROPHILUS, AMELUS, BASSANES, LEMOPHIL, *and* GRONEAS.
CALANTHA *goes and kneels before the altar, the rest stand off, the women*
kneeling behind. Cease recorders, during her devotions. Soft music.
CALANTHA *and the rest rise, doing obeisance to the altar.* (5.3)

After this procession and the display of her heartfelt protestations
of reverence, Calantha turns to the crowned corpse, 'thou shadow
| Of my contracted lord', and places on its finger her mother's
wedding ring (5.3.62). The frisson evoked from this gruesome
scene owes it power not only to the marriage of the living to the
dead, but to her being wed to the only proper and appropriate
object of her love, which is not simply Ithocles, but Ithocles in
death—and, at the same time, Ithocles *as* King Death, emblematically rendered with his costume of sovereignty.[27]

> Thus I new-marry him whose wife I am;
> Death shall not separate us. Oh, my lords,
> I but deceived your eyes with antic gesture,
> When one news straight came huddling on another
> Of death, and death, and death. Still I danced forward;
> But it struck home, and here, and in an instant.
> Be such mere women, who with shrieks and outcries
> Can vow a present end to all their sorrows,
> Yet live to vow new pleasures, and outlive them.
> They are the silent griefs which cut the heart-strings;
> Let me die smiling.
>
> (5.3.66–76)

[27] See Michael Neill, *Issues of Death: Mortality and Identity in English
Renaissance Tragedy* (Oxford: Clarendon Press, 1997), 354–74, esp. 363 on
Calantha's 'artful dying'; also see Colin Gibson, ' "The Stage of my Mortality":
Ford's Poetry of Death', and Harriett Hawkins, 'Mortality, Morality, and
Modernity in *The Broken Heart*', both in Michael Neill (ed.), *John Ford: Critical
Re-visions* (Cambridge and New York: Cambridge University Press, 1988).

Death shall not separate them indeed, for like Proserpine in Kyd's *Spanish Tragedy*, she has given up her earthly dominion for a life among shades, and has been wedded to Death. And so it is, she dies (as she had hoped) smiling; but only after kissing the 'cold lips' of the shadow of her beloved, following a melancholy dirge reminding those on stage, and beyond it as well, of the transience of mortal glories. The dirge concludes with lines which sum the substance of the play: 'Love only reigns in death, though art | Can find no comfort for a broken heart' (5.3.93–4).

These words having been sung, Calantha, with no more words of her own, dies.[28] Whether she is shown smiling or not, a strong message is conveyed to the audience either way, since her words are so ironically resonant: 'They are the silent griefs which cut the heart-strings; | Let me die smiling.' If the scene is staged so that she can be seen to smile as she dies, it could be construed both as her contentment with the end of her fortune, and also as a mirror image of the rictus-grin of the corpse beside her. Traditionally, the decaying mouth, caught in a silent sardonic laugh, was moralized as mocking viewers with an image of that to which we all must come. Thus *The Broken Heart* offers what, according to Neill, 'now seems like a nostalgic retrospect of Renaissance drama's confrontation with death, even as it writes a *ne plus ultra* to the path of tragic discovery'.[29]

What is discovered, though, and yet what is easy to lose sight of once it has been symbolically brought into our purview, is that love may well reign in death; and yet, as Ford's spectacle demonstrates through an aestheticized allegory that modernizes and outstrips the union of Pluto and Proserpine (like that depicted in *The Spanish Tragedy*), it is perhaps beyond the power of art to provide an antidote to this extreme state of affairs, where beauty is represented as being beyond death itself.[30] And, through the use of spectacle and the memorable framing of an emblematically charmed, sacred space, this allegory of love reigning in death declares itself to be beyond beauty, to be beyond 'Calantha'. Her marriage to a corpse presents a tableau that is eerie and strange enough to qualify as an effective and long-lasting memory image.

---

[28] Neill, *Issues of Death*, 367.   [29] Ibid. 374.   [30] Ibid. 313.

It is at once wondrously foul and also wondrously fair. She hon-
ours and elevates, sacramentalizes and ennobles, extreme faithfulness in love. The episode is so pathetic that it borders on the
incredible; and yet it takes its source from Iberian history: Don
Pedro exhumed the body of his murdered wife, Ines, to crown her
queen.[31] This is more than a case of 'truth being stranger than fiction'. To be sure, the dramatization and celebration of love reigning in death reflects the baroque tendency to venerate ruins in
general, and to adorn and crown corpses in particular.[32]

Such striking images that are at once excellently fair and
exceedingly foul, to return to Fulwood's description of a decorous
memory image, when evoked in Renaissance dramas like
those discussed here, created and occupied a charmed space
which called forth cunning double perspective glasses. We cannot
dismiss them as being merely macabre and sensational stage-
business (though, to be sure, they are), since so much of the plot
hinges on reconfiguring these traditional emblematic structures
involving the face of death. We see in these fatal perspectives that
'the greater the implied significance, the greater the subjection to
death'.[33]

By such means, cunning dramatists evoked and represented
fatal perspectives by tapping into age-old cultural reservoirs of
memory images. And in doing so, like conjurers—whether
malignant or benign—they called into being theurgically charged
spaces in plays of mourning, such as *The Revenger's Tragedy* and
The Broken Heart, by virtue of using emblematic vignettes that
exposed and commented on the limits of staged illusions. In cases
like those just examined, mnemonic emblems bodied forth, and
themselves became, evanescent *tableaux vivants* designed to remain impressed on the inner lid of the mind's eye of the audience.
English tragic dramas like *The White Devil*, *Bussy D'Ambois*, and
The Broken Heart variously displayed spectacles of silent death to

---

[31] Shanti Padhi, '*The Broken Heart* and *The Second Maiden's Tragedy*: Ford's
Main Source for the Corpse's Coronation', *Notes & Queries*, 31: 2 (June 1984),
237; Verna Ann Foster and Stephen Ford, 'Structure and History in *The Broken
Heart*', *English Literary Renaissance*, 18: 2 (Spring 1988), 305–28.

[32] Luca Quattrocchi, 'Pearls of Eternity', in 'Something rich and strange',
FMR (English Edition), 28 (Sept.–Oct. 1987), 94.

[33] Benjamin, *Origin of German Tragic Drama*, 166.

evoke multiple perspectives on-stage, and in doing so pointed toward the end of the play—where, once again, end indicates both the play's inexorable conclusion and also its principal aesthetic aim: namely, to provide a portal to another space, to a charmed and highly charged mnemonic place, one which we are in part relieved to leave behind once the spectacle is over but which, to some extent (owing to how images tend to find places in the theatres of our minds), we still manage to recover and take away with us. Perhaps the greatest illusion about the illusion of theatrical distance is that we think we can entertain such cunning entities for a time only and then send them away. But the charm is wound; the spell has begun to weave its work.

But there is still more than meets the eye with regard to the mechanisms underlying the translation of substance to shadow, whether on the stage or in the realm of language or through lived experience. Indeed, there is a larger-than-life, intoxicating sense of theatre's translative capacity associated with the high rhetoric of the stage.[34] So too Memory was held to move shades of thought, transporting them from spirit, to picture, to word, and then out into the world:

To the memorie there belongeth iiii. Mouvnges. The fyrst is a mouinge of the spirites which transporteth figures or similitudes from the Cogitatyue to the Memoratiue. The seconde is a picturing and faininge of fygures in the same memories. The thyrd is a reportation of carrying againe of the spirites from the memoratiue to the cogitatiue or rationcinatiue. The fourth is that action by whych the cogitatiue considereth and knoweth thinges perfectly, the whiche is properly called the Memorie.[35]

This idea of translation—whether of ideas, words, or bodies—through 'faininge of figures', effectively characterizes how charms, and charmed words of the theatre especially, bring about the transference of meaning and power through art and in social

---

[34] Michael Neill, 'The World Beyond: Shakespeare and the Tropes of Translation' in R. B. Parker and S. P. Zitner (eds.), *Elizabethan Theatre: Essays in Honor of S. Schoenbaum* (Newark: University of Delaware Press, 1996), 291.

[35] William Fulwood, *Castel of Memorie* (London, 1573), sig. E7ᵛ.

relations. This is true, irrespective of the form it takes, whether on the stage or across a page, as a reflection of the way the world goes. Accordingly, the next chapter will explore how the self-conscious feigning of kinetic figures gave shape to, and animated, the mnemonically driven world of words in the Renaissance poetic imagination.

PART II

The True Work of Translation

3

'Now as touching my translation': Linguistic Decorum and Memory's Domain

> *Cæsar.* I fauori della corti sono come i Sereni dell'inuerno,
> & nuvoi della state, & la corte anticamente fù detta
> morte.
>
> *Tiberio.* Tuttauia è corte per i vitiosi, ma morte per i
> virtuosi, literati, & dotti.
>
> *Cæsar.* The fauors of the court are like faire weather in
> winter, or cloudes in summer, and court in former times
> was called death.
>
> *Tiberio.* It is still court for the vicious, but death for the
> vertuous, learned, and wise.
>
> (John Florio, *Second Frutes* (1591), sig. V1ᵛ–V2)

The rhyming wordplay of 'corte/morte' does not come through in
the English, 'court/death'. In the Italian, however, only one letter
keeps the words from becoming the other. Still, the translation
makes the sententious meaning clear: in former times the court
was called death because the vicious thrived, and it is still fatal for
the virtuous. This was certainly the case with the honourable
women mentioned in Part I, Antonio's wife, Bracciano's Isabella,
and Calantha; and it was the case as well for those who were
sinned against perhaps more than they sinned, like Tamyra and
the Duchess of Malfi. Still, the witty pairing of 'corte/morte' was
sufficiently sonorous and memorable to make John Florio include
it in his dual-language phrase-book which mixes platitudes and

puns, everyday matters of interest and obscure references. Part II
stands between *corte* and *morte*, between two chapters on drama
and two chapters on history, and seeks to bridge them. Appropriately, then, it concerns the work of translation as that which moves
mortal meanings from one shore to the other. In doing so, it anticipates the Conclusion, in which Charon's barque, while never
actually mentioned, is understood to slip its way across the River
Lethe, carrying the sheeted dead from one shore to their place of
rest—the restless dead, unable to speak and, in time, unable to remember where they came from or who they were. Charon trans-
ports the dead to the court of Pluto, where, as we saw in the case
of Andrea's shade, judgement is passed.

The transporting of bodies or words is the work of translation.
Metaphor, in the Renaissance, was itself metaphorized as being
'the figure of transport'.[1] Such a transporting, then, was understood not only as a word denoting transposition, but also as a
process connoting transformation. Bound up in the work of translation is a sense of faithfulness to the original—whether ideas or
images, words or deeds—toward which one has an obligation
and with which one tacitly enters into a relationship. Among the
Elizabethan translators who took this task to heart was Richard
Harrison: 'Now as touching my translation, although I have not
made him speak with like grace in English as hee dooth in Latine:
yet have I not chaunged his meaning, nor altered his matter,
endeavouring myself rather to make thee understand what thou
readest, then to smoothe and pollish it with fine & picked words.'[2]

The shades he was interested in translating and presenting to
his readers were grounded in the common stock of accumulated
popular lore and theological studies of those who had come
before him. But there is another kind of shade that he manages to
convey as well, the kind mentioned in the Introduction: 'the
shadow of anything'—in this case, the shadow of intended mean-

---

[1] George Puttenham, *The Arte of English Poesie* (1589), facsimile reprint
(Kent, Ohio: Kent State University Press, 1970), 189; Lee A. Sonnino, *A Handbook to Sixteenth-Century Rhetoric* (London: Routledge & Kegan Paul, 1968),
181–3.

[2] R.H. [Richard Harrison], *Of Ghosts and Spirites, Walking by Night. One
Book by Lewes Lauraterus of Tigurine translated by R.H.* (London, 1596), sig.
a3ᵛ–a4. An earlier edition appeared in 1570.

ing. This author is aware that there is something haunting the gap between what the text says in its original and what he is able to bring out in English. Like spirits denied access to speech, these shades of meaning, though unable to declare their presence, come to our attention because something happens to remind us that they are on the verge of slipping into oblivion. The author seems aware that they are buried—but not yet beyond being recovered— and though he lacks the means to conjure them to speak once more in their original voice, he would try to find a way to exorcise them. The true work of translation invites just such a fantastic, and poetic, way of thinking about shades of memory.

At the end of the last chapter I considered the intoxicating sense of theatre's translative capacity associated with the high rhetoric of the stage. In this chapter, however, the main drama, such as it is, is expressed through the work of the translator, and is seen in terms of the theatrical miming—or feigning—of habits of speech befitting one who would go places. In the Renaissance going from place to place, as has been seen, could mean, on the one hand, movement or commerce in the world and, on the other, movement in a landscape or a building within an artificial memory scheme.

But me thynketh it a verye easye thinge to deuise and imagine not onelye an hundreth but also infinite places, seeing no man is ignorant of where he was borne, or in whiche he hath long dwelled. Therefore when the mynde entreth in at the gate, while it considereth the diversities of wayes, directing and leading to diuers countries, and whiles it remembereth frendes houses, publicke dwellinge places, Palaces, or common places of Judgement, it shall fynde out a marueylous number of places. Hereto also it maye imagine great courtes or places of larger roume, wherein it may deeuise as great a number of places as it liketh, so that euery thinge may be written therein that he will haue.[3]

Whether moving, or travelling, in the world or within a mnemonic landscape, one was transported from the familiar to the foreign, even while engaged in translating foreign elements into familiar terms. As was seen in the Introduction, regarding Quarles's frontispiece, nothing less than one's soul is at stake in one's being translated 'by this to that', from this world to the

---

[3] William Fulwood, *Castel of Memorie* (London 1573), sig. F7.

other, from the earthly realm of imperfection and multiplicities, to the heavenly realm of perfection and divine unity. Even when construed in a more mundane, less theological way, words that allow one to translate ideas into language express one's character—one's spirit—in the world.

The translator in the Renaissance entered into a relationship both with the original work and his own cunning, with the goal of being as true to both as possible. The stakes remain the same: nothing less than one's soul, though not necessarily in a strict theological sense. There are other ways to conceive of the soul, or spirit, of a thing during the period. Accordingly, John Florio's translation 'Of giving the lie' in his *Essayes of Montaigne* (II. 18) indicates the reality, no less than the theurgic possibilities and power—the spirit—that Florio perceived to inhere in words: 'Our intelligence being onely conducted by the Word: Who so falsifieth the same, betraieth publik society. It is the onely instrument, by means wherof our wils and thoughts are communicated: it is the interpretour of our soules: If that faile us we hold our selves no more, we enterknow one another no longer' (sig. Kk2v). With words as the interpreter of the soul, since speech brings forth one's will and thoughts, the social dimension of the spirit is thus revealed. Florio raises here, as elsewhere, fundamental issues not only about linguistic forms—say, curses or proverbs—culled from a large field of possibilities, but also about the social, ethical, and ultimately the mysterious—we might even say the magical—work of language.

'A SHADOW OF A SUBSTANCE'

Harrison's apology touching his translation bears comparison with how John Florio began his translation of *Montaigne's Essayes*. Bristling with ingenious wordplay that sets the tone for the book that follows, the Preface proclaims that words, whatever their native tongue, embody and convey specific fields of meanings that reflect the spirit of that language:

Shall I apologize translation? Why but some hold (as for their free-hold) that such conversion is the subversion of Universities. God holde with them, and withholde them from impeach of empaire. It were an ill turne, the turning of Bookes should be the overturning of Libraries. Yea my old fellow Nolano [Giordano Bruno] tolde me, and taught publickly, that from translation all Science had it's of-spring. . . .

But . . . let me confesse . . . and let confession make halfe amends, that every language hath it's Genius and inseparable forme; without Pythagoras his Metempsychosis it can not rightly be translated. The Tuscan altiloquence, the Venus of the French, the sharpe state of the Spanish, the strong significancy of the Dutch cannot from heere be drawne to life. The sense may keepe forme: the sentence is disfigured; the fineness, fitnesse, featenesse diminished: as much as artes nature is short of natures arte, a picture of a body, a shadow of a substance.[4]

Judith Anderson has observed of this passage from Florio that 'the picture, the inferior imitation, is the rendering in one language of another language rather than a direct depiction of nature'.[5] Her analysis of Florio's craft recovers some important ground-rules about how we should be thinking about Renaissance ideas concerning the true work of translation:

Logically in Florio's statement, the original language is therefore comparable to 'natures arte', ' a body', and 'a substance.' The language of translation then appears to be at two removes from nature and implicitly, at least, the original language at one. . . . He sees that each language has a different character, a different perspective, or in Florio's words a different 'forme' and 'Genius.' . . . The world of words that Florio as dictionary-maker translates, and that he imagines, is not so very different from the world that, as a translator of Montaigne, he must try to recreate. Both have a kind of integrity or autonomy of their own. . . . Florio's pages evidence against the sense that words occupy a room of their own rather than simply stand for things. This is the essentially artistic, the poetic . . . awareness of words . . . (pp. 68–70)

The 'world of words' that Florio imagines (and, incidentally, this is the title given to his 1611 dictionary) becomes the medium through which his art grounds itself, and seeks truthfully to effect the work of translation. Thus we are no longer in a world where the vernacular simply is a shadow of the original, whether Latin or French or what-have-you, for this world of words embraces the

---

[4] John Florio, 'Preface', *Essayes of Michel Lord of Montaigne* (London, 1603).

[5] Judith H. Anderson, *Words that Matter: Linguistic Perception in Renaissance England* (Stanford: Stanford University Press, 1996), 68–70.

view that words themselves are translations of ideas partaking of a higher order of Being, in a Neoplatonic sense. With Florio we are in a world of words that subsumes previous notions of first-order or second-order degrees of truth-telling, for this world of words is animated by a genius of its own—a World-Soul or Spirit. In this sense, we have come upon a different kind of shade of memory here, and one that will attempt to speak through Florio's phrase-books.

His conception and conceit of a world of words is coextensive with his *World of Words*. It makes way for, and indeed creates, a space previously absent from the realm of social and linguistic relations in Renaissance England. And it is in this regard that, as Anderson puts it: 'the space that it inhabits is conceptual, but it is constructed from visible words, and it is perceived as being real in some sense. Moreover, it coexists with—here, in fact, emerges from—the lexical fixing of language' (p. 70). So too with the construction and comprehension of the truth of our being, which is bound up with and known through (and in terms of) words that are projected onto the material world. In the process of being thus set to work, words can be seen to leave a residual trace of their lineage, of where previously they have been along that metaphorical route or river-way, or crossing, traversing idea and thing, linking shadow and substance. Words, of course, are an essential feature of the art of poetry no less than of the work of translation.

Ben Jonson, in his own way, was committed to representing the truth that poetry could reveal to his readers, who might otherwise not get it without him.[6] His approach to poetry (whether his own, like the arresting elegy on the death of his son; or his strong, epigrammatic translations from Latin poets), like his approach to staged artifice (whether comedies of manners for the populace, or his stately masques for members of the royal court), led him to give cogent expression to the commonplace of Renaissance thought that language is the mirror of the soul—by which he meant one's truest form and inmost being. According to the terms

---

[6] Jonas Barish, *The Antitheatrical Prejudice* (Berkeley, Los Angeles, and London: University of California Press, 198), 133; Robert C. Evans, *Habits of Mind: Evidence and Effects of Ben Jonson's Reading* (Lewisburg: Bucknell University Press, 1995), 37–8.

of this analogy, which he copied out and commented on in his famous notebook, words expose rather than conceal what really is: 'Language most shewes a man: speake that I may see thee. It springs out of the most retired, and inmost parts of us, and is the Image of the Parent of it, the mind. No glasse renders a mans forme, or likenesse, so true as his speech. Nay, it is likened to a man; and as we consider feature, and composition in a man; so words in Language.'[7] Jonson elsewhere was concerned with translation as a process by which the truths of human life were exposed and expressed through words. In his notes under the commonplace heading 'De orationis dignitate', he commented that the 'propriety' of words rests in one's ability to 'draw them forth to their own just strength and nature, by way of Translation, or *Metaphore*'. During the Renaissance the rhetorical device known as *metaphora* was credited with conveying meanings from one place to another. The 'Englished' term for *metaphor* was a translation of the Greek word for 'translation'. And the word 'translation' itself, derived from the Latin *transfero*, meaning 'bear across', has, as Neill reminds us, 'as much to do with changing places as with shifting speech; it embraces the negotiation of all sorts of boundaries'.[8]

Florio embraces all of this and more in his phrase-books, collections of proverbs, and dictionaries, which, when taken together, can be seen to reflect the true work of the translator. He caters to, and further buttresses, a special kind of 'artificial memory' that was popular during the day. The notebook method of accumulating commonplaces, championed by Florio, is characteristic of Renaissance attitudes toward the translation not only of words and ideas in everyday commerce, but also of the body and soul on a journey toward death and beyond.[9] Accordingly, in what follows, I will examine the uses to which such an approach to recording the quotidian and seeing in it universal truths were put,

[7] Ben Jonson, *Timber: Or Discoveries: made upon men and matter* (London, 1641), under the heading 'Oratio imago animi'; see the edition by G. B. Harrison (London, 1923), 78.

[8] Michael Neill, 'The World Beyond: Shakespeare and the Tropes of Translation', in R. B. Parker and S. P. Zitner (eds.), *Elizabethan Theatre: Essays in Honor of S. Schoenbaum* (Newark: University of Delaware Press, 1996), 291.

[9] Engel, *Mapping Mortality*, 67–8.

taking as a focus the pre-eminent phrase-maker, sometime militant Protestant, and egregious Italian-about-London John Florio,
and the work of his literary successor John Torriano.[10]

MNEMONIC ASPECTS OF PROVERBS

When prospective travellers mulled over phrases, proverbs, and
word-lists before going abroad, they imagined themselves in that
foreign land—and did so by means of, and within, a discourse that
reflected a wealth of accumulated, if commonplace, experiences.
Prospective travellers anticipated what *will have been seen* once
the journey had been undertaken and they were safely back home.
For as the old adage aptly says—and it is recorded, among other
places, in the popular continuation of Florio's gathering of 6,000
Italian proverbs—'Che và e tourna fà buon viaggio' ('He who goes
and returns makes a good voyage').[11] Florio collected and gave
a new life to thousands of proverbs, and thereby displayed his
cunning no less than his essentially poetic awareness of words.

Words of proverbial wisdom are stabilized and linguistically
preserved in the form of old saws and catchphrases. Ultimately
they are grounded in, and initially they are derived from, lived
experience. It is in this respect that Florio's didactic transformation of the commonplace took part in the ideals of humanist cos-
mopolitanism while, at the same time, providing the traveller with
a linguistic passport to the everyday, the mundane.[12] Such proverbs
at times were contextualized as highly mannered, often rhymed
speech, and at other times as the street cant of South London.
Whatever form it took, though, in the end, for Florio, travel was

[10] See R. C. Simonini, introduction to Florio's *Second Frutes* (Gainesville:
Scholars' Facsimiles & Reprints, 1953); twelve Italian grammars and dialogue
manuals (and four attempts at dictionaries) were published during the Tudor-
Stuart period, and four were by John Florio: *First Fruites* (1578), *Second Frutes*
(1591), *Worlde of Wordes* (1598), and *Queen Anna's World of Words* (1611); two
more, by Giovanni Torriano, were either adaptations or augmentations of
Florio's scholarship, *Italian Tutor* (1640) and *Vocabolario Italiano & Inglese*
(1659).
[11] Giovanni Torriano, *Vocabolario Italiano & Inglese* (London, 1659),
sig. Kk2.
[12] Cf. James Samford, *The Garden of Pleasure* (London, 1573), and Claudius
Hollybande, *The French Schoole-Maister* (London, 1573).

seen as a way to cultivate and exhibit one's character through and by means of language.

Conversational commonplaces set side-by-side in Italian and English gave would-be-sojourners a way to explore for themselves, and while abroad to reveal (though some might rather be seeking to obscure and conceal) aspects of themselves through spoken words. For every act of showing at the same time implies that something else has had to be put in reserve and is, at least temporarily, not being shown (or said) about the composite truth of one's being. This dual sense of revealing and concealing the truth of who one is, which has been analysed in other contexts as 'self-fashioning',[13] is echoed in Jonson's formula, 'language most shows a man'. Implicit in Jonson's use of the word 'shows' is the double sense of both genuine disclosure as well as, alternatively, the staging of studied artifice.

This aspect of our scripting, through commonplace language, what we would project of ourselves abroad is built into the formal structure of dual-language phrase-books. While it has long been recognized that such popular lesson manuals brought together the medieval debate form, Latin colloquy, and French *manière de langage*, we need to take into account the classical Art of Memory as well. Mnemonic and dramatic turns of mind converged and surfaced in Renaissance writings about how a traveller might want to speak . . . and, thereby, bespeak himself.

Florio, like an urbane traveller who sets his sights on new lands, projected—and laboured to create—a lingering and resolute image of himself, through his translations of others' words and his foreign-language dialogues riddled with proverbs and aphorisms. This image would stand over and above his origins as the son of a refugee,[14] and would assume a commanding presence in Elizabethan London.[15] But what are we to make of the

---

[13] Cf. Stephen Greenblatt, *Renaissance Self-Fashioning From More to Shakespeare* (Chicago: University of Chicago Press, 1982); and Wayne A. Rebhorn, *The Emperor of Men's Minds: Literature and the Renaissance Discourse of Rhetoric* (Ithaca and London: Cornell University Press, 1995).

[14] Frances A. Yates, *John Florio: The Life of an Italian in Shakespeare's England* (Cambridge, 1934), 2–6.

[15] Ibid. 334–6; cf. Arthur Acheson, *Shakespeare's Lost Years in London* (1920; repr. New York: Haskell House, 1971), 181–222.

contributions of a man like Florio, who made a living and a name for himself by trading primarily in words during the English literary Renaissance? Although he was born in England in the beginning of the reign of Edward VI, he banked on his foreignness throughout his life, and yet never went to Italy.[16] This may help to explain why Florio's dialogues are set, for the most part, in and around London.

Still, it is the imaginative staging of one's activities, with the student-traveller anticipating being the particular speaker of a universal and memorable phrase, that brings texts like Florio's in line with the *vade mecum*, the commonplace book, the *enchiridion*, which conventionally was filled with notable sentences and witty sayings. In the process of using such a book, the student imagined himself in situations that drew on communally derived wisdom—situations that might at some time in the future become his present reality. Thus, books of travellers' dialogues and handy phrases are of the same order as those relating to the Memory Arts, in that they lead to the creation and use of artificial memory systems, whether notebooks or Memory Palaces.

In the extended demonstration and analysis that follows, one needs to attend not only to similarities in form and in specific terms and phrases, but also those pertaining to function and to the principles underlying the targetted use of such books—especially the projective kind of memory they both depend on, and which they set in place. For example, in *Italian Revived*, Torriano said that, for the benefit of his readers, he decided to include: 'some small Histories, Fables, and Jests, cull'd and colected out of several of our Italian Authors, namely such as I thought might have most Propriety of Language in them, transitions and Links of Discourse, fit for Imitation; and all I presume, more or less, useful, delightful' (sig. A2v).

The same topics and rationale are used as well by John Willis, who, in summarizing the accepted decorum of a Memory Theatre, as was seen in Part I, advocated that one should reduce and store 'All Histories, Actions, Fables, common Affaires'.[17] He advised further that all kinds 'of *Hyeroglyphicks*, and innumer-

---

[16] Yates, *Florio*, 12, 15, 21.   [17] Willis, *Mnemonica*, 74.

able sentences ingenuously exemplified, may be reposited in *Repositories*' (p. 78); and gives a comprehensive account of how one might use commonplace books to collect, for future use, 'sentences worthy of Memory'—such sentences 'as we desire to preserve not onely in paper, but in our hearts, because of their singular Elegancy, serious Gravity, concise brevity, or witty ingenuity' (p. 11). He also advocates that such information be collected and stored under apt headings:

in a Manual every kind in a particular place: Epigrams by themselves, Anagrams by themselves, so Proverbs, Epitaphs, Jests, Riddles, Observations, &c. by themselves: This *Enchiridion* wherein you write such remarkable sentences, ought always to be carryed about you, (and may therefore be called, *Vade mecum*), that you may peruse the same at leisure-hours when you are abroad, not having other employments; by which means, Time, most precious of all things, will not be unprofitably spent.

While Willis did not break new ground, he sums up well the practical application of humanist rhetorical training, and the ways in which such collections were viewed and used. By the same token Torriano, like Florio before him, conceived of his *Select Italian Proverbs* in the same way that Willis speaks of the practical mnemonic uses for commonplaces: 'And for the conveniency of making this book a *Vade mecum*; I have placed the Italian first with the English interpretation immediately underneath it' (sigs. A3v–A4).

For the same reasons that there was a booming market for printed commonplace books during the period to help people identify and study generally useful sayings and deeds for use in public and domestic affairs,[18] there was also a demand for dual-language dialogues to help travellers learn what was considered useful abroad. Both kinds of collection, of remarkable sentences worthy of memory and of handy Italian phrases, make the information available in ways that are easy to use. Printing made available neatly arranged anthologies and thesauruses of

---

[18] See Louis B. Wright, *Middle Class Culture in Elizabethan England* (1935; repr. London, 1958), 145–53; and Joan Marie Lechner, *Renaissance Concepts of the Commonplaces* (New York: Pageant Press, 1962).

commonplaces, whether *sententiae* culled from classical works or phrases from foreign-language texts.[19] And like the jurist or orator, or simply like the person who wanted to be deemed witty 'at table', the traveller needed to make the most of his time and have ready phrases close at hand. How fitting, then, it was for him to draw on the humanist rhetorical tradition and on the time-tried mnemonic methods that already had proven to be so commodious for organizing a vast array of useful information, which he might need to draw on at a moment's notice, depending on what the situation required.

Frances Yates gives a history of the mnemonic techniques based on strolling, or travelling, from place to place as one retrieved previously stored bits of information, but she does not address the connection between travel books and the *ars memorativa*.[20] Still, we do not have to look far in collections of proverbs associated with foreign-language acquisition to find these two traditions overlapping one another. For example, Florio's *Second Frutes* contains an explicit reference to a Memory Palace, as a background image suitable for storing bits of information that had been emblematically reduced and placed, perhaps, as statues in niches along the walls.[21] The reference seems to have been as commonplace as the mundane topics covered in the dialogues. With an English audience in mind, the storyline concerns Italians in

[19] A bridge between the private and the printed systems of collecting and preserving 'sentences worthy of Memory' is John Foxe's *Pandectae locorum communium* (1572), which was a fill-in-the-blank workbook with printed topical headings and a few typical examples to suggest a pattern for the book's owner to follow. See John G. Rechtien, 'John Foxe's *Comprehensive Collection of Commonplaces*: A Renaissance Memory System for Students and Theologians', *Sixteenth Century Journal*, 9 : 1 (1978), 83–9.

[20] Cf. *Rhetorica ad Herennium*, III. xvii–xx, and Quintilian, *Institutio Oratoria*, XI. ii. 17–41. See also Carruthers, *Book of Memory*, 122–55.

[21] Cicero, *De oratore*, II. lxxxvii. 358. On the revival of interest in the *Domus locorum* in the Renaissance, see Volkmann, *Ars Memorativa*, 163–5; and, on such multi-tiered mnemonic devices, see Guilio Camillo, *L'Idea del Theatro* (Florence, 1550) and Lodovico Dolce, *La Memoria* (Venice, 1586). The pragmatic application of this kind of interior architecture is evident, among other places, in Teresa of Avila, *The Interior Castle*, trans. Kieran Kavanaugh and Otilio Rodrigues (New York: Paulist Press, 1979); see Fernando de la Flor, *Teatro de la Memoria: siente ensayos sombre mnemotecnia Española de los siglos XVII y XVIII* (Salamanca: Junta de Castilla y Leon, 1988), 91–8.

London, for example, going to see a comedy at the Bull Theatre, walking with a friend to the Exchange, or catching a boat at Paul's wharf. Florio put everyday conversation above learned disputation, and never strayed from this goal. He sought to provide his readers with the tools for effecting their own transformation, with respect both to language and character. The Art of Memory is all part of this programme, though, naturally enough given Florio's goals, it is not an end in itself.

The reference to a background memory image comes in *Second Frutes* (sigs. B3v–C), in the midst of a section that reads like stage-banter between a straight-man and a clown, between Torquato and his servant Ruspa.[22] These characters show up in many of the dialogues and thus become memorable, even endearing figures to the reader. Typical of books that follow a diurnal patterning sequence, the first dialogue concerns 'rising in the morning'. At the same time though, it can be seen as an implicit address to the reader-pupil regarding the author-tutor's ideas behind his pedagogic method, at once memorably amusing and also drawing on mnemonic methods of edification. This sets the tone and pace for the rest of the book. Further, one of the speakers in other sections, identified as 'Nolano', undoubtedly is the Italian polymath Giordano Bruno, a chief advocate of the Renaissance *ars memorativa*, who was residing in London at the time and was Florio's close friend.[23] In this colloquy, Torquato and his madcap servant Ruspa prepare to leave the house. Their dialogue is given in Italian on the left-hand page, and an English translation on the right:

R. Io non sò trouar la chiaue.	R. I cannot finde the key.
T. Doue l'hai posta, trascurato che sei?	T. Where hast thou layd it? thou careles as thou art.
R. Stamane l'ho messa nella scarsella, o io l'ho.	R. I put it in my pocket this morning. Oh I have it.

---

[22] For an analysis of the backlog of social anxieties underlying this kind of an interchange, although without direct reference to Florio's Ruspa and Torquato, see Mark Thornton Burnett, *Masters and Servants in English Renaissance Drama and Culture: Authority And Obedience* (Basingstoke and New York: Macmillan and St Martin's Press, 1997), 5.

[23] Yates, *Florio*, 87–123; Yates, *Art of Memory*, 197–309; and Frances A. Yates, *Giordano Bruno and the Hermetic Tradition* (Chicago and London: University Of Chicago Press, 1964), 205–56.

T. Sei tu cosi pouero di memoria?

R. Io non mi ricordo dai naso alla bocca.

T. * Tu non farai mai statuti, ne casa da tre solari.

R. Pur che io ne faccia da uno.

T. Tre arbori, ti basteranno à far ciò.

R. Molti grandi vengono a star in case cosi basse.

T. Al corpo di, ch'io non uuo dire, che s'io metto mano ad un bastone, io ti farò ben star in ceruello.

R. Io non saprei farci altro.

T. Tu vuoi ch'io dij di piglio à qualche pezzo di legno per perstarti le ossa.

R. Ciò non vorrei già io.

T. * Hora vedo che chi l'ha da ratura, sin ala fossa dura.

T. Art thou so short of memory.

R. No man more forgetfull than I.

T. Thou wilt neuer make statues, nor houses, with three stories.

R. I would I might make any with one.

T. Three trees will serve thee doo that.

R. Many great men come to dwell in as lowe houses.

T. By the bodie of. I will not sweare. If I take a cudgell in hand, I will make thee looke to thy selfe.

R. I cannot do with all.

T. Thou longest to haue mee take a staffe in hand to swaddle thy bones with all.

R. Nay mary would I not.

T. Now I see that what is bred in the bone, will neuer out of the flesh.

The allusion to a Memory Palace ('Thou wilt neuer make statues, nor houses, with three stories'), suggests how we are to approach this exemplary Italian–English phrase-book. The three-tiered building is of the same order as Sidney's reference to a 'certain room divided into many places' as a convenient way to work with poetry and other bits of edifying knowledge.[24] The same can be said of proverbs, which are poetic ways of arranging everyday speech in memorable and generally useful ways. Furthermore, Florio's line referring to 'statui' in a 'casa da tre solari', like those adorning typical Memory Palaces of the day,[25] is marked with an asterisk, on the Italian side only, to signal that it is a sentence

---

[24] This passage was discussed in another context in Ch. 1. Florio was well acquainted with Sidney's views on the subject; in fact, he was commissioned to transcribe Sidney's main texts at the same time as he was composing *Second Frutes* (see Yates, *Florio*, 200–7).

[25] Yates, *Art of Memory*, 18, 310–29.

worthy of being recording in one's commonplace book and reserved for future, practical use.[26]

Throughout the text, many such memorable phrases are thus marked, the better for the reader to collect and find suitable places for them in his own artificial memory system, using places or *loci* on some background image, irrespective of what specific form it took—whether a notebook, hand mnemonic diagram, three-levelled house, Memory Palace, or City of Memory like that described by Fulwood, with its 'publicke dwellinge places, Palaces, or common places of Judgement' discussed at the beginning of this chapter.[27] By the same token, Florio's later *Worlde of Wordes* was not simply designed to help Englishmen work their way through popular Italian literature, as had been the case with some other authors' earlier efforts. It was much more than this, and thereby served to substantiate his claim as a serious scholar.[28] Further, the revised edition of *Vocabolario Italiano & Inglese* remained the standard dictionary throughout the seventeenth century, and formed a basis upon which its successors were built.

Among the characteristic features of this work is the inclusion of proverbs—advertised as enabling 'the speedy attaining to the Italian Tongue'. We can gain insight into the rationale for this approach to language acquisition, especially as it pertains to the culling and arranging of proverbs with an eye toward creating a handy Table of Memory, by looking at Torriano's address 'To the courteous Reader' in *Select Italian Proverbs*:[29]

It is generally conceived, that by Proverbs and proverbiall sentences be they of what language soever, the nature and genius of the Nation is easily discovered: and the reason may be, because they are built upon

---

[26] On this conventional printing practice, especially as it pertains to texts that recorded 'staged speech', see G. K. Hunter, 'The Marking of *Sententiae* in Elizabethan Printed Plays, Poems, and Romances', *The Library*, 5th series, 6: 3/4 (Dec. 1951), 171–3.

[27] On the range and application of such memory schemes, see Claire Richter Sherman, *Writing on Hands: Memory and Knowledge in Early Modern Europe* (Seattle: University of Washington Press 2000), 148–83; and Engel, *Mapping Mortality*, 17–54.

[28] Yates, *Florio*, 189–90.

[29] The systematic arrangement of information in charts and tables is, axiomatically, mnemonic; e.g. multiplication tables and the Periodic Table of Elements.

experience, and the long observation of passages by a whole Nation, one man being not sufficient to bring up a Proverb, but a multitude; nor one year, but one or more ages. By the precepts and cautions contained in them, they become profitable; by their varietie and conceits, delightfull. (sig. A3v)

Further, as a way of making more serviceable later versions of his book, which Torriano conceived of and called a *vade mecum*, he arranged the phrases not 'by way of heads or commonplaces', but by 'a kind of Alphabeticall way for the speedier finding out of the Italian Proverb' (sig. A4). Florio likewise rationalized his reliance on and his special way of arranging adages in his *Second Frutes*: 'Proverbs are the pith, the proprieties, the proofs, the purities, the elegancies, as the commonest so the commendablest phrases of a language. To use them is a grace, to understand them a good, but to gather them a paine to me, though gaine to thee' (sig. *2).

Still, in his previous book of dialogue language instruction, *First Fruites*, Florio exuberantly cribbed proverbs and anecdotes from already published collections, often merely translating them.[30] His motivation for serving up these already well-known platitudes stemmed from his desire to attract the attention and patronage of members of the Sidney circle by appealing to their militant Protestant leanings.[31] And while his attention to prayer-forms and polemical issues assumed a less prominent place in *Worlde of Wordes*, he never gave up his love of extended conceits and euphonious doublets. Florio understood thought-patterns primarily in terms of sound-patterns.[32] Accordingly, in the dedication of this work, he relates why his Muse named his book as she did:

since as the Univers contains all things, digested in best equipaged order, embellisht with innumerable ornaments by the universall creator. And as *Tipocosmia* imagined by *Allessandro Cittolini*, and *Fabrica del mondo*,

[30] Yates, *Florio*, 38.
[31] See e.g. Florio, *First Fruites* (London, 1578), sig. V2, with the Italian on the left-hand column, the English on the right: 'Oh glorious militant Church, which art nought else but gold in drosse, a rose amongst thornes, grain amidst straw, marrow amidst bones, pearle amidst the sea shells . . . God for his grace long tyme maintaine and defend thee.'
[32] Yates, *Florio*, 227.

framed by *Francesco Alunno*, and *Piazza universale* set out by *Thomaso Garzoni* tooke their names of the universall worlde, in words to represent things of the world: as words are types of things, and everie man by him-selfe a little world in some resemblances; so thought she, she did see as great capacitie, and as meete method in this, as in those latter, and (as much as there might be in Italian and English) a modell of the former, and therefore as good cause so to entitle it. If looking into it, it looke like the Sporades, or scattered Ilands, rather than one well-joynted or close-joyned bodie, or one coherent orbe: your Honors knowe, an armie ranged in files is fitter for muster, then in a ring; and jewels are sooner found in several boxes, then in one bagge. If in these rankes the English out-number the Italian, congratulate the copie and varietie of our sweete-mother-toong.[33]

From this passage, among other things, we learn that Florio considered his work to be in the same sphere as that of the leading Renaissance treatises on knowledge, including one that had an entire chapter devoted to the *ars memorativa*—Garzoni's *Piazza Universale* (1578). In fact, as Yates has pointed out, though not with regard to Florio, Garzoni sought to produce a universal memory system that combined the techniques of Rossellius and Lull.[34] Such systems, even those less grand in scale and intent, were designed to hold back the flood of oblivion and keep ignorance from inundating us. Using the principles associated with mnemotechnics was a viable, even a decorous, response to our ineluctable mortality. And so, finally, in a way that was perhaps unanticipated by Florio, dictionaries and foreign-language phrase-books are expressions of, and responses to, our mortal temporality.

'I FEIGN AN ITALIAN': THE TRUTH OF SIMULATED SPEECH

The thrust of Florio's language lessons, and indeed his philosophy of language, can be seen in his approach to compiling and pub-lishing his books. Specifically, even though later editions of the dictionary contain detailed grammar rules, the emphasis on being

---

[33] Florio, *Worlde of Wordes* (1598), sig. a5.
[34] Yates, *Art of Memory*, 206.

able to speak readily and colloquially, if floridly, takes precedence
over the general acquisition of the fundamentals of Italian composition. Florio's practice reveals that he was in sympathy with a
pedagogical view ripe for a nation on the go: the aim of language
acquisition in Elizabethan England was to get the student speaking as soon and as proverbially as possible.[35]

This explains in part why Florio favoured the colloquy, and why
the grammar portion was truncated and consigned to an appendix. Of course, as can be seen in his faulty translations of
some passages in Montaigne, Florio's knowledge of grammar—
whether French or his native Italian—was defective.[36] Still, with an
English audience in mind, his dialogues take the form mainly of
conversations between Italians in London. Following in this spirit,
Torriano says in his address 'to all who desire to learn the Italian
Tongue' that his present dialogues were made 'for the Meridian of
England':

> to teach the English Nation Italian; not intending, as some might imag-
> ine, by a reverst method, to teach an Italian, or any other Forreighner
> English . . . wherefor I have made the Italian to lead all along: I feign an
> Italian, though not the same person alwaies, to have had some Friendship
> or Acquaintance at least with some English man in Italy, not the same
> person neither, and so the Italian coming over into England, meets the
> one occasionally, another by purposely visits, and entertains discourse
> with him. (sig. A3)

And so the stage is set for the first dialogue in which, as Torriano
reports: 'I suppose an Italian newly come to a Person or Ordinary
. . . renew their former acquaintance.' He feigns and he supposes;
just as Florio modelled his dialogues on social and linguistic
circumstances that men might encounter. But we must note that
Florio and, to a lesser extent, Torriano, were given to extended
conceits, euphuistic extravagances of language, and ever-evolving
staged repartee and maxims.

And so what stands out here is the staged aspect of the memorable language lessons, made more so because of their obvious
debt to the principles of the *ars memorativa*. The stage with its

---

[35] Yates, *Florio*, 139.
[36] See del Re, *Florio's 'First Fruites'*, p. liv; and Yates, *Florio*, 238.

balconies and cellarage, like Torquato's three-tiered house, was ideally suited to serve as an artificial, or local, memory system within which one might encounter proverbs and other emblematic modes of expression.[37] This typical Elizabethan view of the mnemonic efficacy of the staging of dialogues and the recreation of deeds that men might play gives us further insight into, and to some extent helps us give an account of, why Florio was partial to simulated speech.

The dialogue format is effective for learning a language precisely because it sets up mini-narratives and situations that resemble those of stage plays, filled with memorable verbal exchanges. The better to help the pupil assimilate the words and order of the linguistic episodes, whether in mere lists or in the more elaborately scripted dialogues, Torriano in the *Vocabolario Italiano*, like Florio before him, kept to mainstream language: 'in this Dictionary I have shun'd and avoided (as near as could be) obsolete and forc'd words, and have chosen to put only such as are obvious to the understanding, preferring good plain currant Money before gawdy Medals' (sig. 3U2v).

From Florio's earliest work as well, this same theme is couched in the vernacular commonplace of the humanist tradition; namely, that it is through speech that a person 'expresseth and sheweth foorth his thoughts, and conceits of his mind', and that 'that kinde of writing is most perfect, that most perfectly can shew forth and express the liuely meaning of speache'.[38] Perfect writing, then, represents not speech itself, but the lively meaning of speech, which is to say the soul or spirit that animates, that quickens and gives life to, the body of thought. It is like a shade on the other side of the River Lethe waiting for the blood offering at last that will give breath to this shadow and life to his or her words.[39] It was through simulated proverbial discourse, and through his ebullient translations, and his ever-growing collections of

---

[37] See Yates, *Theatre of the World*, 136–40. Torriano retains Florio's entry for 'memória locále' as late as the 1688 edition of *Vocabolario* (sig. Nn3ᵛ).

[38] Florio, *First Fruites*, fo.113ᵛ.

[39] Sarah Iles Johnston, *Restless Dead: Encounters Between the Living and the Dead in Ancient Greece* (Berkeley, Los Angeles, and London: University of California Press, 1999), 9–16.

proverbs, that Florio succeeded in expanding for everyday use the Elizabethan world of words—and memory links them all.

Artificial memory schemes, like those known to Florio and his contemporaries, can aid in making sense of the confusion of one's experiences. The effective use of any mnemonic design, though, depends on the relative ease with which we can regain both our points of access and our cues for retrieving what we previously had singled out as being important. Only then can we build on it and do something with it that moves beyond mere recollection, so as to see how it might be a bridge to other areas of endeavour. Memory in this sense implies much more than merely getting facts in place and setting the record straight, though to be sure these activities are important in and of themselves. Memory is also to be understood here as a means poetically to forge ahead and begin to build anew, in the face of our inevitable decline. In Ruspa having forgotten where he put the key, Florio allegorizes the place of memory as that which bestows the material we need to preserve the world thus opened up through simulated speech. In the end, this is a key that unlocks not only the tongues of foreign lands but also the Temple of the Muses—and thus checks oblivion.

Thus, through repetition and practice, we are taught to think afresh, albeit from within the core of proverbial wisdom. In so doing we can begin to think through, and from within, that common stock of words, words that historically have been used so often and at times so willy-nilly that they can seem to lose their ability to signify in decisive and meaningful ways. And yet something along the lines of Florio's self-conscious and repetitive deployment of the proverbial makes us aware of the lineage of the commonplace. Such a practice thereby allows us to see proverbs from the inside out and refracted, yet again, through the filter of other languages. In this way we can begin to see in, and through, those words—and then beyond them—toward new horizons and new possibilities for future translations.

As Florio's practice bears out, words show us not only aspects of our own past, but also they give us a place to go—a destination. Words can show us where we are heading. Like maps and like guidebooks, which give travellers a sense of their route and what they are likely to encounter, words give us a destination. And yet, in thus setting out before us our destination, the end of that journey is prefigured; indeed, our own end is thus prefigured. Words in this sense not only provide us with a destination, but also they predestine what subsequently we can come to know about what we do day-to-day, insofar as they present us with a view of a course or path—and it is translated, and thus apprehended, as a memory-picture. To some extent, then, scrutiny of commonplace proverbs, adages, or other memorable sentences allows us to see, through their repetition, where they came from. In the glimpse we get of their origins, real or imagined, we look back to their lineage and forward towards their varied implications. In the process, we come to see something of ourselves reflected there, something of our history as individuals within a larger culture, and also with respect to the universal sentiment expressed in the proverb. Further, we come to see something of our common history, no matter what our origins or cultural heritage, real or imagined, construed or constructed. In this sense, words create new worlds of thought that are given life through our activities in the world; they do not merely store or translate meanings from thought-images into verbal expressions that we use in daily and social commerce. There is thus a generative element in Florio's understanding of the power of words to be interpreters of our souls. It is through our becoming aware of, if not also to some extent recovering, the residual trace of cultural and historical memory embedded within commonplace phrases and clusters of proverbial wisdom that our ideas are propelled toward the end of history.

But how, through proverbs and other elementary structures constitutive of the Memory Arts, are we to understand the end, the goal or aim, of that history? And how, in the seventeenth century, was the end of history made comprehensible with respect to the place of memory? These questions, once answered, or at least confronted and recast, will provide us with the words we need to speak about dead and final things; words, which are not just the interpreters of our souls, but are also (insofar as they become agents of transformation in their own right, which set in motion memory's ongoing engagement with oblivion) translators of the soul of history.

PART III

The Marrow and Moral of History

The example of diuine providence, everywhere found (the
first diuine Histories being nothing else but a continuation
of such examples) haue perswaded me to fetch my beginning
from the beginning of all things; to wit, Creation.

(Walter Ralegh, *History of the World* (1614), sig. B7^v)

History is like a watch-Tower on which we may see dangers
farre off, and so avoid them; and what can be more pleasant
than to see a Tragedie acted to the life; which onely is to be
seen in History; for here we shall see the whole world, but as
a Stage on which men of all sorts have acted their parts.

(Alexander Ross, *History of the World: The Second Part*
(1652), sig. b2)

PART II

The Matter and Mode of History

4

'O eloquent, iust, and mighty Death!': Ending *The History of the World*

THE MEMORY THEATRE OF DIVINE JUSTICE

> When I looked for good, then euill came vnto mee: and when I waited for light, there came darknes. | My bowels boyled and rested not: the dayes of affliction preuented mee. | I went mourning without the Sunne: I stood vp, *and* I cried in the Congregation. | I am a brother to dragons, and a companion to owls. | My skinne is blacke vpon mee, and my bones are burnt with heat. | My harpe also is turned to mourning, and my organe into the voyce of them that weepe.
>
> (Job 30: 26, 29–31)

It is with this last sentence that Ralegh concluded his monumental *History of the World*, but using the Latin Vulgate and not the King James English translation, as quoted here (see the Appendix). How did it come to this? What did Ralegh seek to communicate by making this biblical sentence serve, quite literally, as the last word of his *History*? What sorts of assumptions in his own day would have been made about this cunning conclusion? And to what extent did it reflect cunning, in the sense of the term discussed in Part I?

Ralegh's view of the end of *The History of the World*, where 'end' means goal or aim, as well as achievement or termination, parallels his view of the end, or trajectory, of history itself. Despite the reliance on platitudes and familiar themes of medieval and Renaissance historical theory, Ralegh's *History* stands out from other works of the day which likewise show a fascination with death, decay, impiety, and folly.[1] But Ralegh's self-conscious—we might even say, metatheatrical—approach to the subject brings it into line with the underlying principles of the Aesthetic of Decline, which, as we have seen, marked other literary forms of expression during the period. Ultimately though, rather than dwell on how his book is on the one hand unique, and on the other, typical or exemplary, I have made Ralegh the focus of this chapter because of his unexpected use of the Memory Arts in creating a monument to the Renaissance Aesthetic of Decline that exemplifies 'the work of translation' like that discussed in Part II.

In particular, his literary cunning, leaning on the principles associated with the Memory Arts, implicitly revives the ancient sense of terminus—a stone pillar marking the end, the border, the farthest boundary.[2] The sentence from holy writ at the end of his book is at once like a tombstone inscribed with 'Hic iacet' (see Appendix), and also like the classical terminus pillars showing the extent of how far one can go. There is an additional meaning here, coming from beyond the grave as it were, along the lines of the emblematic messages conveyed through staged tableaux that portended fatal destiny in Part I.

Ralegh's literary terminus, in keeping with his essentially pessimistic philosophy of construing and representing the soul of history, bespeaks the emerging possibilities of the Memory Arts in the early modern period, projected onto the world stage in the form of memory-pictures, condensed into historical and scriptural *exempla*. The world of human affairs and fatal destiny thus portrayed in *The History of the World*, as is made clear through the cunning terminus, is a memory theatre of divine justice—and judgement. It is no wonder, then, that Job should figure as the proper end for this work. But before looking at the conditions occasioning Ralegh's *History*, and at the temporal territory mnemonically marked out to be moralized in his treatise, let us consider the Renaissance idea of terminus as a marker

---

[1] D. R. Woolf, *The Idea of History in Early Stuart England* (Toronto: University of Toronto Press, 1990), 54.
[2] Ovid, *Fasti*, II. XXIII. 639–84; Terminus is 'the god who marks the boundaries'.

of that place toward which we hasten and beyond which we can go no further. For, in this end, it is the terminus that puts us in our place.

Francis Thynne's poem, entitled 'Our terme or limit of life not removeable', recalls traditional expressions of the vanitas theme.[3] This 'naked emblem', as he calls it, because it is 'not clothed with engraven pictures' (p. 2), opens with a standard description of the mental image, or memory-picture, that Terminus would have conjured up in the minds of Elizabethans: 'ffrom neck it hath the humane shape, | the rest a pillar stone: | Thus *Terminus* the god is made, | of all the godds alone.'[4] Jove 'willd him to departe the feilde, | and leaue him the place', but Terminus says: 'I yeald to none.' The moral point of this encounter is brought home for the reader with a sententious rhyme: 'Soe are the fixed bonds which god | doth limit to our daies, | not to be changed or removed, | to lengthe them anie waies' (ll. 17–20).

Henry Peacham's emblem with the motto 'Terminus' (Fig. 8) shows Jove turning back from the pillar after he is told by this god: 'I giue place to none: I am the bound of things.'[5] And Erasmus, while impatient with conceits that were either too trite or too obscure, adopted the figure of Terminus as his own emblem, and had it struck as a medal with the motto 'Concedo Nvlli'. In about 1535 Hans Holbein executed a woodcut of Erasmus, his hand resting on a bust of Terminus, thus reflecting the currency of this emblem as well as exemplifying the Renaissance art of suggesting a thought by withholding it.[6] Moreover, the portrait indicates how additional levels of meaning come into focus when something like an emblematic bust, or sententious word, is incorporated into a larger work. Thus, putting the image of Terminus in a portrait is comparable to putting words from Job into a historical compendium. These words take on special significance in whatever transposed context they might appear, but especially so when they

[3] Francis Thynne, *Emblemes and Epigrams*, ed. F. J. Furnivall, Early English Text Society, 64 (London, 1876), 30.

[4] Cf. Andreas Alciato, *Emblematum libellus* (Venice, 1546), 33[r].

[5] Henry Peacham, *Minerva Britannia* (London, 1612), 193.

[6] Edgar Wind, 'Aenigma Termini', *Journal of the Warburg and Courtauld Institute*, 1 (1937), 66.

Fig. 8. Terminus

are placed at the end of the author's farewell. They bespeak a final
leave-taking in several senses: the author bidding adieu to the
reader, to his book, and to the writing of history—and to the
world itself, having come to that point in his journey where (to
speak emblematically), though he might have wished it otherwise,
he comes face to face with his end. And so Ralegh places Job at
this boundary, like a pillar of Terminus at the furthest extent of
the Roman world. Any step further would put the sojourner in
unfamiliar, even hostile, territory. However, nothing stops one
from looking beyond that marker at what stretches towards the
horizon.

The implications of Terminus, as the personified boundary
beyond which neither mortals nor gods can cross, include reso-
luteness and fixity. With or without Christian connotations superimposed onto the Roman deity, the emblem of Terminus expresses
the theme of not budging, owing to justice rather than stubborn-

ness.[7] Ralegh's witty terminus brings together the range of meanings implied in emblems like 'Our terme or limit of life not removeable', the implications of Job's situation (as discussed in the Introduction), and Ralegh's own 'fixd bonds'. Such an end was prefigured when Ralegh first began writing his *History of the World*, shortly after he was tried and condemned to death in 1603, the first year of James's reign, ostensibly for conspiring with the Spanish to upset the English succession. Ralegh spent about twelve years confined to the Tower of London, and was finally executed in 1618.

His *History* was popular from the start, going through eight editions[8] after initially being suppressed.[9] Though much admired by Henry Stuart, heir to the throne, his father James I, in 1615, with due cause judged it 'too sawcie in censuring princes'.[10] Indeed, there is little room for prevarication in statements like that made in the Preface: 'Kings live in the World & not above it.' As Jenny Wilson has observed further: 'Ralegh's demystification of royal power was both cumulative and condemning; it was also wryly ironic coming from a man who has spent some of his best years as an instrument of Tudor mystification in the service of Diana, Belphoebe and Cynthia (he sometimes called her Elizabeth).'[11] Even so, James was very much attuned to such potential sedition, being the son of Mary, Queen of Scots, who had been executed after spending eighteen years in English

---

[7] Cf. George Wither, *Collection of Emblems* (London, 1635), 161, where Terminus is used as a way to compare Christ to a border-stone, confining all and confined by none.

[8] John Racin, Jr., *Sir Walter Ralegh as Historian* (Salzburg, 1974), 7.

[9] John Racin, Jr., 'The Early Editions of Sir Walter Ralegh's *The History of the World*', *Studies in Bibliography*, 17 (1964), 199–209; Anna R. Beer, ' "Left to the world without a Maister": Sir Walter Ralegh's *The History of the World* as a Public Text', *Studies in Philology*, 91: 4 (Fall 1994), 461; *The Poems of Sir Walter Ralegh: A Historical Edition*, ed. Michael Rudik (Tempe, Ariz.: Renaissance English Text Society, 1999), 169.

[10] See *State Papers Domestic, 1603–1618*, cited by Jenny Wilson, 'Ralegh's *History of the World*: its Purpose and Political Significance', Durham Thomas Harriot Seminar, Occasional Paper, No. 28 (n.d.). This correspondence from John Chamberlain to Sir Dudley Carleton, 5 Jan. 1615, is also discussed by C. A. Patrides, *Sir Walter Ralegh, 'The History of the World'* (New York: Macmillan, 1971), 11, n. 4.

[11] Wilson, 'Ralegh's *History of the World*', 15.

prisons, on the orders of Ralegh's beloved sovereign Elizabeth, to whom he wrote his extended verse commendation *The Ocean to Cynthia*. And while the government called in *History of the World* within weeks of its publication, it enjoyed a wide readership.[12]

One reason for its staying in circulation was that, from the first to the last—indeed, on the opening pages of the Preface as on the final page of the text—Ralegh's *History* was linked to Prince Henry, his patron, who had far more militant Protestant policies than did James: 'For it was for the service of that inestimable Prince Henry, the successive hope, and one of the greatest of the Christian World, that I undertooke this Worke. It pleased him to peruse some part thereof, and to pardon what was amisse.'[13] It is also true, as Anna Beer has pointed out, that this and other invocations of the dead prince provide something of a buffer between Ralegh and his critics; which is to say: 'if they are not convinced of his innocence, perhaps they will respect its ghostly protector, the ghostly Master of this masterless text.'[14]

Building on the important implications of his calling on the name of Henry, complex but fairly obvious double meanings are embedded in the terms 'successive' and 'pardon'. As such, they point the way toward recovering the veiled meanings associated with Ralegh's use of *sententiae* and biblical passages. Sequestered from the affairs of court, Ralegh had the enforced leisure to write his book, which could pave the way toward a royal *pardon*. The *succession* of events leading to his liberty depended on the intercession of the *successor* to the English throne, Prince Henry. The historical validity of this claim is not in dispute; what is of interest, though, is the degree to which Ralegh ingeniously conveyed such coded messages at various junctures in his book while at the same time crafting a work of popular historiography—one esteemed throughout the next century and which inspired, among other statesmen and poets, John Milton.

Ralegh, 'a legally dead writer', found a way to make his voice heard and to remind the world of his existence, by calling on a

---

[12] Anna R. Beer, *Sir Walter Ralegh and his Readers in the Seventeenth Century: Speaking to the People* (Basingstoke: Macmillan, 1997), 31.

[13] Walter Ralegh, *The History of the World* (London, 1614), sig. C4ᵛ.

[14] Beer, *Sir Walter Ralegh*, 30.

genre designed to preserve memory and convey advice to leaders; indeed, the publication of this history of the world can be seen as 'a political act, both in terms of Ralegh's individual career and within the larger framework of cultural and political developments'.[15] He cloaked his message in the attire of history, which, like Erasmus's understanding of a witty conceit, enables a meaning to be conveyed while being withheld. This was wholly appropriate considering, as I will argue, that King James was the main person for whom his book was covertly intended. So too Prince Henry, Ralegh's patron in this endeavour and the book's dedicatee, dressed himself in bellicose attire to publicize to the world his willingness to take on all comers, at a time when James wanted more than anything else to placate fears of foreign incursions. As Stephen Orgel has discussed, Henry, Prince of Wales, 'commissioned from Jonson and Jones two entertainments designed to restore to life the world of ancient British chivalry. . . . But the martial side of the prince's nature apparently disturbed King James, who vetoed a similar project for the next year.'[16]

It was at around this same time that Henry was visiting Ralegh in the Tower; and, as is well known, they shared many of the same views and values. For example, in *Prince Henry's Barriers* (1610), a chivalric romance of Jonson's making, in which the young king is summoned by Merlin and King Arthur to revitalize English knighthood, Henry played the role of Meliadus, lover of The Lady of the Lake, and 'the production centered about feats of arms in which Henry distinguished himself'.[17] But while Henry had access to theatrical attire and chivalric displays to express his intentions, Ralegh was more limited in his means of self-expression. And so he turned, in his writing, to the covert language of select *sententiae*, one of the main reservoirs of cultural commonplaces

---

[15] Ibid. 22.

[16] Stephen Orgel, *The Illusion of Power: Political Theater in The English Renaissance* (Berkeley, Los Angeles, and London: University of California Press, 1975), 66–7.

[17] Ibid. See also Stephen Orgel and Roy Strong, *Inigo Jones* (Berkeley, Los Angeles, and London: University of California Press, 1973), i. 159: 'A contemporary spectator records that "the Prince performed this challenge with wondrous skill and courage, to the great joy and admiration of all the beholders, the Prince not being full sixteene years of age." '

associated with the effective use of the Memory Arts. This is like a code-sheet for retrieving from obscurity many of the cloudy digressions and double meanings found in Ralegh's *History*. For example, although the book follows a chronological plan, spanning the Creation to 168 BC (where Ralegh broke off work on it), an expansive work like this one filled with sententious digressions just as easily could have ended with any period and practically any topic. And yet there is an underlying plan at work here, though it is not a straightforward or linear one. The work's ending reflects the logic of decline, with its accompanying aesthetic specifications. It is this which above all else characterizes and gives shape to *The History of the World*.

To be sure, the book's conclusion is asserted purposefully in the face of the unalterable, namely, the death of Prince Henry, and in the face of the inevitable, Ralegh's own impending execution; both of which are to be seen against the emblematic backdrop of human mortality in general, but especially that of statesmen and kings. Moreover, the view of history that emerges from Ralegh's book is one of man seeing examples of the past and knowing what he should do, but where the chronicler realizes, and is obliged to comment on the fact, that people in authority will never see that they are subject to the perennial traps and pitfalls of tyranny.

According to such a view, human nature is at odds with the ideal of Reason.[18] And though he would have it be otherwise, in the world of human affairs Ralegh fears that Aristotle, as he was taught in the Schools, still carries the day over Plato. Ralegh is at great pains to discuss 'second causes' and tries to demonstrate the grounds for his belief that God did not 'shut up all light of Learning in the lanthorne of Aristotle's braines' (sig. B6ᵛ). In conveying this theme he remains true to his humanist training by tapping into the reservoirs of the time-honoured wells of select *exempla* and *sententiae*, of notable deeds and memorable sayings. In the

---

[18] Cf. Christopher Hill, *Intellectual Origins of the English Revolution* (1965; repr. Oxford, 1982), 150–1; Stephen Greenblatt, *Sir Walter Ralegh: The Renaissance Man and His Roles* (New Haven: Yale University Press, 1973), 7–14; Gerald Hammond, *Sir Walter Ralegh: Selected Writings* (1984; repr. Harmondsworth: Penguin Books, 1986), 20; and D. R. Woolf, *The Idea of History in Early Stuart England* (Toronto: University of Toronto Press, 1990), 55.

opening fifty pages we find the usual roll-call: Aristotle, Virgil, Pliny, Seneca, Plutarch; but, owing to Ralegh's visits to hermeticists in Elizabethan London, his association with the Harriot Circle, and his admiration for Neoplatonism, we find as well Plato, Pythagoras, Hermes Trismegistus, Pico della Mirandola, and Ficino. More specifically still, given the recurrent theme of Providence in Ralegh's view of human history, it is hardly surprising to find words by the Apostles, Gregory, Isidore of Seville, Augustine, Lactantius, and the usual quotations from Isaiah and from Solomon, 'The Preacher' of Ecclesiastes. What stands out most though, are the citations from Job, which are six times more frequent than those from, say, Isaiah.

Job, then, as a character known for his patience in the face of undeserved suffering, and Job the book, renowned for its direct questioning of the wisdom of the Supreme Sovereign, parallel Ralegh's view of himself in his writing of *The History of the World* and his long view of the history in the world. Treating the story of Job as a fact of history, as well as an extended exemplum, Ralegh was at pains to locate Job in time and place, even though he concludes that these things must be left to conjecture.[19] But more important for Ralegh's project, and the end to which Job is put in his *History*, the trials of Job gave ready expression to some deep-seated, everyday concerns in Ralegh's world. Biblical caches of wisdom, like those found in Job, provided a ready way to expostulate on mortal strife and the vagaries of life.

This much can be heard in the words, and seen in the memory-images, which Ralegh arranged with great care at the end of *The History of the World* (see Appendix). There is a decisive accent on the vocative, on the tacit, and on giving voice to things in ways other than the familiar: 'O eloquent . . . Death'; 'this Booke . . . calls itself'; 'discouragement persuading my silence'; 'unspeakable . . . loss'; 'taught me to say'; and the Latin *in vocem* (into the voice of). Further, Ralegh uses a series of theatrical metaphors which evoke the *theatrum mundi* motif as well as images associated with a typical Memory Theatre, to characterize our place in the world and in history.[20]

[19] Ralegh, *History*, 2.10.7, p.336.
[20] This aspect of the *theatrum mundi* motif was broached in the Introduction.

For example, in the Preface alone we are described as being 'tragicall actors'; 'We are all (in effect) become Comedians . . . in the course of our lives we renounce our Persons, and the parts wee play'; 'For seeing God, Who is the Author of all our tragedies, hath written out for us and appointed us all the parts we are to play'; 'That the change of Fortune on the Great Theatre, is but a change of garments on the lesse. For when on the one and the other, every man wears but his own skin, the Players are all alike'; 'For seeing Death in the end of the Play, takes from all, whatsoever Fortune or Force takes from any one'; the world is a 'great theatre'; 'Death [ushers us out] at the end of the Play' . . . And there are more, many more, such references until, literally, the last word, which recalls the ending of a historical tragedy or some other printed work of drama: 'FINIS.'

These references suffice to show how Ralegh chose to chronicle human history in a poetic way that invoked ideas of the stage. In so doing he exceeded, and took to new heights, the 'Mirror for Princes' tradition, by virtue of a kind of sententious 'sauciness' that James could only begin to imagine. Not unlike the Book of Job itself, Ralegh's *History* epitomizes a special view of the world through particular events, seen and expressed in terms of the poetic drama of human history. Irrespective of what episode or incident is being described, it becomes, in essence, a page in Everyman's history. But Ralegh is not engaged in imitating or replicating any simple understanding of allegory; he is not seeking to write in a way that only mirrors religious truths. Rather, it is characteristic of Ralegh to write prose in a way that distills human history into the logic of poetry and thus can bespeak the truths of the world and the mysterious work of translation. When he is committing such thoughts to poetry proper, however, he keeps to the same simple set of theatrical conceits that he uses in the Preface.

> What is our life? A play of passion.
> And what our mirth but music of division?
> Our mother's wombs the tiring-houses be
> Where we are dressed for this short comedy.
> Heaven the judicious sharp spectator is

> That sits and marks what here we do amiss.[21]
> The graves that hide us from the searching Sun,
> Are like drawn curtains when the play is done.
> Thus march we playing to our latest rest,
> Only we die, in earnest, [and] that's no jest.

The six texts attributing this poem to Ralegh contain enough variations among themselves to represent most of the forms in which the poem circulated in some sixty other copies;[22] twenty list it as 'anonymous' or ascribe it to other writers. Insofar as the images and conceits are so shopworn as to be cliché rather than mere commonplaces, they serve to reinforce the point that this poem might just as well have been written by anyone in the period. Though the history of this poem is uncertain, its poetic truth about Death's ultimate role in our lives, like that rehearsed over and over in Ralegh's *History of the World*, is undeniable. The exact text and punctuation of the poem are even less certain—and yet, all of this serves to indicate its exemplarity, and to set the stage for the evanescent business of recovering the truths of literary history. The necessary logic of decline, which in the Renaissance was realized as an aesthetic impulse that informed and, to a large extent, governed Ralegh's *History*, was the logic of poesy.

Such a way of thinking about and writing history brings Ralegh further into line with what was said about Florio's poetic awareness of words in Part II. But whereas Florio relied on staged dialogues and proverbs, Ralegh turned to the stage of history and its store of *exempla*.[23] For we know that history can be made to illustrate any of a number of universal truths—this is, after all, the aim and charge of *exempla*. Erasmus describes *exempla* along with similitudes and *sententiae* as the chief rhetorical strategies, which he discusses in terms of the 'eleventh method of enriching', which 'depends on the copious accumulation of proofs'.[24] Although the

---

[21] Cf. Ralegh, *History of the World*, sig. C4ᵛ: 'It pleased [Prince Henry] to peruse some part thereof, and to pardon what was *amisse* [emphasis added].'

[22] *Poems of Sir Walter Ralegh*, 164.

[23] See Philip Sidney, *A Defence of Poetry*, ed. J. A. van Dorsten (1966; repr. Oxford University Press, 1975), 35.

[24] Desiderius Erasmus, *De Utramque Verborum ac Rerum Copia*, ed. Donald B. King and David Rix (Milwaukee: Marquette University Press, 1963), 66.

history of these devices was ancient, having enjoyed a revival in the Latin Middle Ages, by the late sixteenth century fairly standard uses were assigned to the *exemplum* and *sententia*. Mnemonic in their character, they were understood to be interpolated deeds or sayings serving as an illustration, and which then were elaborated or embellished toward a didactic end.[25]

RALEGH'S CUNNING TERMINUS: REVISITING JOB

The History of the World ends with words borrowed from Job, but not those taken from the 1611 translation carried out under the aegis of King James I, at whose pleasure Ralegh was imprisoned. The Bible preferred by most scholarly writers of the day, Milton included, was the Latin Vulgate (or 'the Vulgar', as Ralegh calls it). In Jerome's version, the line reads: *Versa est in Luctum Cithera mea, et Organum meum in vocem flentium* ('My harp is turned to mourning, and my organ into the voice of them that weep').[26] As biblical scholars have pointed out, this line, like several others in this series of paralleling statements (especially verse 26), is a chiasmus—a figure of symmetrical patterning used often, and tellingly, by Latin and Greek poets.[27] In the line from verse 30 with which Ralegh closes his *History*, 'Luctum' and 'flentium' link mourning and weeping, thus forming the outer markers, the extremes of the sentiment being expressed. 'Cithera' and 'Organum', the two instruments used to express this extreme state of affairs, form the inner core. The chiasmus here is especially significant, for the order of the words calls attention to the contrast

---

[25] Cf. Richard Regosin, 'Le Miroüer vague: Reflections of the Example in Montaigne's *Essais*', in *Oeuvres & Critiques*, 8: 1/2 (1983), 78; and Jacques Le Goff, *The Medieval Imagination*, trans. Arthur Goldhammer (Chicago: University of Chicago Press, 1988), 78–80.

[26] Cf. Thomas Connolly, *Mourning into Joy: Music, Raphael, and Saint Cecilia* (New Haven and London: Yale University Press, 1994), ch. 4.

[27] I am indebted to Ward Allen for this point, specifically regarding the significance of the chiasmus in verse 26: '*expectabam* bona et **venerunt** mihi mala; **praestolabar** lucem et *eruperunt tenebrae*' [emphasis added]: 'When I looked for good, then euill came vnto me: and when I waited for light, there came darknes.' Moreover, 'lucem' (light) sets up a future echo of 'luctum' (mourning) in verse 32, thus linking these verses through a form of jarring antithesis, a crossing over of the meanings from within the chiasmus by virtue of the sonorous iteration.

between cithera and pipe, or organ depending on one's translation of the Latin. 'Versa est' is in the perfect passive, which emphasizes that for the one whose cithera is turned to mourning and whose organ into 'them that weep', there is no going back to the way things were. Ralegh's prose leading up to this verse, like Job's lament, is a rhetorical *tour de force* in its own right; and, further, like the passage from Job, it draws on age-old mnemonic techniques associated with oratory and oral poetry. Ralegh's use of the vocative, 'O eloquent, iust, and mighty Death' (see Appendix), reinforces the rhetorical ethos of his own summation argument, or peroration, of his lament concerning the futility of mortal strivings against the backdrop of universal history, no less than with respect to his own situation with regard to the death of his patron and best hope for restoration, Prince Henry.

The verse from Job was aptly suited to serve as Ralegh's final, resonant—indeed poetic—excursus on his place in the Theatre of Divine Judgement, which finds its visual counterpoint in the architectural frontispiece, insofar as it is a Memory Theatre of the larger themes associated with Ralegh's overriding view of God's providential design, represented by the open eye at the top of the page, that oversees, but does not interfere with, the events resulting from the various kinds of mortal learning represented on the four pillars (Fig. 9). According to the poem accompanying the first edition of *The History of the World*, and attributed to Ben Jonson, the robed figure of 'History', labelled *Magistra Vitae*, 'The Mistress of Man's Life', steps on 'Death and dark Oblivion', and raises 'the World to good, or Evil fame, | Doth vindicate it to Eternity'.

Among the other reasons why this Latin version of Job 30: 31 so aptly brings Ralegh's *History* to a close, is because of the range of meanings afforded by 'organon'—from 'organum' in Latin and ὄργανον in Greek. The implications packed into the Greek, which are brought along within the Latin, include an instrument, whether musical or medical, and an implement or tool for making or doing something. In the Vulgate the sense of the term, of course, initially implies the changing of musical instruments, the giving over of one for the other. But the speaker is using metaphors in an effort to express the extent of his sense of loss and grief. So

Fig. 9. History trampling Death and Oblivion

some other sense of instrumentality evoked in the passage from Job is already in place. To readers in Ralegh's day, however, the Latin 'organon' acquired an additional set of associations, relating to the *Novum organon* fashioned by Francis Bacon to be used against Aristotle. Knowledge of Bacon's 'new instrument' was widespread, certainly among those such as Ralegh, with whom he shared many of the same interests and friends; in fact, Bacon's friend and chronicler, Dr William Rawley, reports that he had seen no fewer than twelve drafts of it in Bacon's own handwriting, rewritten from year to year, and at last published in 1620 as the second part of his *Great Instauration*.

Whether or not Ralegh hoped his readers would hear in 'Organum' an echo of Bacon's instrument designed to realize a great 'restoration' in the province of Reason, the reader is alerted that some other register of thought is being tried out here, something other than, and beyond, what is usually evoked in the biblical use of the term. And so an additional association surfaces here: in this passage, 'pipe' or 'organ' extends to imply one's mortal being, which is emblematized during the Renaissance as viscera or the windpipe.[28] This sense is preserved in Golding's translation of Calvin's sermon on the same passage: 'My harp is turned to weeping, and myne *organs* to the voice of lamenting [emphasis added].'[29] And Calvin's commentary takes on added resonance if we link James to God on High, and Ralegh in the Tower to Job on the dung-heap: 'though he should kill vs, yet we would hope still for his mercy, and fight aginst the battailes of death, and grounding ourselves upon his promises, and hold our owne still and continue steadfast in the middest of all our adversities' (p. 52). After all, in the Preface to *The History* Ralegh wrote: 'For Prosperity and Adversity have evermore tyed and untied vulgar affectations.' It is not a stretch of the imagination to entertain the possibility that Ralegh saw his case mirrored in Job's: adopting a stance of steadfastness and seeking to maintain one's integrity despite adversity, while hoping for a reprieve from the Sovereign in whose hands his life is held.

Going back now to the Hebrew, upon which the King James

---

[28] Cf. Neill, *Issues of Death*, 230.   [29] *Sermons of . . . Calvin*, sig. Ll2ᵛ.

translation is to a large extent based,[30] we get the following modern translation: 'Therefore is my harp turned to mourning, | And my pipe into the voice of them that weep.' In the Vulgate, which was the Bible of choice for most humanists even after the appearance of the 'authorized' King James version (even for those with a decidedly Protestant agenda, like Ralegh and later Milton),[31] this entire section is written in a form of poetry as well. In what editors after Jerome call the 'conclusio sermonum Iob', every other line begins formulaically with 'Et', thus preserving the spirit if not the letter of the original poetry, even in translation. The Hebrew original is in verse form, though we must recall that Biblical Hebrew 'poetry' does use rhyme or regular metrical patterning in ways that correlate readily to Renaissance ideas of versification. As in earlier oral traditions, like the Anglo-Saxon, poetry consisted rather of parallelism and thought rhythms, often realized as synonymous or antithetical couplings, like those which we saw in Florio's ebullient prose, which also displayed a poetic awareness of words. And so too with Ralegh's sense of 'poesy', the logic according to which *The History of the World* is composed and in the light of which it is to be interpreted. It is this sense of biblical versification in the abstract, and the resulting thought-cadences in particular, that lends coherence to Ralegh's design in general, and his cunning conclusion in particular. Seeing it in this way explains some of the more extravagant passages, and implies a purpose behind the book's strangely digressive structure. Ralegh modelled his Preface, and certain key parts of his extended narrative, on the poetical form as well as the thematic content of that part of the Old Testament canonically grouped as the 'Books of Wisdom', consisting of Job, Psalms, Proverbs, Ecclesiastes, and the Song of Solomon.

---

[30] See David Daiches, *The King James Version of the English Bible: An Account of the Development and Sources of the English Bible of 1611 With Special Reference to the Hebrew Tradition* (1941; repr. Chicago: University of Chicago Press, 1968); and Ward Allen, *Translating for King James: Being a True Copy of the Only Notes Made By a Translator of the King James Bible* (Nashville: Vanderbilt University Press, 1969).

[31] Alister McGrath, *In the Beginning: The Story of the King James Bible and How it Changed a Nation, a Language and a Culture* (New York: Doubleday, 2000).

Job is the first in this group; and Job is the speaker whom Ralegh names as being the voice chosen to pronounce the last word of his own *History*. Job taught him to say 'Versa est . . .'. Not just at the end though, for throughout the narrative there are many such parallel expressions of dramatic turnings (modelled on the turning of one's harp to mourning or weeping), seen as changes in fortune, which come into focus through the lens of the Renaissance Aesthetic of Decline, set against the backdrop of the vast span of Ralegh's chronicle, even as he projects his moralizing eye across the expanse of human history.

This, in effect, allows Ralegh to set himself up, vis-à-vis James, in a series of parallel scenes which tacitly mirror his own situation; and it is a series that traverses time and place and which enables him, implicitly, to present his own situation for others to see, to note, to pity, and—it is hoped—to urge pardon. The desired result then is a *turning* from his present *sentence*, to a liberal *pardon* by virtue of his Sovereign's grace, before it is too late. Thus, amidst the litany of maimings, beheadings, and general cruelties perpetrated by the 'French kings' in the wake of Charlemagne's death, we can find a timely warning pertinent to Ralegh's own situation:

> Yet did he that which few kings doe; namely repent of his cruelty. For among many other things, which he performed in the General Assembly . . . he did openly confess himself to have erred, and following the example of the Emperor Theodosius he underwent voluntary penance. This he did: and it was praiseworthy. But the blood that is unjustly spilt, is not again gathered up from the ground by repentance. These medicines ministered to the dead, have but dead rewards (sig. A6).

Here, as elsewhere in Ralegh's book, his practice bears out his claim in the Preface that 'the sea of examples hath no bottome' (p. 5). Indeed, by using historical parallels with *exemplum* set atop *exemplum* (as here in the case of Louis the Pious and Theodosius), Ralegh's book is an admonishing, allegorical mirror set up for, and held up to, the reigning monarch, James. From the Middle Ages on, the mirror itself had a particular association with death and mortality.[32] Ralegh sees himself therein, mirrored in the faces

---

[32] Jane H. M. Taylor, 'Un Miroer Salutaire', in Jane H. M. Taylor (ed.), *Dies Illa: Death in the Middle Ages* (Liverpool: Francis Cairns, 1984), 37.

of those whose blood was spilled, never to be recovered. This is a
'Mirrovr which Flatters not', [33] for it is not Ralegh's intent to flat-
ter either himself or his sovereign, but to urge another kind of
response, one that might lead still to his release. Speaking ostensibly about King Henry VIII, Ralegh sums up the events warranting
the epithet, 'if all the pictures and patternes of a mercilesse Prince
were lost in the World, they might all again be painted to the life,
out of the story of this King' (A5ᵛ), and gently, if wryly, concludes
the section: 'I could say much more of the Kings Maiesty, without
flatterie: did I not feare the imputation of presumption' (A7ᵛ).

Looking more deeply into the mirror of such *exampla*, the
image looking back at Ralegh, and indeed at all of us, is the face of
Death. At the time he was writing there was still a chance that
James might do what Ralegh had asked of Prince Henry: to
'pardon what was amiss'. And so, in an effort to teach the
Sovereign how to recognize this and act accordingly, Ralegh tried
on the part of Job, the trappings of which he acquired in the tiring
house of the Tower, that he might be taught to speak words of
sincere lamentation. As has already been intimated, Ralegh's own
'story' in some salient respects parallels that of Job, who was
sorely tested and tried, and who for a time questioned and railed
against the Highest Power.

It is tempting to substitute 'Ralegh' for Job, and 'James' for
God, especially given James's penchant for stressing the Divine
Rights of Kings. According to such an analogical perspective, the
king was given a way to save face because, in the Job-story, it was
not God who tormented Job, but the Adversary, allowed to do so
by the Sovereign's own laws to test a servant of the Lord whose life,
in the end, is spared. Ralegh's appropriation of patient Job's
words in his book runs more deeply still. Henry, we will recall,
wanted to portray a chivalric knight in masques involving King
Arthur in 1610 and 1611, but ended up playing instead in *Oberon,
The Fairy Prince*. As Orgel has pointed out: 'The king, for all his
pacific policies (which in any case were not especially popular)
was awkward and largely without charm. Henry's death in 1612

[33] The popular emblematic title-page, *The Mirrour which flatters not*
(London, 1639), shows King Death holding a reflective glass. See Neill, *Issues of
Death*, 5–7.

robbed England not only of a patron for her poets and artists, but of a romantic hero as well' (p. 70). Ralegh began writing his *History of the World* with Henry in mind, and with the death of the Prince, Ralegh broke off the narrative at that part which he was researching at the time, the entries for 168 BC. Although he had ample opportunities to do so, he never returned to it. For all intents and purposes the book was finished in 1612, and so too were Ralegh's hopes for a royal reprieve gained through this avenue of approach (Guyana being another story, another failed scheme). Still, with his decision to leave off writing his *History* came a final, last-ditch effort. It showed up in the conclusion to his book which, though James publicly disavowed it, he still seems to have read closely.[34]

In the end, Ralegh made this his final poetic call for a reprieve with the words of Job—by what is said, as well as what is assumed although not said. Ralegh identified with, and perhaps found some measure of consolation in, Job's plight and reversal in fortune. He would claim for himself the same patience and penitence, whether or not his character would allow for such sentiments. The Job story is comparable to Ralegh's own history after the ascension of James in 1603, and further is mirrored in much of the Scriptural narrative covered by Ralegh (after all, the only part of the *History* he completed includes the biblical sections up to the Maccabean revolt).

The Job story is an extended meditation on the decline and ruin of all things. In response to the awful inequities and injustices of life, the Job-author, like Ralegh, questioned how God could permit human suffering and why so much of it seemed to fall on those who did not deserve it. This is our key to understanding the place of the sententious words from Job tacked on to the end of Ralegh's narrative. These words, no less than the way they are couched, leave the door of reconciliation open while maintaining one's innocence. The line quoted comes at the very moment when Job screws up his courage, as if convinced by his own line of reasoning which justifies his lamentation, for one final and resonant protestation of his innocence' (chs. 26–31). These are the last

---

[34] John Racin, Jr., *Sir Walter Ralegh as Historian* (Salzburg, 1974), 7.

words Job speaks prior to the Lord's direct response and challenge to Job (chs. 38–41), in which his chief wisdom was in the use of words which concealed rather than made plain his meaning.[35] It is significant that Ralegh sets up a tacit mnemonic placeholder for the speech in which Job protests his innocence, rather than the culminating, if brief, expression of his repentance leading to his restoration (ch. 42). The end for Ralegh is less certain at this stage of his writing than it was for Job, who is blessed by God in his old age with magnificent rewards (42: 12–17).

Ralegh's calling attention to Job's last speech is, in effect, his final literary appeal for his own restoration. Northrop Frye has referred to his passage as the 'climax of the poem', and as the 'magnificent conclusion of Job's summarization speech'.[36] He notes further that 'nowhere in literature is there a more powerful statement of the essence of human dignity in an alien world than we get from this miserable creature'. Undoubtedly Ralegh sensed something of the same, and could say with Job: 'till I die, I will not remoue my integritie from me' (Job 27: 5).

The context of the entire passage, especially what comes just before and after Job 30: 31, brings into focus something further that Ralegh may well have set out to convey by evoking, and thereby demonstrating he had been taught by, and learned to speak through, the voice of Job. As his audience would have known, in the lines immediately prior to 'turning his harp to mourning', Job declares, in the King James Version, that he is 'a brother to dragons'. The Vulgate renders the phrase 'frater fui draconum'. To say with Job that he is a brother to dragons—albeit in a section left understood and not actually recorded in the *History*—provides a fitting end to Ralegh's unapologetic history of, and in, the world of court affairs.

And so while the death of Henry, Prince of Wales, was a great blow to his bid for a reprieve, there is perhaps something more here that Ralegh hoped to recover, especially when it is recalled that the Welsh flag bears a red dragon. Dragons, in English popu-

---

[35] Henry H. Halley, *Bible Handbook*, 24th edn. (Grand Rapids, Mich.: Regency, 1965), 244.

[36] Northrop Frye, *The Great Code: The Bible and Literature* (1981; repr. New York: Harcourt, Brace, & Jovanovich, 1983), 195.

lar mythology, were respectable, even noble, beasts. Henry VII marched behind the Welsh dragon of Cadwalader, the emblem of his Tudor ancestors, to gain the English crown at the Battle of Bosworth; he later made a dragon one of the supporters on his royal arms—as did Henry VIII and Edward VI.[37] What is more, dragons adorned the heraldic arms of other powerful English houses, thus putting some bite into the claim of being 'brother to dragons'. The image of a dragon possibly being left behind in the reader's mind, like Ralegh's more explicit use of Job, standing like a pillar of Terminus, past which we can project our gaze, speaks volumes about the cunning end of this solitary, censorious, and cynical chronicler of kings, who was himself a dogged reminder of Cynthia's golden, glorious, and bygone regime.

[37] Brian Barker, *The Symbols of Sovereignty* (North Pomfret, Vt.: David & Charles, 1979), 98–9.

5

'More easie to the readers memory': Using *The History of the World*

There was an ancient sage Philosopher,
That had read Alexander Ross over,
And swore the world, as he could prove,
Was made of Fighting and of Love.
(Butler, *Hudibras*, II. 1–4)

ALEXANDER ROSS'S VIEW OF HISTORY

Such a jest at Ross's expense was more likely the rule than exception when *Hudibras* first appeared in the decade after Ross's death. But during his own lifetime, and well into the Enlightenment, his writings were remarkably popular. This was due, in part, to the fact that, as the jest implies, Ross tended to reduce things, through allegory, into their simplest components, thereby making even the most complex topics easily comprehensible. Further, Ross recognized the affective power of the Memory Arts, especially when the soul of history was at stake. He hit upon a method of using memory pictures that complemented his narrative style, and it seems to have been a winning combination, for he grew rich off his writing.

Alexander Ross was born on 1 January 1590/1 to an old Scottish family. Like many other talented Scots seeking preferment, he travelled south when James VI left Scotland to assume the English throne. Ordained as a chaplain, he did not specialize in any single discipline, ranging freely over the intellectual landscape of the time. Ross wrote upward of 125 works and left a considerable for-tune.[1] He is best remembered today, if not for the gibe in *Hudibras*, then for his continuation of Ralegh's *The History of the World*. However, in addition to the usual sermons and exegetical tracts typical of clergymen seeking preferment, he also wrote a thirteen-book verse epic covering 'virtually the whole of sacred history from both Testaments' composed out of fragments from Virgil; the first English translation of the Qur'an (from French), which went through no fewer than five editions between 1649 and 1719; the first home-grown English interpretative handbook of classical mythography; and a survey of the world's great religions (it went through six editions during his lifetime and was translated into Dutch, German, and French).[2]

Ross also achieved notoriety for his critical engagement with every significant thinker of his time, including Hobbes, Bacon, Browne, Copernicus, Digby, and Ralegh.[3] His contrary attitude toward new developments in politics, science, and religion seems to have intrigued rather than repelled his countrymen. He remained a staunch Aristotelian and Royalist until his death on 23 February 1653/4, and lived long enough to write voluminously about his views, which, while heterodox by any standard, reflect a strange sense of backward-looking orthodoxy.

Looking backward was something Ross did well, and so his choice to focus on history at the height of his literary career seems only natural. His pessimistic view of history is grounded in Ralegh's work, and yet he is no slavish adherent to his predecessor. In fact, given the many corrections he made to *The History of the World*, and the patronizing tone in which he discussed them, there is no doubt that he was unimpressed with Ralegh's scholarship, or lack of it.[4] What, then, was accomplished through correcting and digesting, continuing and completing, Ralegh's monumental

[1]   Alexander Ross, *Mystagogus Poeticus, Or The Muses Interpreter*, ed. John R. Glenn (New York and London: Garland, 1987), 35. Citations are to this edition unless otherwise noted.

[2]   Ross, *Mystagogus Poeticus*, 11; see also Glenn's treatment of Ross's literary career (pp. 4–38), and a complete list of the various editions of his many works (pp. 618–29).

[3]   Hill, *Intellectual Origins of the English Revolution*, 36.

[4]   Beer, *Sir Walter Ralegh*, 170.

project? Why did he turn to Ralegh's book, which clearly required so much work to get from the second century before Christ up through the sixteen centuries after his crucifixion?

First, Ralegh's work still had literary cachet in the market-place.[5] Ross could count on people buying his digests and annotations. Further, he later speculated—correctly, as it turns out—that enough readers wanted to see how Ralegh would have ended the chronology had he lived. But beyond the commercial interests, there was also a compelling scholarly rationale for Ross's effort to resume Ralegh's project. Ralegh supplied Ross with an organum that enabled him to cultivate and express, in a kind of coded short-hand, his own intellectual temperament and his affinity with the failed Royalist cause. Furthermore, mnemonic principles of cognition and organization are visible in his text, no less than in his discussion of the end of history. As in the previous chapter 'end' here implies an aim or trajectory, as pertains to great deeds and sayings from the past seen against the backdrop of a blood-spattered memory-picture of political events; and, it also refers to a culminating moment, after a long period of decline—a view that Ross expressed explicitly as early as 1617.[6]

Ross is scrupulously attentive to his source-material in *History of the World: The Second Part* (1652). After compiling a faithful epitome of Ralegh's popular text, *The Marrow of Historie* (1650), which treated history as a series of object lessons in transience, Ross seems to have decided that returning to what Ralegh had started could give him a way to epitomize his own literary career: it enabled him to cut to, and represent, the marrow of his contentions, strivings, and overall melancholy view of history. Nearly 650 folio pages, despite its voluminous size and narrative digressions Ross still thought of this work as a digest, or epitome, of *The History of the World* (1614).

Given the numerous possibilities for polemical digressions, and considering the interpretative liberties in which he might have indulged, Ross's treatment of events from the last Macedonian war to 1640 is remarkably even-handed and, one might even say,

    [5] Beer, *Sir Walter Ralegh*, 153–4.
    [6] See the dedicatory epistle to *Rerum Iudicarum Memoriabiliorun . . . Liber Secundus* (1617), mentioned by Glenn (pp. 8, 45).

objective. In fact, showing more prudence than in his previous (often caustic) attacks on contemporary astronomers, physicians, clerics, and statesmen, Ross carefully sidesteps the political controversies of the day. He notes tentatively that the 'bright day' of Charles's reign is now 'overcast with a dark and dismal cloud'. Rather than clarify this image in terms of local events, though, he moves in the other direction, toward universalizing the theme. He lets Seneca speak for him, which has the effect of distancing himself further from the particulars to which he alludes, and his use of moral commonplaces personalizes it for every reader irrespective of his or her view of the Civil War:

> Who'll dote on Kingdoms? O mans vanitie!
> What mischiefs under smiling faces lie?
> As storms rage most on Hills, and as Rocks
> Which part the Sea, and subject to its knocks:
> So highest Principalities and Crowns
> Are liable to angry fortunes frowns.[7]

Then, musing on the winds of change, he concludes in prose: 'being arrived into the wish'd for Harbour . . . I have sailed over a great Sea, and its time to cast anchor. I will not venture upon the stormy rocks, quick-sands, contrary tides, and whirlpools of these last ten years, lest I make ship-wrack, and so be forced to hang up my wet cloaths in Neptune's temple' (p. 647).[8] It was also with a nautical conceit that he launched his book: 'I had scarce cast Anchor in the Harbour, and finished my Navigation in the Sea of Sir Walter Ralegh's History, which I bounded within the narrow Streights of an Epitome, when I was sollicited by some of my Friends, to hoist Sail again, and to launch into the Ocean of the Generall History of the World, that I might finish what he had begun' (sig. a3). He navigates the potentially treacherous barriers

---

[7] Ross, *History of the World: The Second Part*, sig.4H4.

[8] The same set of conceits is used to characterize his effort in *Animadversions . . . upon Sr. Walter Raleigh's Historie of the World* (London, 1653), ***3–***4: 'I could touch divers other passages in his Book, but that I am imploied in a greater voyage through the Vast Ocean of Historie from the Second Macedonian War to these our Modern times; conteining all remarkable passages of these last two thousand years of the World; which voyage I hope to end in a shorter time then Drake did his, being almost within four hundred leagues of our own shore.'

to his enterprise with skill. Even though his party had been defeated and the Church government built by his patron from sunnier days, Archbishop Laud, had been dismantled, he managed to compose a text that cut across religious and political lines, and ride out the present storms.

And so he ends his continuation of the *History of the World* with a closing prayer, which is a fairly conventional way to conclude a book of this sort. And yet, as his predecessor Ralegh did with Job, Ross encodes a series of messages through biblical references, which are unobjectionable on the surface and yet which speak volumes about the current situation. Nautical imagery recurs, and, even though he refers to the New Testament, the shadow of Neptune and all that this conjures up in Ross's mnemonic shorthand is not far behind:

let us beseech Almighty God, who hath set bounds to the Sea, and to its proud waves . . . that he will be pleased to appease this storm which hath lasted so many years among us, and to asswage this tempestuous wind, worse than Euroclydon, which vexed St. Paul and his passengers; that he would bring again the Sun and Stars so long hid from us, and that he would conduct the weather-beaten ship of this Church and State into the Harbor of Tranquility; that at last enjoying some serenity and Halcion dayes, we may sit securely under our Vines and Fig-trees, and sing the songs of Sion in our own Land. *Amen.* (sig. 4H4, p. 647)

The theme of sitting safely under one's vines and fig trees refers to bygone days of prosperity (1 Kings 4: 25), and singing songs of Zion in our own land refers to the Babylonian captivity (Psalms 137). But there is more that needs deciphering here. The passage from 1 Kings, a book which Ross knew well and with which he had a close affinity, refers to the prosperous days of living under a wise king, in this case Solomon, when the country, then consisting of Judah and Israel, was united and not in the midst of civil war.[9] This would have been known to any who attended Ross's sermons or who had more than a passing familiarity with the historical parts of the Bible. For the even more adept interpreters of the

---

[9] The biblical commonplace of every man sitting under his vine and under his fig tree, when spoken by a prophet rather than a chronicler, conveys a sense of anticipated messianic prophecy; see e.g. Micah 4: 4.

Bible, however, there is a deeper, hidden meaning in the reference to 'under your vines and fig trees'. Used as a formula signifying contentment, this phrase shows up in Isaiah, and gives Ross a way to caution his readers that, while peace is important, they should be wary of paying too high a price for it. The rhetorical trope is used by Rabshakeh who, during the siege of Jerusalem, is sent into the city by the Assyrian King Sennacherib, and 'by blasphemous perswasions solliciteth the people to reuolt' against the lawful king Hezekiah. He urges them to make an agreement with him to be resettled in a land like their own, 'and come out to mee: and eate yee euery one of his vine, and euery one of his figge tree' (Isaiah 36: 16). On the one hand, there is an earthly settlement, and on the other, there is the holy way sanctioned by the Lord who will deliver the people of Israel.

The book ends with a reference to singing songs of Zion, from Psalm 137, but here as well there is another encoded message.[10] The passage concerns the time when the Jewish people were in exile and sat down by the rivers of Babylon and 'wept: when we remembered Zion'. But the captives are mocked by their oppressors and told to sing of their homeland: 'and they that wasted us, required of us mirth: saying, Sing us one of those songs of Zion.' The lament continues: 'How shall we sing the Lord's song in a strange land?' The implication, for Ross, living in England, is that his own land is not his own until the old order is restored. In effect then, he closes his book by praying for a time when he, and others like him, will be able to rejoice in the way they did in former times, and sing the old songs—of the Anglican Church.

Even though he had made his peace with the Presbyters, there can be no doubt that Ross longed for a restoration of the 'weather-beaten' Episcopacy under which he had fared so successfully for thirty years in the south of England. Further, it seems clear that the Sun 'so long hid from us' refers to the son of the defeated king, Prince Charles in exile, and the 'Stars' to the young Duke of York

---

[10] This psalm was one of the most widely known biblical texts in Renaissance England. It gave writers such as Shakespeare, Spenser, and Milton language in which to express spiritual and political exile, especially since, as Hannibal Hamlin has shown, 'the psalm troped alienation as the inability to sing'; see 'Psalm Culture in Renaissance England', *Renaissance Quarterly*, 55: 1 (Spring 2002), 224.

(the future James II) and the Stuart cabal of advisers. Ross's alluding to Neptune's power, to which all mariners are subject, including Paul, is not a blasphemous mixing of pagan and Christian figures. In Ross's mind Neptune is understood to mean 'the divine power of nature of the sea'; and, moreover, Neptune is even equated with Christ: 'Our Savior Christ is the true Neptune, the God of the sea, whom both winds and seas obey.'[11] But in other contexts Neptune allegorically shadows forth the Pope: 'We fitly apply this fiction to the Pope, who is another Neptune, and with his Trident or threefold power that he hath in Heaven, Earth, and Purgatory, shakes the earth, and moves Kingdoms by Civil Wars.'[12] And since the extremes of religion—radical reformers no less than Catholics—were linked in Ross's mind as deviations from the True Church, they could all be subsumed in the figure of Neptune. As is always the case with Ross, the reader is at the mercy of his poetic logic—and though it is at times dizzying, it is always entertaining to see where he will go next. For example, it is Christ, not Neptune, who is said to have the 'true Trident, or full power of heaven and earth' (p. 450).

In his translation of Ovid's *Metamorphoses*, Joseph Addison remarked that 'the pious Commentator, Alexander Ross, had dived deeper into our Author's design than any of the rest; for he discovers in him the greatest mysteries of the Christian religion and finds almost in every page some typical representations of the World, the Flesh, and the Devil'.[13] To be sure, Ross is a latter-day Scholastic apologist, but he is more than this, for his unspoken mission seems to have been to rewrite the way we should be viewing the history of the world by excerpting and reconfiguring the words and works of others. And he did so according to his own

---

[11] Ross, *Mystagogus Poeticus*, 443, 449–50. Ross becomes even more ingenious as he reaches for the resounding finale to this entry: 'as the Greeks called Neptune *Posidona*, that is ποιῶν εἶδος making the image, because of all the elements, water onely represents or makes images, by reason of its smoothnesse and clearnesse; so it was Christ that made us at first to the image of God, and afterward repaired this image being decayed in us; a fit work for him who is the expresse and essentiall image of his Father.'

[12] Ross, *Mystagogus Poeticus* (London, 1648), sig. X4ᵛ.

[13] Joseph Addison, *Works*, 2nd edn. (London, 1730), i. 221, sig. 2F3; cf. Glenn's commentary in Ross, *Mystagogus Poeticus*, 174, 177.

conceit and with a sense of mission—or rather, as we shall see in what follows, *destiny*.

In the several years separating *Gnomologicon Poeticum* (1647) and his *History* (1652), Ross seems to undergo a sea-change of his own. The decade-by-decade chronology of his continuation of *The History of The World*, appended to the volume and advertised as being a major part of it, gives the reader a welcome sense of order and organization. And unlike the numbers slapped on before each of the interpretations of classical deities in his *Mystagogus Poeticus*, these numbers serve as mnemonic hooks in the Temple of History. Ross begins with 158 BC and leaves off at 1630, with each decade clearly marked off and glossed (Fig. 10). The conclusion of the section devoted to 'Affairs of State' reads simply: 'The Scots Presbyterians enter into a Covenant, and raise Arms: Preparation in England and Ireland against them, both by Sea and Land' (sig. 4U4). This is typical of the restraint shown throughout Ross's *History of the World: The Second Part*, for in his other works we are told in very direct terms that sectarianism—indeed, anything deviating from conservative Anglican theology—is the same as 'popery' because it threatens the integrity of the sovereign English nation and true Church.

Ross came to view his task as the maintenance and protection of true and certain knowledge. This, he believed, was doubly grounded in the wisdom of the ancients and in the revealed word of God, which he understood to mean the Anglican Episcopacy and along with it a king by divine right. His literary voice served as a mouthpiece for what was becoming lost in time, fast vanishing, losing ground in the present—whether Aristotle, Ovid, or the Stuarts. Ross prided himself on speaking for, and defending, the words of long-deceased guardians of wisdom from bygone years. But, as when watching a ventriloquist perform, because of his conspicuous posturing we are often fascinated more by his skill and vocal effects than by what is being said.

Ross devoted his life to resurrecting, and translating, the bodies of texts and seeking to smooth over the rough places and remark on their venerable beauty. The popularity of many of his works, if nothing else, attests to the power of an intellectual nostalgia during times of political and religious turmoil. But there is more

	Iea. bef.Chr.
JOnathas brother to *Judas* is made General of the Jewes. Demetrius encroacheth on his Neighboure, is overcome and ſlain by A-lexander the ſuppoſed ſon of *Epiphanes.* The *Dalmatian* War, and then the *Spaniſh* under *Claudius*, *Lucullus*, and *Scipio.*	⌇⌇⌇ 158
Simon ſucceedeth *Jonathas*, he takes *Gaza*, raſeth *Sion*, &c. is ſlain with his two ſons *Mattathias* and *Judas* : *John* eſcapeth. *Ptolomy Phyſcon* or *Evergetes* marrieth *Cleopatra* the mother, kills her ſon, and then marrieth her daughter. The third Punic War, and *Carthage* deſtroyed.	— 148
John Hyrcanus ſucceeds his father, beſiegeth *Ptolomy*, makes peace with *Antiochus Pius*, demoliſheth the Temple on Mount *Garixims*, reneweth the League with the Romans, beſiegeth and takes *Samaria.* The Servil war in *Sicily*. *Numantia* deſtroyed.	— 138
Demetrius freed from the *Parthian* captivity, to him ſucceeds his ſon *Antiochus Gryphus.* *Fabius* recovereth *Luſitania*, and cuts off the right hands of all the Rebels. *Pompey* is beaten by the *Numantines.*	— 128
Antiochus Cyxicenus brother to *Gryphus*, makes war againſt him. *Ptolomy Lathurus* or *Lamyrus* reigns four years with his Mother, by whom he is expelled. The Romans make war againſt the Thracians, and Dalmatians, and *Mithridates* King of *Pontus* and *Jugurtha.*	— 118
Ariſtobulus the firſt King of *Judea* ſince *Zedechias.* *Ptolomy Lathurus* kills his Mother, and aſſumes again the Government. The Romans make war againſt the Cymbrians.	— 108
Alexander Jannæus ſon of *Hircanus*, brother to *Ariſtobulus*, obtains divers Victories againſt his enemies. *Ptolomy Alexander*, *Cleopatra's* other ſon, is forced by her to marry *Selene*, taken from *Ptolomy Lathurus* by *Cleopatra.* At *Rome*, *Metellus* is baniſhed and revoked. *Marius* raiſeth ſedition at home, and ſtirs up *Mithridates* abroad. *Rutilius* condemned for extortion in *Aſia*. *Livius Druſus* ſlain for raiſing ſedition. The *Marſi* and others in *Italy* make war againſt the Romans.	— 98

Fig. 10. Chronology divided into 'decades'

to Ross's project than this. He is a dogmatic defender of antique learning and the Anglican faith; moreover, he is a compiler of commonplaces—whether mythological, rhetorical, or historical—which he saw as leading us toward truth itself: 'I diswade no man from inventing new; but I would not have him therefore forget the old, nor to lose the substance whilst he catches the shadow. . . . As I abridge no man of his liberty to invent new Wayes; so I hope they will not debar me of the like liberty to keep the old paths, so long as I find them more easie and compendious for attaining the end of my journey.'[14] Once he turned his attention to *History of the World*, in what was to be his last decade, it was as if he had come home—to the past. In the opening section he confessed:

I have been hitherto a carefull dispenser of my time, and a Niggard of my dayes, having imployed as few of them as I could in Idleness, and even from my youth I have been more conversant among the dead then the living . . . yet I have found more content among these Dead men then ever I could enjoy among the living. But why should I call those dead, who are now more alive in their Works, then when they were alive in their bodies? (sig. a3ᵛ)

MEMORY PICTURES AND THE SOUL OF HISTORY

Only someone committed to such a course of configuring history for the world to see it in its proper setting—which is to say, an essentially mnemonic setting—and only someone so comfortable with working allegorically with and within an Aesthetic of Decline, could write, and mean it: 'But why should I call those dead, who are now more alive in their Works, then when they were alive in their bodies?' Turning to Ralegh's effort gave Ross a licence to accomplish and realize his life-work: his task was to record, by way of examples, how it is we should be viewing the history of the world. Ross accomplished this by excerpting, translating, and reconfiguring the words and works of others. And he did so, self-consciously, according to mnemonic features of style that animated his sense of poetic enterprise and heroic mission.

---

[14] Alexander Ross, *Arcana Microcosmi* (London, 1652), sig. A2.

What is more, he found noble precedent for his endeavour in the patterns evident in various books of the Bible, whether following a chiastic or ring structure (like that discussed in the previous chapter), numerological subtleties, or an alpha-numeric arrangement.[15] Further, some later books of Hebrew Scripture, most notably Lamentations, were composed with at least these three structuring patterns in mind.[16] After the twelfth century, when chapter-and-verse numbering of the book of the Bible became fairly standard, it was possible to gloss and comment on sections of the Bible in a way that was easy to reproduce and recall.[17] While Ross did not necessarily have any cosmic parallels in mind when he arranged his *History* according to easy-to-recall patterns,[18] like many other writers of his day he was aware of the powerful aid to memory made possible through marking various stages running between microcosm and macrocosm.[19] In Ross's case his ingenuity with respect to biblical *sententiae* and *exempla* is applied not so much to encode hidden designs as it is to conceal messages that communicate his view of history, which overlaps with his view of his own times as being in a state of steady decay.[20] His dark conceits conceal his true intent from all except those with eyes to see. In this regard, his emblematic and mnemonic approach to com-

[15] See Max Nänny, 'Chiastic Structures in Literature: Some Forms and Functions', in Edo Fries (ed.), *The Structure of Texts* (Tübingen: Gunter Narr, 1987), 75–6; Phyllis Portnoy, 'Ring Composition and the Digression of *Exodus*', *English Studies*, 82: 4 (Aug. 2001), 289–307; Maren-Sofie Røstvig, 'Structure as Prophecy: The Influence of Biblical Exegesis Upon Theories of Literary Structure', in Alastair Fowler (ed.), *Silent Poetry* (London, 1970), 32–72; John MacQueen, *Numerology: Theory and Outline History of a Literary Mode* (Edinburgh: University of Edinburgh Press, 1983), 1–25, 47–65.

[16] Using the numerical values of Hebrew letters to interpret the text has been a mainstay of mystical biblical exegesis for centuries. The more commonplace understanding of alphabetic acrostic structure is simply that it 'was a favorite form of Hebrew poetry, adopted to help the memory' (Halley, *Bible Handbook*, 320).

[17] Beryl Smalley, *The Study of the Bible in the Middle Ages* (Notre Dame, Ind.: University of Notre Dame Press, 1964), 222.

[18] Russell Peck, 'Number as Cosmic Language', in Caroline D. Eckhardt (ed.), *Essays in the Numerical Criticism of Medieval Literature* (Lewisburg, Penn.: Bucknell University Press, 1980), 15–64.

[19] S. K. Heninger, Jr., *Touches of Sweet Harmony* (San Marino, Calif.: Huntington Library Press, 1974), 364–93.

[20] Ross, *Mystagogus Poeticus*, 8.

position helped him realize his own heroic destiny as a uniquely gifted chronicler.

His *History* bears out that Ross was conscious of the way that words could give a destination to things that were already on their way—in line with how words can be said to predestine what we subsequently come to ask about a topic and thereby come to know about it. Further, he was adept at recognizing and making the most of the way words can predetermine what we end up finding in and through history as an expression of mortal striving. For example, he concludes his 'Briefe Chronologie of the Principal Passages Faln out in the World . . . Divided into 180 Decades, containing 1800 years' in the following way:

AND thus (Good Reader) in this History and Chronologie, as in two small Maps, thou mayest behold the Microcosme of Mankinde, in so many Hundred years, acted over & over again the same Tragi-Comedies: Thou seest new Persons and Visards, but the same Scene, and the same Things acted: Thou mayest behold some hence, as Charon did from the top of Parnassus in Lucian, a Clod of Earth full of Bee-hives an Ant-hill full of Emmets, or a Pool full of Bubbles, some bigger, some lesser, puff'd with aire, and tossed up and down with the winds, till they all break, and turn into their original Vapours. And what is it thou seest acted here? Nothing almost but Treacheries, Murthers, Incests, Adulteries . . . Toylings, Battels, Law-suits, and a thousand such Vexations, all for a Handfull of Earth . . . And what is the cause of all this mischief? Truly Pride, Ambition, Couvetousnesse . . . And above all things, Injustice, for which the World hath suffered so many changes: Justice is the Pillar on which States and Kingdoms stand; Remove that and down falls the Temple of all Government . . . Lastly, In this Chronologie, as in an Epitome, you shall se all the heretical Opinions which have been spued out in so many Ages, now lick'd up by the Fanatical spirits of this Age. (sig. 4u4ᵛ)

In addition to using the commonplace metaphor of the world as a stage, where the same tragicomedies are acted out over and over again, Ross builds on the compelling analogy of History and Chronology as two small maps. Following the logic of the conceit brings into focus how the Memory Arts enabled Ross to realize his destiny as a chronicler writing in the style of a Hebraic scriptural redactor working on books such as 2 Kings and 2 Chronicles, relating who reigned or rebelled when, and whether and the extent to which they acted in the sight of the Lord. Ross writes: 'The compendiousnesse of this Chronological History, or Historicall Chronologie (call it what you wil for it containes both) wil be useful and acceptable to most sorts of men . . .' (sig. b4ᵛ). Then he lists how each of the five types of readers can benefit—the middle way being of special interest here: 'this Book will be as a Table, Index, or Remembrancer' to 'those who already have ready the Histories at large':

I have for the greater ease of the Reader, subjoyned a Chronologie to this Historie, wherein as in a small Map may be seen the chief memorable Passages that have fallen out in the World. . . . I have not digested this Chronologie as others do, according to each particular year, but have reduced the whole time into so many Decads or Tens, so that we see at one view what hath fallen out every ten years; which way is more ready to be found, and more easie to the Readers memory.

This is consonant with the accepted practices of the Memory Arts from the time and teachings of Cicero, where sets of fives, usually paired into decades, are visualized.

We shall need to study with special care the backgrounds we have adopted so that they may cling lastingly in our memory, for the images, like letters, are effaced when we make no use of them, but the backgrounds, like wax tablets, should abide. And that we may by no chance err in the number of backgrounds, each fifth background should be marked. For example, if in the fifth we should set a golden hand, and in the tenth some acquaintance whose first name is Decimus, it will then be easy to station like marks in each successive fifth background.[21]

In addition to following this technique for making of History a vast Memory Theatre, in this case of God's inscrutable Judgement, Ross also follows Cicero's view that History bears witness to the passing ages, is the light of truth, life of memory, the judge of life, herald of antiquity (outlined as part of the 'Mind of the Front' accompanying the frontispiece to Ralegh's *History of the World* (see Fig. 9),[22] to which he alludes in passing (sig. a6ᵛ).

[21] *Ad Herennium*, III. xvii. 31, p. 211.
[22] See Margery Corbett and Ronald Lightbown, *The Comely Frontispiece: The Emblematic Title-Page in England, 1550–1660* (London: Routledge & Kegan Paul, 1979), 129–35.

After turning history into such a place, from which one can see the chief memorable passages laid out in neat decades, Ross takes this metaphor a step further in his dedication to Henry, Earl of Arundel and Surrey, thus showing the extent to which history functions as a *place*, at once mnemonic and metaphoric, from which one can see chief memorable passages laid out in neat decades: 'History is a necessity to all, but chiefly to those who are set upon the Pinnacle of Honor. . . . Who being placed upon the Watch-Towers, had need of better eyes, and a longer Perspective than those who live below; Now History is the perspective that lets them see the dangers a far off' (sig. a1ᵛ).[23]

So, in addition to Ross's corrections of Ralegh's errors in a treatise dating from the 1650s, and having practised and perfected the art of distillation from his experience digesting Ralegh's tome throughout the 1650s as *The Marrow of History* (1650), his continuation and extension of the project, *History of the World: The Second Part* (1652), contains the Chronology mentioned above (Fig. 10), as well as careful catalogues of useful information with dates, concerning, for example, universities, knights, religious orders, and, as we might expect from the likes of Ross, heretics. There is also an Alphabetical Table, Summary, and Contents of the matters 'intreated'. What emerges from within this 700-page folio is a variety of memory cues for the uses of history and his *History*, moving in increments from microcosm to macrocosm, as in a Tower where one can either go up or down, finding extensive renditions or more compact excerpts, in Ross's *History*—or in one's own version of history, using Ross as a model (Fig. 11). In this range of duplicated efforts, to offer many entry points into the work, we find an elaborate network of memory cues for the use of history and of his *History*. We do not have to look far for such a model in the work that Ross spent so much time reading over and excerpting, Ralegh's *History*. In the section entitled 'That man is (as it were) a little World: with a digression touching our mortalities', we read that 'Man, thus compounded and formed by God, was an abstract or model, or briefe Storie of the Vniuersall: in whom God concluded the Creation, and the worke of the World'

---

[23] Cf. Spenser's *Faerie Queene*, III. ii. 19–21.

MEMORY IMAGE
(whether head-letter;
'Adonis'; two small maps;
books sweating blood)

'SUMMARIE'
book-by-book matter 'Intreated'

CONTENTS
Chapter by chapter topics covered

ALPHABETICAL TABLE
another way of locating and linking events

APPENDED *CHRONOLOGIE*:
'Divided into 180 Decades, containing 1800 years'

History of the World, The Second Part –
Ross's synthesis, but avoiding digressions

CATALOGUE OF HIS SOURCES
cited by Ross as redactor, as Chronicler ...

The raw matter of HISTORY, as examples:
'Principal Passages Faln out in the World'

HISTORICAL KNOWLEDGE

Fig. 11. Ross's project seen as a 'Watch Tower'

(p. 25). Taking to heart such a metaphor, we see that the ends and means, the content and the form, of Ross's *History of the World: Second Part* collapse and coalesce. The moral and the mnemonic unavoidably converge and overlap here. This can be seen as both a theme and as the predominating textual practice. For example, also in the Preface, Ross resumes the conceit of history being a tower, and urges us to consider further the wider implications of the theatrical metaphor: 'here we shall see the whole world, but as a stage on which men of all sorts have acted their parts; Princes, Prelates, Peasants, of all ages acting the same things, on the same stage; who after they have laid aside their discriminating vizards, and performing garments, they are all alike, as they were before they put them on' (sig. b2). Not only is the Theatre of God's Judgement being evoked here in his use of this commonplace, but so too is the typical Renaissance Memory Theatre, which involved the mental staging of what one wanted to excerpt and encode for future use.

Throughout his career, Ross was devoted to methods of systematizing information into compact, ready-to-use formats. For example, his compendium of Latin grammar, *Isagoge Grammatica* (1648), is rendered in hexameter verses explicitly as an *aide-mémoire*; and also he wrote four Latin *florilegia*, consisting of memorable phrases, emblems and *sententiae*, and colloquia. Similarly, as was discussed in the first part of this book, John Willis advocated that all kinds of '*Hyeroglyphicks*, and innumerable sentences' be situated in 'an imaginary house or building'; and Willis approved making use of things 'expressed in action upon the stage', like an 'armed Knight bearing his Scutcheon and imprese written therein' (p. 47). The images that are used, though, have to remain distinct, for, as Fulwood made clear: 'cruell, iniurious, merueilous, excellently faire, or excedingly foule things do change and moue ye senses, & better styre up the Memorie.'

In retracing these steps of mnemonic decorum, we can consider in a new light the extent to which Ross revived these principles to accomplish his end as a historian. Ross found in the image of the Memory Theatre more than a mere metaphor. The staging of maimings and vexations in prose, like those Ralegh and Ross favoured in the telling of history, brings together the practical applications of the Memory Arts and the vast repository of images charged with emblematic significance. English tragic dramas, such as those discussed in Part I, evoked, and themselves became, melancholy Memory Theatres. In typical plays of blood-revenge, like *The Revenger's Tragedy* and *The Spanish Tragedy*, we find the exemplary juxtaposing of merry, cruel, injurious, and marvellous acts; the staging of the excellently fair and the excellently foul overlap, and bleed one into the other, once memory images have been invoked.

Some of the scenes of cruelty Ross describes stand out more vividly than other events covered in his *History*. They thus become landmarks and not simply grisly occurrences; they become beacons, enabling us to travel from one of these shimmering spots to another within his text, and in the process, to ascribe some sense of coherence to the commonplace events encountered in between. This way of telling history seems to have been taken to heart by a contemporary reader who, in the margin, drew a hand, index finger extended, pointing out scenes that are especially marvellous or cruel. Once such points were set in mind, they could serve as 'landmarks', as it were, on a mnemonic map of the terrain of history:

[1624] This year strange things were seen in Germany, portending yet more troubles. For in divers Po[o]les water was congealed into blood, drops of blood fell from the beams and rafters of some houses, the bread, the tables, and books in some places sweat blood. (sig. 3G3ᵛ)

[1630] The Famin in Pomerania and Rugia, was also great, that some like Caniballs fed on mens flesh. (sig. 3H3ᵛ)

[1450] [S]he in the presence of the Tyrant, thrust a knife into his heart, and ripping up his body, pulls out his liver, which she flung to the dogges. (sig 3I)

Of course, these may simply be passages that appealed to the sensibilities of an impressionable, perhaps young, reader of history; nevertheless, such striking and stirring images conform in style and intensity to those regularly used in Memory Theatres. Whatever the case, the heading of gruesome events seems to be the only thing linking these marked passages. Such a practice gives cogent expression to, and vividly—if grotesquely—exemplifies, the notion that the picture we conceive of History is a memory picture. And further, consonant with the objectives of someone appointing a Memory Theatre, Ross sees the work of the historian to be that of giving the best substance for retention so the matter can be profitably used according to one's projected end: 'Lastly, I have in the Work performed the part of an Historian. . . . Two things are commendable in an Historian; to wit, brevity and simplicity' (sig. b6).

Brevity and simplicity apply as well to the scenes from the drama of European history as Ross renders it. And while there are many hundreds of images evoked, no pictures are used in his text—with the notable exception of only a few head-letters. One of them speaks eloquently, if silently, to the essence of Ross's mission as a historian, distilling and encapsulating it in a striking memory image (Fig. 12).[24] This image shows up, tellingly, in only two places. It appears first at the very beginning, thus visually launching the dedicatory epistle, and it appears, at the beginning of the 'Brief Chronologie', immediately following the citation from Seneca already discussed, which closes the *History* (sig. 4I2). As such, these head-letters stand like heraldic supporters of the noble matter expressed as memory images through the prose commentary. They mirror one another from either side of his *History*, reflecting key themes that Ross would express, one way or the other.

Above the letter 'A' is a Tudor Rose, a symbol of English regal sovereignty—a cause to which, as we have seen, Ross was committed. The crown is supported, on the right, by Prudence, identified by her traditional iconographic attributes of mirror and snake, and on the left, by Justice, with her sword. Reminiscent of the figure of Memory, both Justice and Prudence tread upon a decaying corpse, 'a carcass without life' (to use a phrase from Ross, which will be discussed below), signifying Oblivion. Furthermore, traditional graveyard vipers and worms have taken up residence

---

[24] This head-letter dates back at least as far as Sidney's *The Countesse of Pembrokes Arcadia* (1590), sig. B. Its revival in Ross's day thus evokes a sense of nostalgia for the monarchy, and implicitly links Ross's report on the vagaries of human history to the moral dimension of telling about war and love which characterizes the *Arcadia*.

Fig. 12. History and Prudence trampling Oblivion as Death

in the skull, once the seat of Reason, thus making of the image a
vanitas figure (see again Fig. 1). In a manner consistent with the
book's main themes and driving undercurrent, this image also
evokes the notion of death as the wage of sin. That association
takes on added significance when we consider the author's
farewell to the reader: 'there is no such antidote against the
Infection and Poyson of Sin, as the reading of Historie' (sig. b6ᵛ).

The classical figures, frozen in a moment of time, tread upon
the face of that which at once connotes death and oblivion, and
thus recall the rigid imagery from funerary art. Ross's head-letters
are of the same order as Holbein's subtle letters recalling Death
(Fig. 13), and more explicit reminders, like those in Holbein's
celebrated alphabet of Death (Fig. 14). While availing himself of
the conventions typical of book ornamentation of the day, Ross
manages to convey a message that visually echoes the main theme

CELTOGA
LATIAE SITVS.
CAPVT   VII.
TABVLA. III.   EVROPAE.

ELTOGALATIA
in quatuor diuifa eft puincias,
Aquitaniã, Lugdunenſem, Bel
gicam, & Narbonenſem.
Aquitania fines habet
Ab Occidente Aquitanicum
Oceanum, & iuxta littus deſcriptionem talē.
Poſt Ocaſum Pyrenes promonto. quod con∕
tinet gradus   15   45 ½ ⅓
Aturij fluuij oſtia   16 ½ ¼ 44 ½ ¼
Curianũ promontoriũ   16 ½   46
Igmani flu:oſtia   17   45 ⅓
Garumnæ flu.oſtia   17 ½   46 ½
Media ipſius lõgitudo   18   45 ⅓
Fontes fluuij   19 ½   44   ¼
Santonum promon.   16 ½   47   ¼
Santonum portus   16 ½   46 ½ ¼
                                    Canentelli

*Gallia Comata, A∕
quitaniam Lugdu
nenſem & Belgicã
habet , excepta
Narbonenſi, quæ
Braccata. Togata
eſt Lombardia.
Aquitania, Aremo
rica antè dicta, ho
die Guienne duca
tus, Gaſcongne.*

Le dou.

S.Maria.

la Garona.

Blaye.
La Rochelle.

Fig. 13. Gentle reminder of Death

Fig. 14. Startling reminder of Death

of his book. He is at pains to show us, in a memory-picture, the soul of history, and he will not be content with displaying just the body, for such a body would be a corpse. It is chronology, for Ross, that is associated with life—with extended life: 'History, indeed, is the Body, but Chronologie the Soul of Historical Knowledge; for History without Chronology, or a Relation of things past, without mentioning the Times in which they were Acted, is like a Lump or Embryo without articulation, or a Carcass without Life' (sig. b5).

The animating factor, chronology, is like the breath of life that was blown into Adam, the first body in history; Ralegh, let us recall, begins his *History of the World* with Creation. Ross's carcass without life awaiting articulation finds a Scriptural antecedent in Ezekiel's vision: 'Thus saith the Lord GOD vnto these bones, Behold, I wil cause breath to enter into you, and ye shall liue. And I wil lay sinewes vpon you, and wil bring vp flesh vpon you, and couer you with skinne, and put breath in you, and ye shall liue' (Ezekiel 37: 4–6). Breath comes before, and pushes out into the world, any vocal articulation whatsoever. Breath marks whatever is spoken as being a sure a sign of life. And yet nothing is more fleeting than breath. It comes and goes, in and out, until we breathe no more. Although ephemeral in the extreme, it serves to translate audibly what is on our minds. Following the analogical logic here, which is bound up with the Aesthetic of Decline, an epitome, like Ross's outline of Ralegh's text in *The Marrow of History*, works along similar metaphoric lines: the marrow flows through bones like a river of life, keeping them from drying up; the marrow (the epitome) gives the possibility of life to the bones making up the framework, the skeleton (Ralegh's *History* and Ross's continuation), which gives a shape to the carcass, to the body, namely to history, and which chronology in turn animates.

For Ross, the end of historical knowledge, as it is articulated by chronology, is conveyed as well by epitomes and digests as by detailed narratives (see again Fig. 11). To what end, then, does he see through the press a 700-page rehearsal of the vanity of mortal strivings? Is it merely to show us how all things in time can be undone and reduced, a theme that Ross conveys in commonplace, if sobering, terms?

If you ask me to what purpose have all these stirs continually bin, and yet are still in the World; I answer, to no other purpose, but that insatiable, covetous, and ambitious Mindes may have more of this earthly Turf to crawl and domineer upon (as if they wanted elbow-room) and some more clods of earth, whereof a little will content them, when their vast and ambitious thoughts are laid low as their carcasses; then shall a short and narrow coffin contain those, whom one or more kingdoms will not content [b2] . . .

Why should we dream of long continuance here, when we see the great Empires, Monarchies, States, Cities, and Magnificent Buildings of former times all fallen into dust and nothing. Nunc segetes ubi Troja fuit, Troy is a cornfield: Jerusalem a heap of stones, In æternos collapsa cineres, saith Hierom, fallen into perpetual ashes; and Rome is ruine. (sig. b3ᵛ)

At the end of this passage Ross quotes Spenser's translation of Du Bellay's sonnet which begins: 'Thou stranger which for Rome in Rome here seek'st . . .' There can be no doubt that Ross inflects his history with poetry. Reading the world's history, for Ross, is a story, the end of which we know all too well. At stake in this way of telling history, as so many different versions of the same thing leading always to ruin and following a trajectory of decline,[25] where telling takes on the sense of giving a reckoning or account, is nothing less than the preservation of a process of telling our own stories of our tradition leading up to, and collapsing into, our own story—our own histories. What we read in this method, no less than the narrative which serves as the medium for conveying the body (history) from oblivion toward some form of renewed being in the world, is an imitation of the style, and intimation of the vocation, of the Scriptural chroniclers and prophets from the time of Jeroboam's rebellion up to the Babylonian captivity. For the underlying message of the writings from, say, 2 Kings and 2 Chronicles, like that of Ross's *History of the World*, does not stop with the inevitable decline of all things and the vanity of mortal strivings. To speak at once metaphorically, universally, and historically: the destruction of the Temple and the scattering of the people of Judah and Israel recounted through repeated litanies of woe is the final focus. Our eyes are made to look through, and

---

[25] Cf. Ross, *Mystagogus Poeticus*, 45.

past, these heroic struggles and tragicomedies, toward the eventual return to the Promised Land and the rebuilding of the Temple. Through the arduous task of making our way through such an emblematic telling of history, we are brought to a place where we can see, and imagine, a future different from the present, that cycles back to recover what was great and sacred about our past.

Such hopes need not be construed in a strictly messianic way, but of course when viewed typologically and with Christological hindsight such an occurrence does lend itself to interpretation in terms of the resurrection motif. Whether referring to the return from Babylonian captivity or the restoration of the Stuart monarchy, such hopes, in *The History of World*, tacitly are recorded as incidental and incremental moments in the history of the world which, despite the irrevocable declination inherent in all people, cultures, and ultimately of the world itself, bespeak the truth of historical knowledge: that we have something toward which we can, and must, strive. And it is in that striving that we are borne aloft from the tumult of the mischiefs and vexations of the world, so manifestly the mortal destiny of mankind—and of each of us.

As has been seen, Ross's view of history, and the sense of mission he took to heart in recording it, are different from his view and approach to pagan poetry. And yet such allegorical 'typing out' of the closely connected themes of rebirth, resurrection, redemption, and salvation in his *History* recalls Ross's earlier work, *The Muses Interpreter*. But herein lies a clue to what underlies Ross's mnemonically oriented way of thinking and writing throughout his life, and it is reminiscent of what was found in Part II: sound and sense can sometimes unite to produce meanings that we would not have come up with on our own. For example, *Mystagogus Poeticus* is aptly, if cunningly, subtitled: 'historicall Mysteries, or mystical Histories'. As was the case with Bible verses such as Job 30: 27 and 30: 31, a chiastic pattern allows each phrase to supplement and complement the sense of the other. As such, there is a connection being forged here, not only within Ross's title, but also with respect to his other work, namely, his 'Chronological History, or Historical Chronologie'. In *Mystagogus Poeticus* history still remains the form and substance

in question, and chronology remains what ensouls it. For
example, in the chapter on Adonis in Ross's 'historicall Mysteries,
or mystical Histories',[26] after surveying the history of the figure,
understood now as a memory image (Fig. 11, top tier), a tower of
meaning is constructed. The entry has all of the appearance of
being sequential, with its numbered passages, but it is not. The
progression is neither logical nor linear, strictly speaking. Instead
it is organized emblematically, using memory images: each
allegorical association gives rise to another, by virtue of which the
entire sequence can be considered.

5. Adonis is from ἄδων to sing; for beauty and musick are friends to
Venus. 6. Adonis may signifie the good Government of a Commonwealth, which is the beauty thereof, which is killed by Mars in the form of
a boar; for Mars and Wantonnesse are enemies of all Government. 7.
Beautiful Adonis is turned into a fading flower; to shew that Beauty
quickly perisheth. 8. Young and fair Adonis is killed by a Boar; so
Wantonness and Letchery are the destroyers of youth and beauty. 9. Our
resurrection in this may be typed out; for although death kills us, it shall
not annihilate us, but our Beauty shall increase, and we shall spring out
of the ground again, like a beautiful flower in the Resurrection. 10.
Though our bodies die, yet our good name shall flourish, and like a faire
flower, shall live and smell when we are gone. 11. Myrrha of her owne
Father begot this child Adonis . . . 12. Let them remember, who hunt
after too much pleasure, that the Devill is that great boar, who lieth in
wait to kill them. (sig. B4–B5)

The excursus, which accounts for only about a quarter of the
interpretive section (section 11, omitted above, concerns the uses
of myrrh 'as a help to decayed beauty, to a stinking breath, to
procreation, and the vitiocity of the matrix'), concludes with an
explicit admonition to keep the image of the Devil as that great
boar as an enduring memory picture: 'Let them remember . . .'.
While this is a powerful and appropriate image with which to end
the entry on Adonis, and while it might seem like this is the culminating idea of an orderly progression, the entire sequence pro-
ceeds in an associative rather than logical sequence. Indeed,
throughout *Mystagogus Poeticus* each interpretation seems to be
recorded as it came to Ross, and not because of any underlying

[26] This was not in the 1647 edition, but was added in 1648.

narrative plan.[27] The rationale for what comes next has more to do
with principles of poetic truth and the work of translation than
anything that might be implied by the numbers prefixed to each
interpretation of the classical figure. In this, as in his *History*—
both with respect to the matter conveyed as well as the way in
which it is communicated in a series of stages moving from microcosm to macrocosm—Ross treated history as poetry and poetry
as history. While the order may appear to be self-evident, because
of the numbers placed before an interpretation in *Mystagogus
Poeticus* or beside an event in *History of the World*, the numbers
are simply a convenient system of notation, a handy way to organize memorable matters. Much in the same way that Ralegh's
History was organized after a terminally oriented logic consistent
with its own ends, Ross's works—whether concerning history or
poetry or religion—deploy a logic of poetry that is derived from,
and which speaks to, an Aesthetic of Decline.

Further, much in the same way *History of the World: The Second Part* has a grander sense of purpose than did his earlier
Animadversions, Ross's *Mystagogus Poeticus* has a sense of coherence that it did not have in its first form. The original collection
of poems was more akin to a miscellany of notes gathered under
convenient headings, initially published as *Mel Heliconium*
(1642). Each section ends with an admonitory poem, and Ross
used those memorable poems—which were dropped from *The
Muses Interpreter*—as the basis for rendering moral and typologi-
cal interpretations of myths in his later, more compendious, and
evidently popular, editions:

> You that hunt after pleasures, eye that Boare
> Who would your health, and wealth, and souls devour.
> Dote not on beauty; beauty's but a flower
> Whose pride and lustre fadeth in an hour.
> Strive that your names may flourish after death,
> Let them out-live Adonis flower, & yeeld a fragrant breath.

Ross is not claiming this to be the textual truth of the pagan
figures, but that these 'mysticall Histories' can enable us to realize
eternal verities—but only if we gather them up in some sort of

---

[27] Cf. Ross, *Mystagogus Poeticus*, 142.

Fig. 15. The trumpet call of Reputation

orderly succession and mnemonic progression. As long as each
main memory picture is conceptualized in terms of a distinct
background, it does not matter how arbitrarily the mnemonic
icons or emblematic tags are disposed within his book. Thus
'Adonis' becomes a heading worthy of numerous digressions and
moralizations (Fig. 11, top tier), ranging from themes of vanitas to
Christ's resurrection to the restoration of the True Church. Ross
considers such pagan figures to be so many 'flowers of usefull,
delightful, and rare Observations'. So too can we conceptualize
the figure of History, with its trumpet corps of repute, whether
good or bad, as portrayed on the frontispiece of Ralegh's *History*
(see again Fig. 9), as well as in other renderings of the theme, like
one by Peacham (Fig. 15) which shows 'living fame' publishing far
and near deeds worthy of praise and memory. This figure applies
to Ross as well, for, as a recorder of history, he is like 'Fama Bona'
and 'Fama Mala' rolled into one; so, in addition to resembling a
chronicler of God's word, he is also History's own scribe, whose

mission it is to publish near and far the vagaries of human activities in the world. His method of recounting 'mystical Histories', like his conveyance of the soul of historical knowledge through a chronology divided into decades, marks his life-work as being concerned with recovering and translating, reviving and transmitting, the truths both of times past and present using the immemorial techniques of the Memory Arts.

However, as we have seen with the emblematic method, and especially when filtered through prose, there is a fine art to suggesting a thought by withholding it; and the persistent thought, or grand theme, Ross suggests and withholds through memory images is that we cannot understand the value of returning from exile and the hope it brings, unless first we have been scattered and scorned. Even the shadow of this idea would have been eagerly received and taken to heart by people living at the time of the English Civil War. Moreover, such a theme, bolstered by the sense of having been redeemed and made stronger by the lessons of history, would have been appealing, even comforting, to Royalist readers between the time of the publication of *The Muses Interpreter* (1647–8), at the nadir of Charles's fortunes leading up to his execution, and that of *The History of the World: The Second Part* (1652), the first years of the Commonwealth, when 'the Rump had been living in fiscal paradise maintained by the sale of confiscated crown, church, and Cavalier lands'.[28] The process of coming back together, of re-massing and returning, is the work of Memory, and it must follow some sort of principle of order or organization, even if it is only the chiastic logic of poetry. And so Ross was equally interested in mystical histories and historical chronology, as part of his plan to publish 'near and far', and to translate, the soul of historical knowledge. Ross's philosophy of composition, as it applies to both domains of knowledge—namely, poetry and history—was steeped in the Memory Arts.

Notwithstanding the local conditions and historical realities conditioning Ross's project, however, his view of history is one bound up with the serious business of recording and representing

---

[28] Lacey B. Smith, *This Realm of England* (Lexington, Mass.: D. C. Heath, 1976), 256.

as accurately as possible a chronology of time's passage. Instead
of showing us so many 'flowers of usefull, delightful, and rare
Observations', as he did with the poetry of the ancients, through
history he shows us admonitory memory pictures designed to
serve both as guide-posts along our journey through the annals of
the past, and as prospective targets for our future actions in the
world. Seen in this way, in Ross's books—whether those interpreting poetry or history—we recover valid and telling manifestations
of a now lost regime of symbols through which the soul or
shadow, indeed a shade, of history showed itself to be engaged
with death. We would expect no less from a person so committed
to recovering the truth of the end of history from those who have
been, and to transmitting it to those of us who have lost access to
that world of words, that he was indeed 'more conversant among
the dead then the living'. And although Ross speaks metaphorically here, there is a literal truth in his confession as well. It will be
fitting, then, in the Conclusion to consider how words are figured
as being brought back, even recovered, from those who have, in the
words from Job quoted in the Introduction, gone 'into the countrie of darknesse and into the shadowe of death, from whence
there is no returning agayne'.

Conclusion
'Simulars of the dead':
A Final Declension

> My dayes are like a shadow, that declineth: & I am withered
> like grasse.
>
> (Psalm 102: 11)

In Florio's *Worlde of Wordes* (1598), the Italian word 'abbassare'
is translated into the common Latin root word and a dozen
English synonyms: 'to abase, to depress, to suppresse, to stoupe,
to incline, to bend downe, to abate, to descend, to humble, to
submit, to prostrate, to alay, to cast down.'[1] A noteworthy shift
takes place a dozen years later, coincident with the passing from
the reign of Elizabeth to that of James—the latter, for Ralegh,
viewed as a period of great decline, but which for Ross was seen
as England's last Golden Age. It is a change that stayed in all sub-
sequent editions, which suggests the meaning became stabilized
in this new word. Florio's expanded dictionary of 1611 gives the
same list of words for the entry on 'abbassare' except for two
scarcely detectable, but potentially revealing, alterations: 'to cast
down' becomes 'to bring low', and, more to the present point, 'to
incline' becomes 'to decline'.[2] Further, in 1659, when Giovanni
Torriano had taken over Florio's *Vocabulario Italiano & Inglese*,
the English word 'decline' is no longer listed as an entry in its own
right, whereas it had been the equivalent for 'abbassare' in Florio's
editions of the early seventeenth century.

  Likewise, the Renaissance Aesthetic of Decline itself was in
decline, coming full circle, having achieved and exceeded itself by

---

[1] John Florio, *Worlde of Wordes, Or Most copious, and exact Dictionaries in
Italian and English* (London, 1598), sig. A1.
[2] John Florio, *Queen Anna's New World of Wordes* (London, 1611), sig. A1ᵛ.

the end of the English Civil War. But this, after all, is to be expected of such an aesthetic movement, modelled as it is upon, and reflecting, the cycle of mortality. Although it is always a tricky business to declare the end of a cultural *mentalité*, a good case can be made that the 1650s in England—with the appearance of Ross's *History of the World: The Second Part*, the second edition of Izaak Walton's much-expanded *The Compleat Angler*, and Thomas Browne's *Urne Buriall* (published in the year of Cromwell's death, 1658), as well as with the winning of rich territories such as Jamaica—bring to a close the Renaissance Aesthetic of Decline. In Ross's case, in the decade following his death the fortunes of Aristotle changed forever with the advent of the Royal Society, and his antiquated notions of kingship would become untenable even in the wake of the restored monarchy; the Temple may have been restored, but the rites were decidedly different from those of the generations before the Captivity and Exile.

There is, however, nothing of a death-knell sounded for the Aesthetic of Decline in the works of Ross or Browne, as their prose allows it to be expressed thoroughly and fully, and to accomplish and achieve its end; and, in doing so, it too passes away, falling away from patterns of poetic thinking and writing—but it does not pass out of sight and memory altogether. The Aesthetic of Decline, from its emergence (as described in Part I), undergoes a steady declension, understood here to imply both an inflection (like that informing the work of translation in Part II) and a descending slope (like that characterizing the world's course in Part III).

It is characteristic of the nature of artistic endeavours to represent, and thereby to re-create in another form, an image of something that will be absent once the work of art is completed or performed, whether a portrait, Persephone in the Underworld, the Crucifixion of Christ, or a foreign cityscape. It is the nature of essentially mimetic art to be engaged with what is absent, as well as with things that are now gone. In this sense, as John Sallis has shown, art is concerned primarily, if not exclusively, with 'pastness'.[3] This theme takes on personified symbolic form in

---

[3] John Sallis, *Stone* (Bloomington and Indianapolis: Indiana University Press, 1994), 31, 99; see also his subtle analysis of *The Winter's Tale*, 117–47.

Shakespeare's Perdita, whose name bespeaks what her character enacts.[4] She is somehow lost to the world and displaced through time, but like her mother Hermione (linked by tradition variously to Harmony, the daughter of Helen and Menelaus, and Aphrodite),[5] can, in part, be restored to her former and proper place in the domestic, civic, and political worlds she once inhabited through enchanted conjuring and theatrical projection. After all, Shakespeare often wants the audience to see a dramatic character, 'in spite of his or her unmistakable individuality, against the archetypal background of a corresponding mythological figure set in the context of its perennial fate'.[6] Further, such a calling upon classical and other culturally accrued meanings draws upon, and serves to illustrate, the main principles of the Memory Arts.[7]

What is brought back, however, whether with respect to the recovery of the compound archetypal signification invested in a figure or regarding a character's identity from within the world of the play, can only be recuperated in terms of something other than—yet which still is hauntingly similar to—what it is modelled on, what it once was. This brings us back to the dynamics of the work of translation, like that discussed in Part II. But, as was seen to be the case with the superadded meanings that cling to proverbs, there is something that gets added in as well. In this process of bringing it back through representational means, other cultural resonances, in the form of accrued tokens of its past, begin to make themselves known. For example, Hermione's name is also linked to the town where Persephone was carried off by the king of the dead.[8] Irrespective of whether such information was generally known to the person watching Hermione in the cele-

---

[4] Inge Leimberg, ' "Golden Apollo, a poor humble swain": A Study of Names in *The Winter's Tale*', in *Deutsche Shakespeare-Gesellschaft West: Jahrbuch* (1991), 150–2.

[5] Inge Leimberg, ' "The Image of Golden Aphrodite": Some Observations on the Name "Hermione" ', in *Deutsche Shakespeare-Gesellschaft West: Jahrbuch* (1988), 136, 141, 146, 148.

[6] Ibid. 149.

[7] Daniel Martin, *Le Triptyque des 'Essais' de Montaigne et l'héraldique des dieux gréco-romains* (Tours: Librairie A.-G. Nizet, 1996), 61–90.

[8] Leimberg, 'The Image of Golden Aphrodite', 130; cf. Sallis, *Stone*, 120.

brated tableau scene, it was carried along nonetheless in the feigning of the figure.

Shakespeare's *The Winter's Tale* thus presents us with a kind of after-image of what always has been before us whether we stopped to recognize it or not—like the immanence of Death, and like the prefiguring of our own end. In the monument scene, Hermione, who is presumed dead, poses as a statue that would resemble her to the life, taking into account the passage of time all the while she has been concealed from sight. One static moment more and she will be brought back into the fold of the court, language, and family relations. The sight of the feigned statue makes Leontes so 'stirr'd' that he would break through the frame of the tableau: 'Let no man mock me, | For I will kiss her.' As the friar had to tell Bussy about the limits of the magic perspective glass, Leontes is instructed by Paulina in the law of this piece of art: 'forbear. | The ruddiness upon her lip is wet; | You'll mar it if you kiss it; stain your own | With oily painting. Shall I draw the curtain?' (5.3.80–3). At the appropriate cue of 'Music! awake her! strike!' (5.3.98), ceremonial strains initiate the solemn transformation of feigned stone into life. She is thus conjured: 'be stone no more.' In this masterful double-reverse of artifice, as she descends, Paulina says to Leontes: 'Start not; her actions shall be holy, as | You hear my spell is lawful. Do not shun her | Until you see her die again, for then | You kill her double' (5.3.104–7).

The spell is wound up and works its wonder, both in the world of the play and also in the play in our world, however professionally or amateurishly it is acted. For *The Winter's Tale*, as Norman Rabkin has discussed, is concerned with the creation of a world in which 'character and destiny are aspects of a cosmos whose laws control the action of the play, and our illusion is that we are participating in a life that has its own full and peculiar integrity'.[9] Theatrical artifice recovers, and discloses, a fundamental truth about the magic of such a combination of impersonation, action, and dialogue. The coming together of these three elements into a special act of invention are likewise prerequisites for 'religious drama', but which, unlike plays of Shakespeare, 'must not be

[9] Norman Rabkin, *Shakespeare and the Problem of Meaning* (Chicago and London: University of Chicago Press, 1981), 118.

thought of as something that emerged of itself by natural process from a complex of vividness, excitement, and human interest'.[10] Shakespeare's evocation of quasi-religious enchantment, though, linked to the theme of redemption through art (rather than through Christ), imbues the closing scene of *The Winter's Tale* with a double perspective of wonder along the lines discussed in Part I, but where what is figured forth is the triumph of life, not death. For Northrop Frye this means that the true subject of the play is its own art, the mirror is held up to art, not nature; thus in *The Winter's Tale* the world we see is the world symbolized by nature's power of renewal, and yet the world the play leaves us with 'is neither an object of knowledge nor of belief'.[11]

And yet what is the nature of this life restored, shown to us through this evocative tableau, if Hermione has lived decades as one dead to the world? What has been lost irreparably and irremediably? One response is that which was seen to be expressed through Ross's work of history: we cannot understand the value of returning from exile and the hope it brings, unless first we have been displaced and left as if hopeless. The Aesthetic of Decline thus involves and evokes a double movement; a looking forward that is always a return to 'pastness'—a double-take on what or who has just passed. This is precisely how Ross views the work of history, and which he discussed in terms of an emblem: 'Antiquity did wittily adumbrate and represent unto us a Wise man, by the fiction of double faced Janus, with a serpent by him, biting his tail; intimating, that hereby wise men take notice, and make use both of things present and past; and withal are not unmindful of their End, expressed by the serpent biting his tail' (sig. a1).

What is distinctive about this for *The Winter's Tale* is that the consummate play of feigned enchantment becomes an affective reality that ushers in the return from exile and the longed-for redemption. This comes about by a double theatrical feigning: the actor (or today, the actress) who feigns Hermione feigning being stone, comes to move and speak. Such kinetic emblems, in and of themselves, communicate things that characters' feigning cannot

---

[10] Craig, *English Religious Drama*, 4.
[11] Northrop Frye, *A Natural Perspective: The Development of Shakespearean Comedy and Romance* (New York: Harcourt, Brace & World, 1965), 8, 116.

convey by words and actions alone. By virtue of the doubled character of theatre's reality, which is to say what it is concretely and what it shows metaphorically, it 'brings to presence something that is dead and gone, if it ever was at all, something *vorbei*, something decisively absent. . . . Theatre brings it back; back to the light of day; back to the domain of the living'.[12] Dramatic artifice, especially where death is involved, brings with it a glimpse of its double nature—and of our own. For when we, like Leontes, are made speechless and are moved by a sense of wonder evoked through the spectacle before us (5.3.21), at the same time we are still left to wonder whether the extent of such a thing ever can be recovered, realized, and instantiated fully. We are left wondering whether the encounter we have with things in the world ever can be anything more than a confirmation, or refutation, of what we expected to find there.

What holds true for dramatic artifice applies as well to things staged in the mind, as memory pictures. And, as has been seen from three perspectives presented in each part of this book, words both condition and facilitate how those meanings come to be stored as mnemonic packets of some sort—whether as emblems, proverbs or *sententiae*, or *exempla*—and then how they are reconstituted and energized and thus able to discharge their meanings. In the same way that oblivion is linked to death and opposed to memory, so gibberish is at odds with language. Oblivion's counterpart in the world of words, especially as it pertains to social commerce, namely the means by which, as Florio put it, we 'enter-know one another', is gibberish. Like death, gibberish confounds our plans for exerting our memorative and creative powers in the world. Gibberish, like death, brings low even the mightiest of the mighty. Gibberish is not just nonsense though, insofar as it undermines our sense of sense (see again Fig. 1). As such it offers unexpected insight into the end of memory with respect to the Renaissance Aesthetic of Decline.

It is for this reason that *Death and Drama* concludes by endeavouring to listen to what the sheeted dead have to tell us about the place of oblivion in our lives.

---

[12] Sallis, *Stone*, 124.

HORATIO: In the most high and palmy state of Rome,
A little ere the mightiest Julius fell,
The graves stood [tenantless] and the sheeted dead,
Did squeak and gibber in the Roman streets.
(Shakespeare, *Hamlet*, 1.1.116–19)

Many cultures imagine that the souls of the dead wander restlessly betwixt and between the Underworld and the upper world, no longer sharing in 'the society of the living and yet . . . not admitted amongst the dead either'.[13] In the English Renaissance the restless dead, among other things, squeak and gibber.

Gibberish is an onomatopoeic word that means to speak rapidly and inarticulately, or to chatter. Cowper's translation of the *Odyssey* relates of the dead suitors that Cyllenian Hermes 'drove them gibbering down into the shade', and that the 'ghosts | Troop'd downward, gibbering all the dreary way' where they enter into the meads of Asphodel 'by shadowy forms possess'd, | simulars of the dead'.[14] A glance at Liddell and Scott's *Greek–English Lexicon* shows that the terms translated into English as 'squeak' and 'gibber' are sounds uttered by animals, usually the chirping of young birds or bats, but 'also applied to the noise made by ghosts'.[15]

Thomas Browne noted that Penelope's paramours, killed by Odysseus and Telemachus at the final banquet of the epic, 'chirped like bats', as they were conducted to the Underworld by Mercury, 'and those which followed *Hercules* 'made a noise but like a flock of birds'.[16] Being at once quite literal in his interpretation and yet open to the power of allegory, Browne commented that the dead in the 'human Hades' of Homer 'seem all alive . . . yet cannot well speak, prophesie, or know the living, except they drink bloud, wherein is the life of man' (p. 161).

Thomas Hobbes's ghosts, in his translation of the *Iliad*, however, do not gibber; they scream: 'Follow all, but screaming fear-

---

[13] Johnston, *Restless Dead*, 9.

[14] *Odyssey* XXIV, in *The Life and Works of William Cowper* (London: Bohn, 1845), vol. 8.

[15] Henry Liddell and Robert Scott, *Greek–English Lexicon* (New York: American Book Co., n.d.), 1575.

[16] Browne, *Urne-Burial*, *Works*, 161.

fully. | So screaming all the souls together fly.' And in his *Odyssey*:
'they after murmuring flock | Like Bats . . . humming fly about | So
Hermes leads them muttering through the broad waies'.[17] Screaming and not gibbering, muttering rather than chirping, they are
portrayed aurally as being rather more human; though no less
restless for this.

John Florio's *Worlde of Wordes* defines the Italian *Balchi*, as 'a
fustian, roguish, gibberish word, used for money'; and Michael
Drayton's *Polyolbion* (1612) associated 'gibbridge' with the sound
made by an infant (xii. 227). Although there are other references
to the term in the Renaissance, these examples suffice to give us
a sense of who was said to gibber: shades, rogues, and infants.
Horatio's shades squeak and gibber, while Calphurnia's 'shriek
and squeal' (*Julius Caesar*, 2.2.24). Shrieking in Shakespeare,
however, is most often attributed to owls,[18] the quintessential
melancholy night-bird, and glossed as such by George Wither (cf.
Fig. 3). From this brief sampling we learn that the sounds made
by ghosts, at least with respect to what the poetry suggests we
imagine we hear, is the squeaking of bats, the shrill cry of young
birds, the shrieking of owls, and murmuring and muttering.
Moreover—and this is crucial to my argument—all of these
sounds, while different in degree but similar in kind, require
breath, the sign of life, to make them audible. Wind, whether
coming through an instrument turned to mourning, as was the
case with Job and Ralegh, or whether coming from the bloodless
mouth of a shade in Hades, or depicted as coming from a horn
played by a spry cadaver in a popular *Danse macabre* (Figs. 16
and 17), symbolizes life and art—it is a response to death and
destiny—even if the lamentable strains or utterances or notes are
jarring, unintelligible, or chaotic.[19]

Sounds made by gibbering shades may not convey specific

[17] Thomas Hobbes, *The Iliads and Odysses of Homer*, 2nd edn. (London,
1677), 289; and Hobbes, *Homer His Odysses* (London, 1665), 351.
[18] See e.g., *Richard II*, 3.3.183; *3 Henry VI*, 5.6.44; *Macbeth*, 2.2.3. Also, hark-
ing back to Ch. 4, in addition to being 'brother to dragons', Job, in the King James
version, is 'a companion to the owls', which is most appropriate for one whose
'organe' is turned 'into the voyce of them that weepe'.
[19] Kathi Meyer-Baer, *Music of the Spheres and The Dance of Death: Studies in
Musical Iconology* (1970; repr. New York: Da Capo Press, 1984), 5.

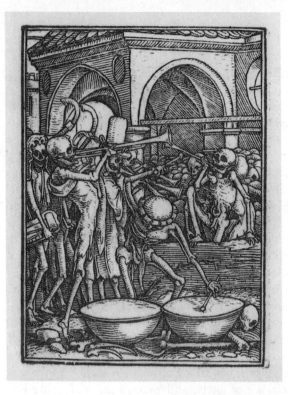

Fig. 16.
Morts
making
music

Fig. 17.
Eviscerated
morts blowing
horns

semantic content, but they still manage to communicate something important about their fate—and our own. The meaning comes from the shades' efforts to make audible their intentions, and thus implies both the longing and striving to form pleas or to shout curses, even while incapable of doing so. The shades, linguistically impaired, are thus reduced to the kind of powerlessness associated with infants and idiots. As Browne points out though, blood, the life of man, empowers the shades to speak. Correlatively it follows then, that the animating element of speech is reason, for it orders and conveys the spirit of one's intentions, thus characterizing one as being part of the human community.

The spirits of Hades, however beset by impotence and perhaps frustration they may be, still embody and convey a sense of uncanny restlessness associated with one who must squeak and gibber. When we encounter a shade in the world of poetry, or a person in the world who, for whatever reason, has been divided from the community of language, we see our own mortality and fragility mirrored in the situation. Those who have crossed over, whether the River Lethe or that crinkle in the brain that controls speech and reason, leave behind their lives and identities—their memories. Having crossed over, they cannot even begin to wonder what has been lost, or what might be recovered if speech and reason were restored, whether through a blood offering as occurs in classical versions of the Underworld, or a pioneering procedure of modern science.

With this in mind, one can consider another version of Memory standing over a figure associated with death and labeled Oblivion (Fig. 18). Memory and Oblivion are bound in a dialectical relation. The same relation is seen in Christian iconography, when God-the-Son, who brings the word of truth into the world, is depicted trampling on bones, defeating death, and winning the final victory for mankind (Fig. 19, bottom right and left corners). In this regard, the classical image of Memory accomplishes in the realm of the mind for Reason, what the Son does in the Christian realm of the Spirit, and which the emblem of History does in Ralegh's project (see again Fig. 9; and cf. Fig. 12). These three victorious figures—involving poesy, religion, and history—succeed

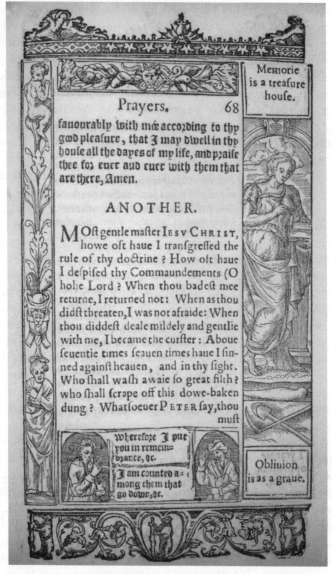

Fig. 18. Memory over Oblivion

Fig. 19. Christ tramples on Death

in bringing about wonderous translations. Memory spares us from declining into gibberish; Christ makes possible one's passage from this world to the next by interceding on our behalf; and 'the Mistress of Man's Life, grave History' (as she is described in the poem explaining Ralegh's frontispiece), vindicates the world to eternity. Although it is awkward to speak of personified virtues needing anything, it can be said that Memory, like History, needs Oblivion to fulfil its function.

Such visual programmes celebrating the power of memory, like trampled-down Oblivion, still take our minds back to their originals whence they were derived—the sheeted, shrouded dead. Such powerful and enduring representations thus give us something to hold on to, and some control over the dreadful prospect of our eventual decline into oblivion. They become like conceptual talismans to which we cling in the face of losing all of our significant, and indeed, our characteristic, worldly aspects of ourselves. As such they are imbued with a sense of desperate immediacy and end up symbolizing, beyond the content they are intended portray, the need for such conceptual vehicles to keep in circulation tokens of our will to endure.

When one seeks to forget something (barring declining age or cerebral injury), it happens not by cancellation but by superimposition, and not by producing absence but by 'multiplying presences'.[20] Just as allegorical depictions of Oblivion evoke and support those of Memory and History, so gibberish (and not so ironically) serves as the key to understanding the structures of thought that link, and enshrine, reason, speech, and memory. These attributes of the properly ordered life recall the emblems in the margins of Queen Elizabeth's Prayer Book (see Fig. 18), which are themselves reminiscent of the statues in niches adorning Memory Palaces.[21] But they can come to our aid only once we acknowledge our mortal, and mental, limitations, and resolve to use them to assist and strengthen our natural memories. In this sense, Oblivion motivates our recreation of Memory. The

---

[20] Umberto Eco, 'An *ars oblivionalis*? Forget it!', *PMLA* 103 (1988), 254–61.
[21] Yates, *Art of Memory*, 18.

prospect of declining into gibberish spirals us toward an abysmal remove from reason and discourse and history, and into another, a dark and dreadful, order of things overseen by Death and shrouded in Oblivion. O but to conjure and latch hold of that memory image, and thus to be propelled 'from hence, by this to that.'

Appendix

In the following transcription of the conclusion to Ralegh's *History of the World* (1614), sig. 5Z4, p. 669, several key words have been emphasized with respect to my argument in Chapter 4 about Ralegh's reliance on emblematic cues and memory images to express an encoded message.

For the rest, if we seeke a reason of the *succession* and continuance of this boundlesse ambition in mortall men, we may add to that which hath beene already said: That the Kings and Princes of the world haue always laid before them, the actions but not the ends, of those great Ones which præceded them. They are always transported with the glorie of the one, but they neuer minde the miserie of the other, till they find the experience in themselues. They neglect the aduice of God, while they enioy life, or hope it; but they follow the counsell of Death, vpon his first approach. It is he that puts into man all the wisedome of the world *without speaking a word*; which God with all the words of his Law, promises, or threats, doth infuse. Death which hateth and destroyeth man, is beleeued: God, which hath made him, and loues him, is alwaies deferred: I have considered (saith Solomon) all the workes that are under the Sunne, and behold, all is vanitie, and vexation of spirit: but who beleeues it, till *Death tells it vs*? It was Death, which opening the conscience of Charles the fift, made him enioyne his sonne Philip to restore Nauarre; and King Francis the first of France, to command that iustice should be done vpon the Murderers of the Protestants in Merindol and Cabrieres, which till then he neglected. It is therefore Death alone that can suddenly make man to know himselfe. *He tells the proud and insolent*, that they are but Abiects, and humbles them at the instant; makes them crie, complaine, and repent, yea, euen to hate their forepassed happinesse. He takes the account of the rich, and proues him a beggar; a naked beggar, which hath interest in nothing, but the grauell that fills his mouth. He holds a Glasse before the eyes of the most beautifull, and makes them see therein, their deformitie and rottennesse; and they acknowledge it.

 O *eloquent*, iust, and mighty *Death*! Whom none could aduise, thou hast perswaded; what none hath dared, thou hast done; and whom all the world hath flattered, thou only hast cast out of the world and despised: thou hast drawne together all the far stretched greatnesse, all the pride, crueltie, and ambition of man, and couered it all over with these two narrow words, *Hic iacet.*

Lastly, whereas *this Booke*, by the title it hath, *calls itselfe* The first part of the General Historie of the World, implying a Second, and Third Volume; which I also intended, and have hewne out; besides many other discouragements, perswading *my silence*; it hath pleased God to take that Glorious Prince out of the world, to whom they were directed; whose *vnspeakable* and neuer enough *lamented losse, hath taught me to say* with Iob, Versa est in Luctum Cithara mea, & Organum meum *in vocem* flentium. FINIS.

Bibliography

PRIMARY SOURCES

ADDISON, JOSEPH, *The Works*, 2nd edn. (London, 1730).
ALCIATO, ANDREAS, *Emblematum libellus* (Venice, 1546).
BACON, FRANCIS, *Advancement of Learning*, ed. Arthur Johnson (Oxford: Oxford University Press, 1980).
——*The Works of Francis Bacon*, eds James Spedding, Robert Leslie Ellis, and Douglas Denon Heath (Boston: Brown and Taggard, 1861–5).
BEAUMONT, FRANCIS and FLETCHER, JOHN, *Works*, ed. Alexander Dyce (London: Edward Moxon, 1846).
Beowulf, ed. C. L. Wrenn (London: George G. Harrap, 1958).
BROWNE, THOMAS, *Works*, ed. Geoffrey Keynes (1928; repro. Chicago: University of Chicago Press, 1964).
BUTLER, SAMUEL, *Hudibras* (London, 1663).
CALVIN, JOHN, *Sermons of Master John Calvin, upon the Booke of IOB translated out of the French by Arthur Golding* (London, 1574).
CAMILLO, GUILIO, *L'Idea del Theatro* (Florence, 1550).
CICERO, *De oratore*, trans. E.W. Sutton and H. Rackham (Cambridge, Mass.: Harvard University Press, 1942).
COWPER, WILLIAM, *The Life and Works of William Cowper* (London: Bohn, 1845).
DOLCE, LODOVICO, *Dialogo . . . nel qvale si ragiona del modo di accrescere & conservar la Memoria* (Venice, 1586).
ERASMUS, DESIDERIUS, *De Utramque Verborum ac Rerum Copia*, ed. Donald B. King and David Rix (Milwaukee: Marquette University Press, 1963).
FEATLEY, DANIEL, *Clavis Mystica* (London, 1636).
FEATLEY, JOHN, *A Fountaine of Teares* (Amsterdam, 1646).
FLORIO, JOHN, *The Essayes of Michel Lord of Montaigne* (London, 1603).
——*First Fruites* (London, 1578).
——*Queen Anna's New World of Words* (London, 1611).
——*Second Frutes* (London, 1591), ed. R. C. Simonini (Gainesville, Fla.: Scholars' Facsimiles & Reprints, 1953).

—— *Worlde of Wordes* (London, 1598).

FORD, JOHN, *The Broken Heart*, ed. Brian Morris (New York: Hill & Wang, 1966).

FULWOOD, WILLIAM, *The Castel of Memorie* (London, 1562).

GOETHE, JOHANN WOLFGANG, *Faust*, trans. Walter Kaufmann (New York: Doubleday, 1961).

GRATAROLI, GUGLIELMO, *De Memoria* (Zurich, 1553).

GREENE, ROBERT, *Friar Bacon and Friar Bungay*, ed. Daniel Seltzer (Lincoln: University of Nebraska Press, 1963).

HOBBES, THOMAS, *Homer His Odysses* (London, 1665).

—— *The Iliads and Odysses of Homer*, 2nd edn. (London, 1677).

HOLLYBANDE, CLAUDIUS, *The French Schoole-Maister* (London, 1573).

Holy Bible, 1611 facsimile edn., King James Version (Nashville: Thomas Nelson, 1982).

Holy Scriptures, According to the Masoretic Text (1917; repr. Philadelphia: Jewish Publication Society of America, 1955).

JONSON, BEN, *The Complete Works*, eds. C. H. Hereford, Percy Simpson, and Evelyn Simpson (Oxford: Oxford University Press, 1927).

—— *Timber: Or Discoveries: made upon men and matter* (London, 1641), ed. G. B. Harrison (London, 1923).

KYD, THOMAS, *The Spanish Tragedy*, ed. J. R. Mulryne (1970; repr. New York: Norton, 1985).

LEPOREUS, GUILELMUS, *Ars memorativa* (Paris, 1520).

MARLOWE, CHRISTOPHER, *The Complete Plays*, ed. Irving Ribner (Indianapolis and New York: Bobbs-Merrill, 1963).

MIDDLETON, THOMAS, *Selected Plays*, ed. David L. Frost (Cambridge: Cambridge University Press, 1987).

MILTON, JOHN, *Complete Poems and Major Prose*, ed. Merritt Y. Hughes (Indianapolis and New York: Bobbs-Merrill, 1957).

OVID, *Fasti*, trans. James G. Frazier; rev. G. P. Goold (Cambridge, Mass.: Harvard University Press, 1989).

—— *Metamorphoses*, trans. Frank Justus Miller, 3rd edn. rev. G. P. Goold (Cambridge, Mass.: Harvard University Press, 1984).

PASTORIUS, FRANCIS, 'Emblematical Recreations', Newberry Library, Chicago, MS W1025.

PEACHAM, HENRY, *Minerva Britannia* (London, 1612).

POOLE, JOSUA, *The English Parnassus: Or a help to English Poesie* (London, 1677).

PUTTENHAM, GEORGE, *The Arte of English Poesie* (Kent, Ohio: Kent State University Press, 1970).

QUARLES, FRANCIS, *Divine Poems* (London, 1632).

QUINTILIAN, *Institutio Oratoria*, trans. H. E. Butler (1922; repr. Cambridge, Mass.: Harvard University Press, 1979).

RALEGH, WALTER, *The History of the World* (London, 1614).

—— *The History of the World*, ed. C. A. Patrides (New York: Macmillan, 1971).

—— *The Poems of Sir Walter Ralegh: A Historical Edition*, ed. Michael Rudick (Tempe, Ariz.: Renaissance English Text Society, 1999).

—— *Sir Walter Ralegh: Selected Writings*, ed. Gerald Hammond (Harmondsworth: Penguin Books, 1986).

'R.H.' [Harrison, Richard], *Of Ghosts and Spirites, Walking by Night . . . by Lewes Lauraterus of Tigurine* (London, 1596).

Rhetorica Ad Herennium, trans. Harry Caplan (Cambridge, Mass: Harvard University Press, 1954).

ROSS, ALEXANDER, *Animadversions . . . upon Sr. Walter Raleigh's Historie of the World* (London, 1653).

—— *Arcana Microcosmi* (London, 1652).

—— *The History of the World: The Second Part* (London, 1652).

—— *The Marrow of History* (London, 1650).

—— *Mel Heliconium* (London, 1642).

—— *Mystagogus Poeticus, Or The Muses Interpreter* (1647 edn.), ed. John R. Glenn (New York and London: Garland Publishing, 1987).

—— *Mystagogus Poeticus* (London, 1648).

—— *Rerum Iudicarum Memoriabiliorun . . . Liber Secundus* (London, 1617).

SAMFORD, JAMES, *The Garden of Pleasure* (London, 1573).

SHAKESPEARE, WILLIAM, *Hamlet*, ed. Harold Jenkins (London and New York: Methuen, 1982).

—— *The Riverside Shakespeare*, ed. G. Blakemore Evans (Boston, Mass.: Houghton Mifflin, 1974).

SIDNEY, PHILIP, *Apology for Poetry*, ed. Geoffrey Shepherd (1965; repr. Manchester: Manchester University Press, 1973).

—— *A Defence of Poetry*, ed. J. A. van Dorsten (1966; repr. Oxford University Press, 1975).

—— *The Countesse of Pembrokes Arcadia* (London, 1590).

SPENSER, BENJAMIN, *Vox Civitatis, or Londons Complaint against her Children in the Country* (London, 1636).

SPENSER, EDMUND, *The Faerie Queene*, ed. Thomas P. Roche (Harmondsworth: Penguin Books, 1987).

TERESA of AVILA, *The Interior Castle*, trans. Kieran Kavanaugh and Otilio Rodrigues (New York: Paulist Press, 1979).

THYNNE, FRANCIS, *Emblemes and Epigrams*, ed. F. J. Furnivall, Early English Text Society, 64 (London, 1876).

TORRIANO, GIOVANNI, *Italian Tutor* (London, 1649).

——*Select Italian Proverbs* (Cambridge, 1649).

——*Vocabolario Italiano & Inglese* (London, 1659).

TOURNEUR, CYRIL, *The Revenger's Tragedy*, ed. Lawrence J. Ross (Lincoln: University of Nebraska Press, 1966).

DE VORAGINE, JACOBUS, *The Golden Legend*, trans. William Granger Ryan (Princeton: Princeton University Press, 1993).

WEBSTER, JOHN, *The White Devil*, ed. John Russell Brown (Manchester: Manchester University Press, 1979).

WILLIS, JOHN, *Art of Memory* (London, 1621).

——*Art of Stenographie, or Short Writing by Spelling Characters* (London, 1602).

——*Mnemonica; or the Art of Memory* (London, 1661).

WITHER, GEORGE, *Collection of Emblems* (London, 1635).

SECONDARY SOURCES

Books

ACHESON, ARTHUR, *Shakespeare's Lost Years in London* (1920; repr. New York: Haskell House, 1971).

ALLEN, WARD, *Translating for King James: Being a True Copy of the Only Notes Made By a Translator of the King James Bible* (Nashville: Vanderbilt University Press, 1969).

ANDERSON, JUDITH H., *Words that Matter: Linguistic Perception in Renaissance England* (Stanford: Stanford University Press, 1996).

BARISH, JONAS, *The Antitheatrical Prejudice* (Berkeley, Los Angeles, and London: University of California Press, 1981).

BARKER, BRIAN, *The Symbols of Sovereignty* (North Pomfret, Vt.: David & Charles, 1979).

BATH, MICHAEL, *Speaking Pictures: English Emblem Books and Renaissance Culture* (London: Longman, 1994).

BEER, ANNA R., *Sir Walter Ralegh and his Readers in the Seventeenth Century: Speaking to the People* (Basingstoke: Macmillan, 1997).

BENJAMIN, WALTER, *The Origin of German Tragic Drama*, trans. John Osborne (London: New Left Books, 1977).

BERGERON, DAVID M., *English Civic Pageantry, 1558–1642* (Columbia: University of South Carolina Press, 1971).

BOLGAR, R. R., *The Classical Heritage and Its Beneficiaries* (1954; repr. Cambridge: Combridge University Press 1958).

BRECHT, BERTOLT, *Brecht on Theatre: The Development of an Aesthetic*, trans. John Willet (New York: Hill and Wang, 1974).

BURKERT, WALTER, *Homo Necans: The Anthropology of Ancient Greek Sacrificial Ritual and Myth*, trans. Peter Bing (1972; repr. Berkeley: University of California Press, 1983).

BURNETT, MARK THORNTON, *Masters and Servants in English Renaissance Drama and Culture: Authority and Obedience* (Basingstoke and New York: Macmillan and St Martin's Press, 1997).

BURY, J. B., *The Idea of Progress* (London: Macmillan, 1920).

BYNUM, CAROLINE WALKER, *The Resurrection of the Body in Western Christianity, 200–1336* (New York: Columbia University Press, 1995).

CARRUTHERS, MARY, *The Book of Memory: A Study of Memory in Medieval Culture* (Cambridge: Cambridge University Press, 1990).

——*The Craft of Thought: Meditation, Rhetoric, and the Making of Images, 400–1200* (Cambridge: Cambridge University Press, 1998).

CASEY, EDWARD S., *The Fate of Place: A Philosophical History* (Berkeley: University of California Press, 1997).

CLEMENTS, ROBERT J., *Picta Poesis: Literary and Humanistic Theory in Renaissance Emblem Books* (Rome: Edizioni di Storia e Letteratura, 1960).

COLIE, ROSALIE L., *Paradoxia Epidemica: The Renaissance Tradition of Paradox* (Princeton: Princeton University Press, 1966).

CONNOLLY, THOMAS, *Mourning into Joy: Music, Raphael, and Saint Cecilia* (New Haven and London: Yale University Press, 1994).

CORBETT, MARGERY and LIGHTBOWN, RONALD, *The Comely Frontispiece: The Emblematic Title-Page in England, 1550–1660* (London: Routledge & Kegan Paul, 1979).

CRAIG, HARDIN, *English Religious Drama of the Middle Ages* (Oxford: Clarendon Press, 1955).

CRESSY, DAVID, *Travesties and Transgression in Tudor and Stuart England* (Oxford: Oxford University Press, 2000).

DAICHES, DAVID, *The King James Version of the English Bible: An Account of the Development and Sources of the English Bible of 1611 With Special Reference to the Hebrew Tradition* (1941; repr. Chicago: University of Chicago Press, 1968).

DALY, PETER M., *Emblem Theory: Recent German Contributions to the Characterization of the Emblem Genre* (Nendeln: KTO Press, 1979).

——*Literature in the Light of the Emblem: Structural Parallels Between the Emblem and Literature in the Sixteenth and Seventeenth Centuries* (Toronto: Toronto University Press, 1973).

DEBORD, GUY, *La Société du spectacle* (Paris, 1967); trans. and rev. (Detroit: Black & Red, 1983).

DENT, R. W., *John Webster's Borrowing* (Berkeley and Los Angeles: University of California Press, 1960).

DOEBLER, JOHN, *Shakespeare's Speaking Pictures: Studies in Iconic Imagery* (Albuquerque: University of New Mexico Press, 1974).

EISENSTEIN, ELIZABETH L., *The Printing Revolution in Early Modern Europe* (1983; repr. Cambridge: Cambridge University Press, 1998).

ENGEL, WILLIAM E., 'Emblems and *Sententiae* in Seventeenth Century Prose: Mystical and Literary Design in Robert Burton and Thomas Browne', Ph.D. thesis, University of California, Berkeley, 1988.

——*Mapping Mortality: The Persistence of Memory and Melancholy in Early Modern England* (Amherst: University of Massachusetts Press, 1995).

EVANS, ROBERT C., *Habits of Mind: Evidence and Effects of Ben Jonson's Reading* (Lewisburg: Bucknell University Press, 1995).

EVETT, DAVID, *Literature and the Visual Arts in Tudor England* (Athens and London: University of Georgia Press, 1990).

FISH, STANLEY, *Self-Consuming Artifacts: The Experience of Seventeenth-Century Literature* (Berkeley: University of California Press, 1972).

DE LA FLOR, FERNANDO, *Teatro de la Memoria: siente ensayos sombre mnemotecnia Española de los siglos XVII y XVIII* (Salamanca: Junta de Castilla y Leon, 1988).

FORKER, CHARLES R., *The Skull Beneath the Skin: The Achievement of John Webster* (Carbondale and Edwardsville: Southern Illinois University Press, 1986).

FOWLER, ALASTAIR, *Time's Purpled Masquers: Stars and the Afterlife in Renaissance English Literature* (Oxford: Clarendon Press, 1996).

FRAZER, JAMES, *The Golden Bough* (1890; repr. Oxford: Oxford University Press, 1994).

FREEMAN, ROSEMARY, *English Emblem Books* (1948; repr. New York: Octagon Press, 1978).

FRYE, NORTHROP, *The Great Code: The Bible and Literature* (1981; repr. New York: Harcourt, Brace, & Jovanovich, 1983).

——*A Natural Perspective: The Development of Shakespearean Comedy and Romance* (New York: Harcourt, Brace & World, 1965).

GIBBON, EDWARD, *The Decline and Fall of the Roman Empire* (London: J. M. Dent & Sons, 1911).

GOMBRICH, E. H., *Aby Warburg: An Intellectual Biography* (Chicago: University of Chicago Press, 1986).

GREEN, HENRY, *Shakespeare and the Emblem Writers: An Exposition of their Similarities of Thought and Expression* (London: Trübner & Co., 1870).

GREENBLATT, STEPHEN, *Renaissance Self-Fashioning From More to Shakespeare* (Chicago: University of Chicago Press, 1982).

——*Sir Walter Ralegh: The Renaissance Man and His Roles* (New Haven: Yale University Press, 1973).

GREENWOOD, JOHN, *Shifting Perspectives and the Stylish Style: Mannerism in Shakespeare and his Jacobean Contemporaries* (Toronto: University of Toronto Press, 1988).

GURR, ANDREW, *The Shakespearean Stage, 1574–1642*, 2nd edn. (Cambridge, 1980).

HALLEY, HENRY H., *Bible Handbook*, 24th edn. (Grand Rapids, Mich.: Regency, 1965).

HARRIS, VICTOR, *All Coherence Gone* (Chicago: University of Chicago Press, 1949).

HENINGER, JR., S. K., *Touches of Sweet Harmony* (San Marino, Calif.: Huntington Library Press, 1974).

HILL, CHRISTOPHER, *Intellectual Origins of the English Revolution* (1965; repr. Oxford: Clarendon Press, 1982).

HUIZINGA, JOHAN, *Homo Ludens: A Study of the Play Element in Culture* (1944; repr. Beacon, 1955).

HULSE, CLARK, *The Rule of Art: Literature and Painting in the Renaissance* (Chicago: University of Chicago Press, 1990).

HUNTINGTON, JOHN, *Ambition, Rank, and Poetry in 1590s England* (Urbana and Chicago: University of Illinois Press, 2001).

JARDINE, LISA, *Francis Bacon: Discovery and the Art of Discourse* (Cambridge: Cambridge University Press 1975).

JOHNSTON, SARAH ILES, *Restless Dead: Encounters Between the Living and the Dead in Ancient Greece* (Berkeley, Los Angeles, and London: University of California Press, 1999).

KANT, IMMANUEL, *Critique of Judgment*, trans. Werner S. Pluhar (Indianapolis: Hackett Publishing, 1987).

KAYSER, WOLFGANG, *The Grotesque in Art and Literature*, trans. Ulrich Weisstein (New York: Columbia University Press, 1981).

KERNODLE, GEORGE R., *From Art to Theatre: Form and Convention in the Renaissance* (Chicago: University of Chicago Press, 1947).

KIEFER, FREDERICK, *Fortune and Elizabethan Tragedy* (San Marino: Huntington Library Press, 1983).

KLOSSOWSKI, PIERRE, *Sade: My Neighbor*, trans. Alphonso Lingis (Evanston: Northwestern University Press, 1991).

KRISTEVA, JULIA, *Powers of Horror*, trans. Leon S. Roudiez (New York: Columbia University Press, 1982).

LECHNER, JOAN MARIE, *Renaissance Concepts of the Commonplaces* (New York: Pageant Press, 1962).

LE GOFF, JACQUES, *The Medieval Imagination*, trans. Arthur Goldhammer (Chicago: University of Chicago Press, 1988).

LÉVINAS, EMMANUEL, *Autrement qu'être ou au-delà de l'essence* (Dordrecht: Martinus Nijhoff, 1974).

——*Time and the Other*, trans. Richard A. Cohen (Pittsburgh: Duquesne University Press, 1987).

LÉVI-STRAUSS, CLAUDE, *Structural Anthropology*, trans. Claire Jacobson and Brooke Grunfest Schoepf (New York: Basic Books, 1963).

LEWALSKI, BARBARA KIEFER, *Milton's Brief Epic: The Genre, Meaning, and Art of 'Paradise Regained'* (Providence: Brown University Press, 1966).

LOWENTHAL, DAVID, *The Past is a Foreign Country* (1985; repr. Cambridge: Cambridge University Press, 1995).

McGRATH, ALISTER, *In the Beginning: The Story of the King James Bible and How it Changed a Nation, a Language and a Culture* (New York: Doubleday, 2000).

MACQUEEN, JOHN, *Numerology: Theory and Outline History of a Literary Mode* (Edinburgh: University of Edinburgh Press, 1983).

MALINOWSKI, BRONISLAW, *Argonauts of the Western Pacific* (1922; repr. Prospect Heights, Ill.: Waveland Press, 1984).

——*Coral Gardens and Their Magic* (1935; repr. Bloomington: Indiana University Press, 1965).

MARAVALL, JOSÉ ANTONIO, *Culture of the Baroque: Analysis of a Historical Structure*, trans. Terry Cochran (1975; repr. Minneapolis: University of Minnesota Press, 1986).

MARTIN, DANIEL, *Le Triptyque des 'Essais' de Montaigne et l'héraldique des dieux gréco-romains* (Tours: Librarie A.-G. Nizet, 1996).

MAZZEO, JOSEPH A., *Renaissance and Revolution: The Remaking of European Thought* (New York: Pantheon Books, 1965).

MEHL, DIETER, *The Elizabethan Dumb Show: The History of a Dramatic Convention* (London: Methuen, 1965).

MEYER-BAER, KATHI, *Music of the Spheres and The Dance of Death: Studies in Musical Iconology* (1970; repr. New York: Da Capo Press, 1984).

MIROLLO, JAMES V., *Mannerism and Renaissance Poetry: Concept, Mode, Inner Design* (New Haven: Yale University Press, 1984).

MOSELEY, CHARLES, *A Century of Emblems: An Introductory Anthology* (Aldershot: Scolar Press, 1989).

NEILL, MICHAEL, *Issues of Death: Mortality and Identity in English Renaissance Tragedy* (Oxford: Clarendon Press, 1997).

NICOLSON, MARJORIE HOPE, *The Breaking of the Circle: Studies on the Effect of the 'New Science' on Seventeenth Century Poetry* (Evanston: Northwestern University Press, 1950).

OLSON, DAVID R., *The World on Paper: The Conceptual and Cognitive Implications of Writing and Reading* (Cambridge: Cambridge University Press, 1994).

ONG, WALTER, *Ramus: Method and the Decay of Dialogue* (1953; repr. Cambridge and London: Harvard University Press, 1983).

ORGEL, STEPHEN, *The Illusion of Power: Political Theater in The English Renaissance* (Berkeley, Los Angeles, and London: University of California Press, 1975).

——and STRONG, ROY, *Inigo Jones* (Berkeley, Los Angeles, and London: University of California Press, 1973).

PANOFSKY, ERWIN, 'Hercules am Scheidewege', *Studien der Biblothek Warburg* (Leipzig, 1930).

PEIRCE, CHARLES SANDERS, *Selected Philosophical Writings, Volume 1 (1867–1893)*, eds. Christian Kloesel and Nathan Houser (Bloomington and Indianapolis: University of Indiana Press, 1992).

PENSKY, MAX, *Melancholy Dialectics: Walter Benjamin and the Play of Mourning* (Amherst: University of Massachusetts Press, 1993).

RABKIN, NORMAN, *Shakespeare and the Problem of Meaning* (Chicago and London: University of Chicago Press, 1981).

RACIN, JOHN, Jr., *Sir Walter Ralegh as Historian* (Salzburg: Institut für Englische Sprache und Literatur Universität Salzburg 1974).

REBHORN, WAYNE A., *The Emperor of Men's Minds: Literature and the Renaissance Discourse of Rhetoric* (Ithaca and London: Cornell University Press, 1995).

ROY, BRUNO and ZUMTHOR, PAUL (eds.), *Jeux de Mémoire: Aspects de la mnémotechnie médiévale* (Montréal: Presses de l'Université de Montréal, 1985).

RUSSELL, DANIEL, *Emblematic Structures in Renaissance French Culture* (Toronto: University of Toronto Press, 1995).

SALLIS, JOHN, *Stone* (Bloomington and Indianapolis: Indiana University Press, 1994).

SCHÖNE, ALBRECHT, *Emblematik und Drama im Zeitalter des Barock* (Munich: Berk, 1968).

SEZNEC, JEAN, *The Survival of the Pagan Gods: The Mythological Tradition and Its Place in Renaissance Humanism and Art*, trans. Barbara F. Sessions (1953; repr. New Haven: Princeton University Press, 1961).

SHERMAN, CLAIRE RICHTER, *Writing on Hands: Memory and Knowledge in Early Modern Europe* (Seattle: University of Washington Press, 2000).

SMALLEY, BERYL, *The Study of the Bible in the Middle Ages* (Notre Dame, Ind.: University of Notre Dame Press, 1964).

SMITH, LACEY B., *This Realm of England* (Lexington, Mass.: D. C. Heath, 1976).

SONNINO, LEE A., *A Handbook to Sixteenth-Century Rhetoric* (London: Routledge & Kegan Paul, 1968).

TRICOMI, ALBERT, *Reading Tudor-Stuart Texts Through Cultural Historicism* (Gainesville: University of Florida Press, 1996).

VOLKMANN, LUDWIG, *Ars Memorativa* (Vienna: Anton Schroll, 1929).

WILLIAMSON, GEORGE, *Seventeenth Century Contexts* (London: Faber & Faber, 1960).

WIND, EDGAR, *Pagan Mysteries in the Renaissance* (1958; repr. New York: W. W. Norton, 1968).

WOOLF, D. R., *The Idea of History in Early Stuart England* (Toronto: University of Toronto Press, 1990).

WRIGHT, LOUIS B., *Middle Class Culture in Elizabethan England* (1935; repr. London, 1958).

YATES, FRANCES A., *The Art of Memory* (1966; repr. Harmondsworth: Penguin Books, 1978).

——*Giordano Bruno and the Hermetic Tradition* (Chicago and London: University of Chicago Press, 1964).

——*Ideas and Ideals in the North European Renaissance, Collected Essays III* (London: Routledge & Kegan Paul, 1984).

——*John Florio: The Life of an Italian in Shakespeare's England* (Cambridge: Cambridge University Press, 1934).

——*Theatre of the World* (Chicago: University of Chicago, 1969).

Articles and Essays

BARISH, JONAS, 'Remembering and Forgetting in Shakespeare', in R. B. Parker and S. P. Zitner (eds.), *Elizabethan Theatre: Essays in Honor of S. Schoenbaum* (Newark: University of Delaware Press, 1996), 214–21.

BATH, MICHAEL, 'Weeping Stages and Melancholy Lovers: The Iconography of *As You Like It*, II.i', *Emblematica*, 1 (1986), 13–52.

BATAILLE, GEORGES, 'The Use Value of D. A. F. de Sade', in Allan Stoekl (ed.), *Visions of Excess, Selected Writings, 1927–1939*, trans. Allan Stoekl, Carl R. Lovitt, and Donald M. Leslie, Jr. (Minneapolis: University of Minnesota, 1985), 91–102.

BAUDRY, JEAN-LOUIS, 'Cinema: effets idéologiques produits par l'appareil de base', *Cinéthique*, 7: 8 (1970), 1–8.

BERSANI, LEO and DUTOIT, ULYSSE, 'Merde Alors', *October*, 13 (1980), 23–35.

BEER, ANNA R., ' "Left to the world without a Maister": Sir Walter Ralegh's *The History of the World* as a Public Text', *Studies in Philology*, 91: 4 (Fall 1994), 432–63.

BOWERS, A. ROBIN, 'Emblem and Rape in Shakespeare's *Lucrece* and *Titus Andronicus*', *Studies in Iconography*, 10 (1985), 79–96.

BRAUNMULLER, A. R., 'The Arts of the Dramatist', in A. R. Braunmuller and Michael Hattaway (eds.), *The Cambridge Companion to English Renaissance Drama* (Cambridge: Cambridge University Press, 1990), 53–90.

BROWN, ARTHUR, 'The Play Within a Play: An Elizabethan Dramatic Device', *Essays and Studies* (1960), 36–48.

CAMDEN, CARROL, 'Memory, The Warder of the Brain', *Philological Quarterly*, 18: 1 (Jan. 1939), 52–72.

CARRUTHERS, MARY, 'Inventional Mnemonics and the Ornaments of Style: The Case of Etymology', *Connotations*, 2: 2 (1992), 103–14.

CODDON, KARIN S., ' "For Show or Useless Property": Necrophilia and *The Revenger's Tragedy*', *English Literary History*, 61 (1994), 71–88.

DALY, PETER M., 'The Cultural Context of English Emblem Books', in Peter M. Daly (ed.), *The English Emblem and the Continental Tradition* (New York: AMS Press, 1988), 1–60.

DORSTEN, JAN VAN, 'Arts of Memory and Poetry', *English Studies*, 48 (1967), 419–25.

ECO, UMBERTO, 'An *ars oblivionalis*? Forget it!', *PMLA* 103 (1988), 254–61.

ENGEL, WILLIAM E., 'Mnemonic Criticism and Renaissance Literature: A Manifesto', *Connotations*, 1 (1991), 12–33.

——'Mnemonic Emblems and the Humanist Discourses of Knowledge', in Peter M. Daly and John Manning (eds.), *Aspects of Renaissance and Baroque Symbol Theory, 1500–1700* (New York: AMS Press, 1999), 125–42.

FOSTER, VERNA ANN and FORD, STEPHEN, 'Structure and History in *The Broken Heart*', *English Literary Renaissance*, 18: 2 (Spring 1988), 305–28.

GIBSON, COLIN, ' "The Stage of My Mortality": Ford's Poetry of Death', in Michael Neill (ed.), *John Ford: Critical Re-visions* (Cambridge and New York: Cambridge University Press, 1988).

GREENFIELD, THELMA N., 'The Language of Process in Ford's *The Broken Heart*', *PMLA* (1987), 397–405.

HAMLIN, HANNIBAL, 'Psalm Culture in the English Renaissance: Readings of Psalm 137 By Shakespeare, Spenser, Milton, and Others', *Renaissance Quarterly*, 55: 1 (Spring 2002), 224–57.

HAMMERSMITH, JAMES P., '*Hamlet* and the Myth of Memory', *English Literary History*, 45 (1978), 597–605.

HAWKINS, HARRIETT, 'Mortality, Morality, and Modernity in *The Broken Heart*', in Michael Neill (ed.), *John Ford: Critical Re-visions* (Cambridge and New York: Cambridge University Press, 1988).

HUNTER, DIANNE, 'Doubling, Mythic Difference and the Scapegoating of Female Power in *Macbeth*', *Psychoanalytic Review*, 75: 1 (1988).

HUNTER, G. K. 'The Marking of *Sententiae* in Elizabethan Printed Plays, Poems, and Romances', *The Library*, 5th series, 6: 3/4 (Dec. 1951), 171–88.

JOHNSTON, SARAH ILES, *Restless Dead: Encounters between the Living and the Dead in Ancient Greece* (Berkeley, Los Angeles, and London: University of California Press, 1999).

KERRIGAN, JOHN, 'Hieronimo, Hamlet, and Remembrance', *Essays in Criticism*, 31: 2 (Apr. 1981), 105–26.

KINNEY, ARTHUR F., 'Speculating Shakespeare, 1605–1016', in R. B. Parker and S. P. Zitner (eds.), *Elizabethan Theatre: Essays in Honor of S. Schoenbaum* (Newark: University of Delaware Press, 1996), 252–70.

KLEIN, ROBERT, 'Théorie de l'expression figurée dans les traités italiens sur les *imprese*, 1555–1612', *Bibliothèque d'Humanisme et Renaissance*, 19 (1957), 320–41.

LE BRUN, ANNIE, 'Sade and the Theatre', in Deepak Narang Sawhney (ed.), *The Divine Sade*, trans. Justin Barton (University of Warwick: PLI, 1994), 35–50.

LEIMBERG, INGE, ' "Golden Apollo, a poor humble swain": A Study of Names in *The Winter's Tale*', in *Deutsche Shakespeare-Gesellschaft West: Jahrbuch* (1991), 135–58.

——' "The Image of Golden Aphrodite": Some Observations on the Name "Hermione" ', in *Deutsche Shakespeare-Gesellschaft West: Jahrbuch* (1988), 130–49.

LILLEY, SAMUEL, 'Robert Recorde and the Idea of Progress: A Hypothesis and Verification', *Renaissance and Modern Studies*, 2 (1957), 3–37.

NÄNNY, MAX, 'Chiastic Structures in Literature: Some Forms and Functions', in Edo Fries (ed.), *The Structure of Texts* (Tübingen: Gunter Narr, 1987), 75–97.

NEILL, MICHAEL, 'Exeunt with a Dead March: Funeral Pageantry on the Shakespearean Stage', in David M. Bergeron (ed.), *Pageantry in the Shakespearean Theatre* (Athens: University of Georgia Press, 1985), 154–93.

——'The Moral Artifice of *The Lovers Melancholy*', *English Literary Renaissance*, 8 (1978), 85–106.

——'The World Beyond: Shakespeare and the Tropes of Translation', in R. B. Parker and S. P. Zitner (eds.), *Elizabethan Theatre: Essays in Honor of S. Schoenbaum* (Newark: University of Delaware Press, 1996), 290–308.

PADHI, SHANTI, '*The Broken Heart* and *The Second Maiden's Tragedy*: Ford's Main Source for the Corpse's Coronation', *Notes & Queries*, 31: 2 (1984), 236–7.

PECHTER, EDWARD, 'Remembering *Hamlet*: Or, How It Feels To Go Like a Crab Backwards', *Shakespeare Survey*, 39 (1987), 135–47.

PECK, RUSSELL, 'Number as Cosmic Language', in Caroline D. Eckhardt (ed.), *Essays in the Numerical Criticism of Medieval Literature* (Lewisburg, Penn.: Bucknell University Press, 1980), 15–64.

PORTNOY, PHYLLIS, 'Ring Composition and the Digression of *Exodus*', *English Studies* 82: 4 (Aug. 2001), 289–307.

QUATTROCCHI, LUCA, 'Pearls of Eternity', in 'Something rich and strange', *FMR* (English Edition), 28 (Sept.–Oct. 1987), 91–6.

RACIN, JOHN, Jr., 'The Early Editions of Sir Walter Ralegh's *The History of the World*', *Studies in Bibliography*, 17 (1964), 199–209.

RECHTIEN, JOHN G., 'John Foxe's *Comprehensive Collection of Commonplaces*: A Renaissance Memory System for Students and Theologians', *Sixteenth Century Journal*, 9: 1 (1978), 83–9.

REGOSIN, RICHARD, 'Le Miroüer vague: Reflections of the Example in Montaigne's *Essais*', in *Oeuvres & Critiques*, 8: 1/2 (1983), 73–86.

RØSTVIG, MAREN-SOFIE, 'Structure as Prophecy: The Influence of Biblical Exegesis Upon Theories of Literary Structure', in Alastair Fowler (ed.), *Silent Poetry* (London, 1970), 32–72.

SCHEFFLER, ISRAEL, 'Words and Pictures—Mention-selection and Mental Process', *Language of Design*, 3 (1995), 45–54.

SPINRAD, PHOEBE S., 'Ceremonies of Complement: The Symbolic Marriage in Ford's *The Broken Heart*', *Philological Quarterly*, 65: 1 (Winter 1986), 23–37.

TAYLOR, JANE H. M., 'Un Miroer Salutaire', in Jane H. M. Taylor (ed.),

Dies Illa: Death in the Middle Ages (Liverpool: Francis Cairns, 1984), 29–44.

WATSON, ROBERT N., 'Tragedy', in A. R. Braunmuller and Michael Hattaway (eds.), *The Cambridge Companion to English Renaissance Drama* (Cambridge: Cambridge University Press, 1990).

WILSON, JENNY, 'Ralegh's *History of the World*: Its Purpose and Political Significance', Durham Thomas Harriot Seminar, Occasional Paper, No. 28 (n.d.).

WIND, EDGAR, 'Aenigma Termini', *Journal of the Warburg and Courtauld Institute*, 1 (1937).

Index

References to illustrations are printed in boldface type.